John Pearson is a renown
won the Author's Club Av
most famous book, *The Profession of Violence*, was acclaimed
on its release, even in the US, where it won the Edgar Allan
Poe Special Award.

By John Pearson

Non-fiction

Bluebird and the Dead Lake
The Persuasion Industry (*with Graham Turner*)
The Life of Ian Fleming
Arena: The Story of the Colosseum
The Profession of Violence
Edward the Rake
Façades: Edith, Osbert and Sacherverell Sitwell
Stags and Serpents: The Cavendish Dukes of Devonshire
The Ultimate Family: The Making of the House of Windsor
Citadel of the Heart: Winston and the Churchill Dynasty
Painfully Rich: J. Paul Getty and His Heirs
Blood Royal: The Story of the Spencers and the Royals
The Cult of Violence

Fiction

Gone to Timbuctoo
The Life of James Bond
The Kindness of Dr Avicenna

JOHN PEARSON

THE CULT OF VIOLENCE
THE UNTOLD STORY OF THE KRAYS

ORION

An Orion paperback

First published in Great Britain in 2001
by Orion
This paperback edition published in 2002
by Orion Books Ltd,
Orion House, 5 Upper St Martin's Lane,
London WC2H 9EA

Pictures supplied by Hulton Deutsch Collection Ltd,
Mirror Syndication, Popperfoto, Topham Picturepoint,
Kate Howard, PA Photos, Mail Syndicate Ltd.

A CIP catalogue record for this book
is available from the British Library.

ISBN 0 75284 794 5

Typeset by Selwood Systems,
Midsomer Norton

Printed and bound in Great Britain by
Clays Ltd, St Ives plc

For Lynette, of course

CONTENTS

Acknowledgements

I would like to express my gratitude and thanks to the following people, who have all helped me in their different ways to research and write this book. Vida Adamoli, Bradley Allardyce, Dr Mufeed Ali, Stephen Berkoff, Jeremy Beadle, James Blackburn, Dave Courtney, Davie Crockett, David Cammell, Duncan Campbell, Roger Daltrey, Frankie Fraser, John Farran, Nick Frankland, Stan Frankland, Peter Gannon, Freddie Gore, Christopher Gibbs, Mark Goldstein, Ralph Haems, Dick Hobbs, Ben Hytner, Daniel Korn, Frank Kurylo, Roberta Kray, Kate Kray, Trevor Linn, Loretta Lay, the Revd Ken Leach, John McVicar, Dr James MacKeith, Colin MacCabe, Cal McCrystal, James Morton, George Melly, Harry Mooney, Wilf Pine, Jocy Pile, Aubrey Powell, Michael Peppiat, Charles Richardson, John Redgrave, Deborah Rogers, John Squibb, Dr Tomroi Sharma, Shura Shirag, Ian Sinclair, Dr Tim Spector, Tom Tanner, Paul Tickell, Harriet Vyner, Francis Wyndham, Snoo Wilson and Michael Young.

I must also thank my agent, Patrick Walsh, for his exuberant support, my splendid publisher, Trevor Dolby, who made the book possible, and his personal assistant, Pandora White, whose charm and efficiency smoothed the way. As usual Edda Tasiemka, of the amazing Tasiemka Archive, was an endless source of invaluable information. Mark Paton saved my sanity whenever my computer

Acknowledgements

betrayed me. Ted Green, though getting old now, did his best. And of course my very special thanks go to my wife, Lynette, who is a wonderful editor and who helped me all the way.

Preface

It is almost thirty-three years now since I first became involved with the Krays and, without knowing very much about them, rather casually agreed to become their 'official' biographer. The result, *The Profession of Violence*, became an international best-seller, and much to my surprise, only the other day, I was informed that, after the Bible, it is the most popular book in HM prisons.

The Cult of Violence is a different book, and tells a very different story. When I met the Krays, I was still a relatively young former newspaper reporter and *The Profession of Violence* was essentially a reporter's book, dealing with my immediate impressions, as I did my best to unravel what I now realise was an extremely complex story. When I wrote it I was also hampered by the fact that I possessed a vast amount of material I could not use – not just material about the Twins themselves, but also lengthy interviews with many who confided in me on the strict understanding that I did not mention them while either of the Twins was still alive. More important still, when I wrote *The Profession of Violence*, what I now believe to be the most important chapters in the Kray Twins' story had barely started. I ended *The Profession of Violence* with the sentence, 'Society was lucky; the Twins destroyed themselves.' But as the Twins would abundantly prove over the next thirty years, I could not have been more wrong.

While they spent the remainder of their lives in captivity 'repaying their debt to society', the Twins also established their reputation as the most celebrated criminals of our time, and created a myth which will probably outlast us all.

This is the story which *The Cult of Violence* seeks to tell. At the same time I have tried to give an explanation of what I think it was that made the Twins unique, and what lay behind the so-called Kray legend. Above all, now that the Twins and all the Kray family are dead, I feel free at last to tell the story of my personal involvement with the Krays and what I genuinely believe to be the truth about them.

ONE

Death of a Celebrity

Andrea (loudly): Unhappy the land that has no heroes.
Galileo: No. Unhappy the land that is in need of heroes.
Bertolt Brecht, *Galileo*

Finally, death kills even murderers. Reg Kray's death, however, was unlike that of any other killer. Although I'd known him for more than thirty years, as soon as I entered the hospital room where he was dying, I got the uneasy feeling I always had with him – that I was in the presence of a celebrity. There he was, gaunt and shrunken, an old murderer with a tube draining toxins from his stomach through his nose, but even on his deathbed, living off a saline drip, fame refused to let him be.

Reg Kray was the most famous criminal in England. And of course he knew it.

In the road outside the hospital, a bored television crew was on deathwatch, waiting for any news about him, as they had been ever since his second major cancer operation the week before. Press cameramen were still making nuisances of themselves, hoping to snatch a picture of his wife Roberta, or of any of the 'celebrated criminals' rumoured to be visiting him later in the day. Since Reg arrived at the hospital on 12 August 2000, there'd been so many enquiries from well-wishers that the switchboard had set up a special line with daily bulletins on his state of health. Most of the callers left personal get-well messages too.

I was shocked at how frail and small he had become since I saw him only ten days earlier. But, as usual, he had all his wits about him and, unlike Jack 'the Hat' McVitie, the fellow gangster he had murdered thirty-four years before, Reg Kray was being given time to die.

'Anything you want?' I asked him.

His smile hadn't changed; it was the same wry, faintly bitter, twisted little grin.

'I'd like a gin and tonic.'

He meant this as a joke. Gin had always been his favourite tipple in the old days, but we both knew he couldn't swallow. I also knew that all that really mattered to him now was how he was going to be remembered. As I expected, he was desperately concerned about his funeral. He was still driven by his lifelong passion for celebrity, even as he lay dying.

This thirst for fame was always crucial to his being. It helped him face his constant fear of death, and blocked off any feelings of regret, still less remorse, for anything he'd done.

'I'd do it all again,' he muttered when I asked him.

Why not? Unlike most of us, he would always be remembered. If anyone remembered poor old Jack 'the Hat' McVitie, it would be because the Krays had murdered him. Reg was the legend, Jack the legend's sacrificial victim. Jack was the price that fame demanded.

Of course the Twins had also had a price to pay – in Reg's case the thirty-two years and four months he had been locked up, with the best years of his life being amputated, year by year, as time dragged by. But throughout those years, most of them spent as a Category A prisoner in maximum security, his passion for celebrity had been at work, and popular fascination grew steadily around him and his identical twin brother, Ron. There were books on them, films, endless articles. Every taxi driver in London knew someone who had known the Krays. By the time Ron died of a heart attack in Broadmoor in 1995, the Twins had become celebrities at the centre of a powerfully promoted cult of violent crime which has influenced the way we think of criminals. Say the two words 'violent criminal' to virtually anyone today, and the response is automatic – 'Krays'.

As the embodiment of so-called 'gangster chic', the Kray Twins had attracted a wide following of young admirers, would-be gangsters and armchair psychopaths. As such they also helped to set the pattern for the current growth of British gangster movies. At the same time they became as firmly part of the dark mythology of British Crime as Dick Turpin, Bill Sykes and Jack the Ripper, while a nostalgic vision of the old East End (where they came from) with its old-style cockney villains gradually grew up around them.

This made them virtually unique as living criminal celebrities. Even America has no comparable example, with the possible exception of the flamboyant Mafia don John Gotti (currently serving three life sentences for murder and extortion).

As I tried to talk to Reg, chatting on about the people from his past that I had known – his old grandfather, his parents, his brother Ron – I remember thinking as I always did when I was with him what an outlandish celebrity he was. What had made this dying man so special, setting him so totally apart from other murderers, and why should the name Kray hold such magic for the media? Was it simply that the Twins had been exceptionally evil, or did some hidden threat they seemed to pose against society fascinate succeeding generations? Did their undoubted skill at courting fame account for the interest they aroused? Or did the answer lie within society itself, which has always been obsessed with violent crime?

In the end when Reg Kray died on 1 October 2000, in the Town House Hotel, Norwich, twenty-four days short of his sixty-seventh birthday, he suffered horribly, his tortured mind and cancer-riddled body bringing an agonising death, but to the very last considerations of his fame and reputation dogged his deathbed. Even then he could not be allowed to die in peace, and – as we shall see – extraordinary events occurred between his wife, the boy he loved and leaders of the old criminal fraternity, all of whom fought for his soul to the moment that it left his body.

I can't say I was shocked by this, any more than I was deeply moved by his departure. Apart from his former cell-mate Bradley Allardyce and his second wife Roberta, both of whom loved him in their different ways, few would genuinely mourn him. Although, with certain reservations, I had grown to like him, I didn't feel remotely sorry for him; for unlike any other convicted murderer I could think of, in his own strange terms his life had been an extraordinary success.

He would have certainly enjoyed the wide attention he received in the press and on television following his death, and although he would have been annoyed at the failure of *The Times* of London to carry his obituary, he would have been amused by the reason given by the editor: 'The only gangsters to whom we give obituaries are those who become heads of state.' In America the *New York Times* felt no such inhibitions, giving him a full half-page obituary, something normally accorded only to important film stars, financiers and politicians. It was the same with the press and television round the world. Strangely, though, none of the obituaries and none of the endless coverage in the press addressed the question that had puzzled me throughout the time I'd known him, and troubled me still as I watched him dying. What was it with the Twins that turned them into criminal celebrities?

Little concerning them was what it seemed, and I knew enough about them by then to understand that hidden away within their lives lay an extraordinarily complex story. Some of the secrets of this story lie hidden in their childhood, and some in the freakish make-up of their twin psychology. Much originated in a hushed-up scandal and the unique chemistry of Swinging London in the 1960s. I still remember sitting through every day in court as their much publicised Old Bailey trial in 1969, which was meant to utterly destroy them, in fact added to their allure. Afterwards I inadvertently played a role in this myself, for without my book, the cult around the Krays would not have grown as it did. Still more of the mysteries of the story reside in a society increasingly obsessed with violence and which, for whatever reason, seems to crave the company of dangerous murderers and can turn them into heroes.

TWO

Getting to Know the Twins

In life you should try everything once – except incest
and country dancing.
Stephen Fry

It was only when the date of Jack McVitie's murder was
given at the Kray Twins' trial at the Old Bailey that I
realised that I first met them eight days later. And only
recently, when re-reading a journal I was keeping at the
time, did I really understand the significance of that meeting in the context of the lives the Twins were living during
the months before they were arrested. That whole episode
explains much of what happened to them later. It also
marked the beginning of one of the strangest periods in my
life, which could have happened with no other criminals
in London, let alone a pair of gangsters who had just
performed their second murder.

In the autumn of 1967, I was living in Rome and totally
oblivious of how their distant crimes were going to affect
my life. So far the sixties had been kind to me. I'd had an
enviable time as a young reporter on the *Sunday Times*. For
a while I had worked in the London office with Ian
Fleming, and had watched as the cinema transformed my
colleague's *recherché* thrillers into the sixties fantasies of the
James Bond movies. After Ian's death I left the paper to
write his authorised biography.

Life seemed dangerously easy. The book took a year to

write, and thanks to the sudden popularity of the Bond movies, earned me far more money than any comparable biography would today. Taking the money and my good fortune very much for granted, I decamped to Rome, where I bought a flat beside the River Tiber. It seemed that luck like this would last for ever, and in a leisurely way I started researching a history of the Roman Colosseum.

It was then that the magic of the sixties started going wrong for me. My *dolce vita* in Rome came to an end. My wife left me for a very young Italian. I began to find the history of the Colosseum deeply depressing. Soon the tourists and the swallows were departing. I was more than ready for a new book and a new adventure.

These came in the unexpected form of my American publisher, Frank Taylor, editor-in-chief of the McGraw-Hill company in New York. Every autumn, like some eighteenth-century patron, Frank would descend on Rome at the start of a commissioning tour of Europe, one of the long-vanished perks of an older breed of New York editor. Out of the blue, one bright October morning, he rang, inviting me to lunch.

Frank was a great charmer but, as Saul Bellow once observed, 'charm is always a bit of a racket', and Frank was a bit of a racketeer himself. Bisexual and outrageous, with the height and grace of an elderly giraffe, he had somehow managed to combine the role of a successful editor with producing one of the classic movies of that magical decade – Arthur Miller's film *The Misfits*, with the legendary trio of Clark Gable, Monty Clift and Marilyn Monroe. In his role as publisher he had also managed to persuade the drunken and depressive writer Malcolm Lowry to complete another sixties' classic, his weird, beleagured novel *Under the Volcano*.

We lunched together at Passetto's, a deeply serious, old-style Roman restaurant, favourite haunt of gastronomes and Roman politicians, and I remember telling him about my discontents over a dish of risotto and white truffles. As always, Frank was sympathetic. When we parted, he promised he would try to think of something more exciting for me to write about than the history of the Colosseum.

From my experience of publishers, I thought that that would be the last I'd hear from Frank until the next time he turned up in Rome, but exactly one week later, he telephoned at breakfast time from Brown's Hotel in London. He sounded ominously excited.

'Listen,' he said, 'I've just had one of *the* most *fantastic* days of my life. I'm extremely rushed as I'm leaving for New York at noon, so there's no time to explain. I've just met the twins who run the London underworld, and they're very anxious to have a book written about them. I told them all about you, and I think that you should come over here at once. There's a ticket waiting for you at Fiumicino airport on the 5.15 p.m. BA flight to London Heathrow. There's also a reservation for you at the Ritz Hotel. Fly over, have dinner, spend the night there. Everything's taken care of. At nine tomorrow morning you'll be collected from the hotel by two men in a silver-grey Mercedes. They'll drive you off to the country for the day, and I think you'll find it one of the most extraordinary experiences of your life. When you meet these people, you may be worried about certain things you've heard about them already. Don't be. You have my *absolute guarantee* for your personal safety. If you think there's a book in them, we'll publish it.'

Before Frank hurried off, I just had time to ask the name of these people he wanted me to meet.

'The name,' Frank said, 'is Kray.'

Sure enough, at Fiumicino there were tickets waiting for

me. First-class return, Rome–London–Rome. And sure enough, at Heathrow it was raining; there were paper bags flying in the wind, piles of the *Evening Standard* at the bookstall and the unforgettable damp smell of an English autumn. I knew that I was back.

At the Ritz, someone had reserved a suite for me. But who? The clerk at reception didn't know, but the bill had been paid already. I took a bath, ate a lonely meal in the empty dining room and went to bed early. It all seemed so absurd that I wondered what would happen on the morrow, as one might at the beginning of a new chapter in an Eric Ambler thriller.

Next morning I had barely finished a full-scale English breakfast in my room when reception rang.

'Two gentlemen to see you downstairs, sir.'

The two men sitting in the hall were unlikely figures for the Ritz. One was very large, and one was very small. They were both called Tom.

'Ready to go then, sir?' said Large Tom, rising to his feet.

'We must get a move on. They're expecting us by midday, and we'd better not be late,' said Small Tom anxiously.

'Where are we going, then?' I asked.

'You'll see,' they both replied, more or less in unison.

A large, silver-grey Mercedes was parked in Arlington Street. We clambered in. With Large Tom at the wheel, we headed north.

Out of London we took the main Newmarket road. Traffic was heavy until we forked off to the right for Suffolk. Later I recognised the famous church at Lavenham, but once in Norfolk we were soon in a maze of country lanes where I lost all sense of direction. I seem to remember large park gates and a leafy drive, and then we crossed a moat around a rambling, pseudo-Elizabethan country house.

The only signs of life were three black swans moving slowly on the silent waters.

We entered a courtyard and parked beside a pale blue Rolls-Royce. Large Tom placed a large hand on the horn and as the echoes died away the iron-studded, mock-medieval front door opened and a short, good-looking man in checked trousers came out to welcome us.

'Good to see you, John. Frank told us all about you. Great guy, Frank Taylor. Come along in and meet the boys. They can't wait to see you.'

Such was my introduction to Geoff Allan, con man extraordinary, arsonist emeritus, compulsive gambler, dedicated womaniser, property tycoon and long-time friend, associate and protector of the Krays.

I could see at once why Frank had been so impressed when he came here, for the mysterious country mansion and the cockney geniality of Geoff Allan's welcome made this the perfect setting for the ultimate English gangster movie.

Then came my unforgettable first meeting with the Krays, in the great oak-panelled dining room, with the requisite portraits of slightly bogus-looking 'ancestors' hanging in gilt frames around the walls. In front of a baronial fireplace large enough to roast a human being stood the three men who would dominate my life for months to come. With their dark blue suits, white shirts and tightly knotted dark silk ties, they looked like three expensive undertakers.

'Meet Charles Kray, the Twins' elder brother, Mr Nice Guy,' said Geoff, and I found myself shaking hands with a tallish, fair-haired man of forty-something with a worried smile.

'And this is Ron.'

Ron Kray would have fascinated Ian Fleming, with his strong yet clammy handshake, the way he spoke as if suffering from a hidden speech impediment, the big gold bracelet watch and eyes that seemed to bulge with painfully suppressed aggression. Here was Dr No and Goldfinger and Mr Big in one extraordinary person.

'And this is Reg,' said Geoff.

Although they were obviously identical twins – the same height, of around five foot ten, the same dark hair and eyes of some gypsy forebear, and much the same mannerisms, Reg Kray was quicker and thinner than his twin, with a certain shifty charm. When we sat down for lunch, it was Reg who did the talking.

It was quite a gathering – besides Geoff Allan and the two Toms there were several other heavy-looking characters – but the Twins were very much in charge. Sadly the food failed to match the grand surroundings. As I soon discovered, English criminals eat badly, and I was lucky to be offered tinned ham and tongue and coleslaw. We drank light ale and a little hock from Yugoslavia.

There were many other uncomfortable things that I would discover about them later and when I look back to that day, my innocence appals me. When Frank told me that they ran the London underworld, I had accepted what he said implicitly. At the back of my mind was a vague memory of a libel action in which one of them – Ronnie? – had been involved with a member of the House of Lords some three or four years earlier, but that was all I could remember.

After my night at the Ritz, and naturally believing that they owned this stately home, I had every reason to believe that they were figures of extraordinary wealth and power in the world of English crime. So when Reg began explaining why he and his brothers wanted me to write their joint biography, the idea had an obvious appeal. Speaking in a rapid, sometimes all-but-inaudible monotone, he explained that he and his brothers were tiring of big-time crime and were planning to retire. As he said this, I could picture them enjoying their illicit wealth in these grand surroundings like robber barons. And, like many top businessmen weary of making money in the rough and tumble of what Ron would probably have called an 'interestin'' career, they wanted someone, he said, to record their achievements.

'So much rubbish gets written in the press about our sort of people, that me an' Ron both think it's time the truth was told for once.'

At the time this seemed reasonable enough, and with Frank Taylor so impressed by the Twins and their story that he was prepared to back me with McGraw's support, the prospect of the book was starting to appear inviting. I had the sense to ask how much they were prepared to tell me.

'Enough,' said Reg. 'We know a lot of people an' we've not been angels, but we've done nothing we're ashamed of. We'd have to hold a few things back so's not to get friends of ours in trouble. But we both think it could be a very interesting book.'

I thought so too, although I got the firm impression that what they wanted, more than a biography, was to have the story of their lives made into a film. They had seen almost every gangster movie ever made, and seemed particularly impressed by the recently released film *Bonnie and Clyde* – 'It's our sort of story,' Reg remarked mysteriously – and they could already see themselves as stars. This helped explain the connection with Frank Taylor.

Later I discovered that Frank's introduction to the Twins came via a Canadian lawyer in New York with Mafia connections and that most of their discussions had related to the film rights to the story of the Kray Twins' lives. They knew about Frank's career and his fame as a film producer, and were particularly impressed by his connection with Marilyn Monroe. As far as I was concerned, they probably liked the thought of sharing biographers with Ian Fleming.

I also later discovered that our meetings with the Twins were part of an elaborate scam that had been carefully arranged on their behalf by Geoff Allan. Far from belonging to the Krays, as Frank and I imagined, the mansion, Gedding Hall, had only recently been purchased at a knockdown price by Geoff. He later set fire to it, claimed on the insurance, restored it and sold it on to the pop celebrity Bill Wyman, whose much-loved stately home it is today. The pale blue Rolls also belonged to Geoff.

But what really mattered was that the Twins themselves were not exactly what they seemed. I had no idea, of course, of their recent murder of McVitie. During lunch I noticed that Reg's hand was bandaged. In fact, during the killing the kitchen knife had slipped and sliced his thumb in his efforts to despatch his victim. I remember mentioning the bandage, as I tried to make conversation.

'How did you hurt your hand?' I asked him brightly.

To which he made his now famous reply, 'Gardenin'.'

I still find it odd that at such a time the Twins were taking part in this elaborate performance for the benefit of Frank and me, while simultaneously keeping clear of the police. They can have barely washed McVitie's blood from their hands and disposed of his body, before they were on the phone to Frank Taylor in New York, finalising details of my trip to Norfolk.

By any standards this was strange behaviour. Ordinary criminals – and through the Krays I was soon to meet a lot of them – simply don't behave like this. Crime is, by necessity, a discreet profession. From your humblest pickpocket to the greatest City swindler, criminals have one important thing in common – they do their best to keep their criminal activities private. Yet here were the Krays, not picking pockets or milking a corporate pension fund but killing people, and setting me up to tell the world about it. For unless they were being even more naive than I was, which I don't believe they were, they must have known that any moderately competent biographer would find out in the end, as of course I did, that among their less endearing qualities was the fact that they were killers.

THREE

The Dungeon

Evil is not something superhuman, it's something less than human. Your criminal is somebody who wants to be important.

Agatha Christie

Once back in Rome, I rang Frank Taylor in New York, reporting on my trip to Gedding Hall.

'Isn't that house of theirs fabulous?' he said. 'And those black swans! Catch an American gangster with black swans, let alone a place like Gedding Hall. That's style. I think those Kray Twins are amazing. Particularly Ronnie. You realise he's gay?'

'I find him rather creepy.'

'But what a character! If you can really get the low-down on him and Reg, you'll have a winner.'

Encouraged by his enthusiasm, I said I'd like to make a longer trip to London and get properly acquainted with the Twins before making up my mind about writing their biography. He agreed.

At Gedding Hall, their brother Charlie had given me a London contact number, which I rang a few days later. He sounded guarded when I talked about my plans, and the thought struck me that the telephone was bugged. When I asked if he could find me somewhere suitable to stay in Bethnal Green, he was not forthcoming. However, perhaps he discussed the subject with his brothers, for he rang me back in an hour with the address of Blackwall Buildings.

* * *

Until they were demolished twenty-seven years ago, the Blackwall Buildings were one of the more depressing landmarks of the old East End. A soot-grimed Victorian block of tiny, two- and three-room flats built in the 1860s to house a fraction of the homeless poor of Bethnal Green, they stood in a small turning off the Bethnal Green Road, like a monument to the ultimate futility of Victorian philanthropy in this part of London. An old friend of the Twins who lived there as a boy used to call them 'barracks for the poor'.

I saw them first one late November Sunday afternoon, a few weeks after meeting the Krays at Gedding Hall. It was still three hours before the pubs opened and unremitting rain was pelting down. Along the road from Aldgate East underground station, the coster stalls stood empty, lashed up against the rain with old tarpaulins. By the look of it, the human race had wisely vanished for the afternoon.

It had clearly given up on the Blackwall Buildings too. No lights were on in any of its grimy windows, and the courtyard was slippery with uncollected refuse.

By the time my taxi-driver found the place, Little Tom was waiting for me on the pavement, looking like a drowning ferret.

'Home sweet home,' he said, taking my smart Italian suitcase and leading me across the courtyard. 'Here you are,' he said, sounding like a hotel porter. 'Flat number two. Easy to remember. Ronnie says he hopes you like it.'

He had to struggle with the door, but finally wrenched it open and turned on the light.

The last time I'd seen a room like this was in a slum in Calcutta. The grey curtains were permanently drawn, the window, I soon discovered, had been boarded up, the light came from a naked light bulb hanging from a mottled ceiling. The room exuded mildew and decay and years of stale tobacco. The Krays, I learned, had christened it 'the Dungeon'; what they had used it for I dread to think. After their arrest, the police took up the floorboards, searching – unsuccessfully – for Jack McVitie's body.

Tom showed me the bedroom. Someone had made up the bed, but I noticed that the iron bedstead had a broken leg and was supported at one corner by a packing case. Tom appeared embarrassed, but I was not particularly disturbed, still believing that a writer worth his salt should be able to endure anything. Besides, I was fascinated by the contrast between Gedding Hall and this. I knew that the Krays were deeply rooted in the old East End, but surely it couldn't be this squalid. I'd have liked to have talked to Little Tom about it, but he was looking nervous and clearly couldn't wait to get away.

'Reg'll be calling for you here around seven o'clock. There's teabags in the cupboard. Make yourself at home. I'll see you later.' With which he was gone.

I had started unpacking when I was interrupted by a timid knocking at the front door. I opened it cautiously but need not have worried. Night was falling and outside in the rain, as wet as a pair of mermaids, stood two of the weirdest women I had ever seen. One was very tall and thin with no front teeth.

'Ullo, I'm Tall Teth,' she whispered.

Her companion was short and round as a dumpling.

'And I'm Trixie. Reggie sent us round. 'E thought you might be lonely.'

I could hardly turn them back into the rain, and any friendly face was welcome at a time like this, so I asked them in. They seemed to know the flat already.

'The bed here'th dreadful,' lisped Tall Tess. 'But we can manage. Do you want me firtht or Trix, or would you like uth both together?'

Not wishing to hurt the two girls' feelings, I declined Tall Tess's offer as politely as possible, and was faintly put out to see that both of them were obviously relieved. Instead of sex we had a nice strong cup of tea. Both girls were great talkers, particularly Tess, but just as with Little Tom, whenever I asked anything about the Krays, they changed the subject, and we ended up chatting about our children. Both girls seemed to be devoted mothers. Tess had a son of eight called Daren. Trixie's two-year-old daughter, Beverley, was already 'into everything'. After half an hour or so, the rain ceased and the girls departed. I was sad to see them go.

It was closer to eight than seven when Reg arrived. Although it was Sunday, he was still in a dark blue suit and clean white shirt, both of which, I learned, were a sort of Kray family livery. He seemed more relaxed than he had been at Gedding Hall. Indeed he was positively affable, and even apologised for the flat.

'It was Ron's idea of a joke. Ron's very humorous.'

I replied that I liked people with a sense of humour.

'Then you'll get on well with Ron,' he said.

Reg's car was a disappointment. I had been hoping for the pale blue Rolls or a bulletproof Cadillac; instead there was an elderly grey Austin with a badly dented bumper. It was driven by a bulky figure introduced as 'Geoff'.

'I've given up on driving,' Reg explained. 'Whenever I drive, the law always tries to fit me up for some motorin' offence or other. I can do without that sort of aggravation.' (In fact, as I discovered later, both he and Ron were such appalling drivers that it was not safe to let either of them loose behind the wheel.)

Our journey took ten minutes and ended at the Old Horns, a tiny pub discreetly tucked away in a narrow turning off the Whitechapel Road. When I followed Reg into the crammed saloon bar, it was like stepping back in time to a tougher, rougher London which has now gone for ever. It seemed packed with hefty-looking characters, most of them in their Sunday best. The tobacco smoke was powerful enough to fumigate a polecat. The noise was just as powerful, most of it coming from a tiny hunch-backed pianist in horn-rimmed spectacles, pounding away at the pub piano like a mad percussionist.

'That's Lil,' shouted Reg above the din. 'Me brother's favourite pianist.'

Not only did Lil play; she also sang, with a strength remarkable in one so small. I listened to the words.

'I'll bring you bluebirds in the spring … But most of all, when shadows fall, I'll bring you *love*.'

As the ballad ended I found myself shaking hands with Ron, but this was a very different Ron Kray from the threatening figure I had met at Gedding Hall. He was smiling gently as he watched the scene before him through his rimless spectacles. I would discover that the Twins could both be deeply sentimental.

'Lovely, ain't she?' he murmured. 'I just think she's lovely. That's my favourite song. She sings it specially for me.'

He was standing at the far end of the bar, a strategic position favoured by old bar fighters, with several already opened bottles of light ale at his elbow – 'Ron has the record for downing light ale. Fifty-four at a sitting,' someone told me. I would rarely see Ron Kray as happy as he was that evening. As he stood there in his favourite pub, surrounded by a servile throng of ageing criminals, he made me think of some weird feudal magnate, surrounded by his followers.

Most impressive of these was Cha-Cha, a former wrestler from Basutoland. He was built like a packing-case. His great square head was completely bald and shiny and although he rarely spoke, he possessed great dignity. Like some old retainer, he addressed the twins as 'Mr Ronald' and 'Mr Reginald'.

Ron had also hired two dwarfs from a local circus for the evening. He beckoned to them, and they came trotting over. One grasped my trouser-leg. 'Just you write the truth about the Twins or we'll kill you,' he shouted in a piping treble. Ron laughed mirthlessly.

The drinks that night were on the house and, as usual, paid for by the Twins, who used the pub as their private club – any stray outsider who had blundered in would have rapidly departed. Marital problems had given me a gastric ulcer, which was as good an excuse as any for drinking nothing more than half a pint of bitter.

I began to realise that the pub was filled exclusively with criminals summoned from the four corners of London to meet the Twins' biographer. It was a strange occasion, conducted with terrible propriety. With Lil now pumping out 'The White Cliffs of Dover' on the piano, Reg did the introductions, and I found myself meeting a gallery of London criminals.

'This is Fred, who robs banks, and Lennie here's the best safe-blower in London.'

Most of them were colourful old-timers. There was Jim, the getaway driver, who once escaped from the police by driving a stolen Bentley at top speed in reverse the length of Bond Street. There were two members of the Hoxton 'whizz-mob', a gang at the bottom of the criminal pecking order, who specialised in working football crowds and picking pockets. There were fences and con men and burglars and a man with a stutter who fixed up stolen cars. As they talked about their different occupations, I was reminded of a Rotarian dinner I once attended. Most of these friendly figures seemed to have the true Rotarian's sense of social worth and dedication to his calling.

I found myself stuck with a former gambler and thief from Whitechapel called Sammy Lederman. He was a voluble little man and a friend of the Twins who claimed to have known most of the famous London criminals over the last half century – the Sabini brothers from Saffron Hill who organised the race-track gangs in the 1930s, their successor, Billie Hill – 'shrewd man Billie, even if he did spend seventeen years inside' – and the celebrated Jack 'Spot' Comer, who at one time 'ruled' the gambling and most of the protection rackets in the West End of London.

'I knew Jack like he was my brother. I was with him when we broke up Mosley's Fascist marches down Cable Street before the war. And when Jack started getting flash, I warned him it would be his downfall. It was then I saw the potential of the Twins, and knew that one day they'd be taking over. I warned Jack, and as usual I was right. But the Twins are different from the others. You know why?'

I shook my head, keen to know their secret.

"They're gentlemen. I've watched those boys from the beginning, and I know the good they've done – the charities they've supported, and them they've helped. Anyone in trouble only had to ask. I'm telling you, one day there'll be a statue here in Bethnal Green to the Twins for what they really are – benefactors. Am I right, Charlie?

This was said to Charlie Clark, a handsome old cat burglar from King's Cross.

'Absolutely,' Charlie said.

The landlord, personable Teddy Berry, also nodded, then changed the subject to the Twins' virtuosity as boxers. His father, old Harry Kid Berry, was a famous East End flyweight who had trained them both as boys at the Repton Boys' Club.

'He always said the Twins were the most promising

boxers he'd ever known. Ronnie had no fear. He wasn't what you'd call a fancy fighter, but he'd take on anyone and he'd take any amount of punishment. He was so strong that nobody could beat him. The elder brother Charlie was a lovely boxer who fought for the Royal Navy. But Reggie was the star, a natural. He had everything it takes to make a champion.'

'Why did he give it up?' I asked.

Did I detect the faintest shadow of a smile on Teddy Berry's battered countenance?

'Ask him,' he answered.

The whole evening was of course a set-up, aimed principally at convincing me of the truth of certain important public relations themes that the Twins were constantly putting round about themselves. Even I could tell that everyone I spoke to had all been carefully rehearsed over what they told me. I was to hear many virtually identical conversations during the months ahead, which would boil down to two key subjects in the end: the Twins' unrivalled early skill as boxers and their role as kind-hearted benefactors to the whole East End community.

I'm not sure how long I spent listening to this, with my solitary glass of bitter, at the Old Horns, but I do remember feeling ravenous, as I'd eaten nothing since leaving Rome that morning. But Ron seemed so happy with his light ales and his faithful followers that it was long after closing time before Reg could lever him away.

Five or six of us piled into two cars parked outside the pub and we headed west. Once again I had no idea where we were going, and was in for another of those culture shocks that seemed to be a feature of life with the Krays.

It was years since I'd been inside the Astor Club in Mayfair. Just off Berkeley Square, it used to be one of the West End's more prestigious nightclubs, favoured haunt of débutantes, young officers from the Cavalry Club and advertising executives trying to seduce their secretaries. But times had changed, and now the Astor was apparently attracting a rather different clientele.

There were six of us by now – the Twins, their brother Charlie, Charlie Clark and genial Geoff Allan, who had appeared quite suddenly, late in the evening. The uniformed doorman greeted the Twins with reverence, and the Mâitre D grovelled in their presence. Neither twin appeared to take the faintest notice. They were clearly as well known here as back in Bethnal Green and seemed perfectly at home. We were shown to what seemed to be their usual table.

I have no recollection of what was said at the meal, but I do remember that the food was delicious – I had artichoke soup, followed by *blanquette de veau*. A bottle of champagne arrived with the compliments of the management. Thanks to my ulcer, I was unable to enjoy it, and I seem to think that Ron was drinking Scotch with very little water, while Reg, now sunk in silent gloom, was consuming neat Gordon's gin in alarming quantities.

It was well after two o'clock before I felt able to leave. Everyone else was drinking heavily by now but Reg, in spite of being very drunk, insisted on seeing me out and making sure I had a taxi.

At 2.30 in the morning, the Buildings were silent as the tomb, and I fell asleep at once on my three-legged bed in that airless little mausoleum.

FOUR

Fort Vallance

The East End was a land of the living dead, a symbol to all of the consequences that befell those unable to partake in the normal activities of capitalism.
Dick Hobbs, *Doing the Business*

The next day I was awakened by the morning noises from the nearby Thames – the distant hoot of a tug passing up river, the wail of a siren from the docks. Then, shortly after eight, someone started banging on my door.

Outside was Little Tom. I was becoming quite attached to him. He was my minder and I liked the way he looked after me as if I was a foreigner of strictly limited intelligence. He waited as I shaved in cold water, then took me, still without a word, for breakfast up the road at Pellici's Caff in Bethnal Green Road. Here, among the down-and-outs and dockers, he purchased for me a mug of strong sweet tea and a ham sandwich wrapped in cellophane.

'What are the plans?' I asked.

'We're visiting Fort Vallance. Reg wants to introduce you to the family.'

'And Ron?' I asked.

'Ron's not an early riser.'

After Gedding Hall I half-pictured Fort Vallance as some turreted Kray stronghold set in the dark recesses of the old East End. So I was disappointed to discover it was just the local nickname for the Kray family home – number 178 Vallance Road.

Like much within their world, it was under sentence of death even as I saw it. Some months earlier the whole of Vallance Road had been condemned as unfit for human habitation, and all the remaining little nineteenth-century terraced houses were scheduled for demolition. Three months later the remaining members of the Kray family living in the neighbourhood were rehoused, and the Twins' parents took possession of a top-floor flat in a nine-storey tower block on the edge of the City, in Bunhill Row – the street where Milton wrote *Paradise Lost* and Defoe was buried, on the edge of what was then a very different London.

This meant that for the Krays, as for so many old inhabitants of Bethnal Green, the core of the family who'd clung together for so many years in Vallance Road was dispersed and lost their corporate identity. What I was seeing that morning was a last glimpse of the family before then, as it had survived the misery of the thirties and the bleakest years of the Dickensian East End.

Reg was already there when we arrived. As I learned later, he had great powers of recovery and seemed none the worse for the previous night's excesses. Gone was the gloomy figure from the Astor Club, drinking to forget whatever was tormenting him, and he was clearly happy to be showing me where he spent his childhood.

Technically, Fort Vallance was a slum – an unhealthy little four-roomed terraced house of the sort that once made up mile upon depressing mile of some of the most frightful housing in the country. There was a yard at the back, half filled with refuse, an outside lavatory, no damp course and no proper bathroom.

Reg was deeply sentimental as he talked about it. 'It's the

only house I've ever lived in where I really felt at home,' he said, and despite the squalor I could understand how safe and positively cosy it must have seemed to him. He clearly felt the same about this whole doomed stretch of Vallance Road. The warren of tiny houses was interspersed with narrow alleyways, the doors were rarely locked and everybody knew his neighbour. At the end of the street was a boundary in the form of the smoke-blackened viaduct which carried the main line into Liverpool Street station, less than five minutes away, but the Krays and the City commuters on the trains could have been living on two separate planets.

Reg showed me the scruffy back yard and pointed out the coal hole.

'That's where we hid our father when he was on the run from the police.'

In the front bedroom there was a meat hook fixed to the floor.

'And that's where he fixed a punch bag for me an' Ron when we was training to be boxers.'

He pointed out the tiny bedroom off the stairs, which the Twins had shared throughout their adolescence. Then he took me to the kitchen, where he introduced me to his mother.

Instead of the blousy harridan I was half expecting, I found myself shaking hands with a cockney Queen of Mothers wearing a smart mauve knitted dress. The colour suited her. She had pale blue eyes and discreetly dyed blonde hair, and although she was now in her early sixties, she had something of the quiet confidence of an older woman who was once good-looking. There was also a warmth about her. I liked her instantly, but then everybody liked Violet Kray – even the police. Although I knew her as the mother of two notable criminals, what struck me was the aura of intense respectability around her.

During the dramas and disasters that soon engulfed her (of which more later), I never saw her show the faintest sign of self-pity or despair. Certainly she never lost her dignity; nor would she lose her absolute devotion to her Twins, who had always been the centre of her world.

But like everyone around the Twins, Violet Kray was not exactly what she seemed, and although I came to know her well, I always found her an enigma. How much did she really know about the Twins' activities, and had she secretly encouraged them? I never knew, although there were those who thought she had.

One thing was obvious about her from the start: in her own quiet way, Violet was one of nature's snobs. She took it for granted, as the mother of two famous sons, that it was perfectly natural for me to be writing a book about them. She couldn't wait to tell me of the celebrities who'd been to Vallance Road, and if she was telling me the truth – and I soon found out that Violet rarely lied, except to the police – along with world-famous boxers such as Joe Louis and Rocky Marciano, there had been several members of the House of Lords, and stars such as Judy Garland and Diana Dors; and she spent several minutes describing how George Raft had called and stayed for tea.

Then she told me the story of how the boys bought her a racehorse called Solway Cross – 'lovely horse. Pity it never won a race' – and how they had taken her on holiday to Majorca. At Reg's prompting, she produced two mammoth cuttings albums in which she'd pasted up the press reports from the Twins' careers, as if they were successful pop stars. Although the cuttings dated back to their earliest days as boxers, she seemed just as proud of the accounts of their crimes, their acts of violence, and their court appearances, all of which she had neatly pasted in.

It was then that I realised what it was about Vi Kray that I found so disconcerting. On the one hand she embodied most of the family values of my own mother – good manners, respectability, faith in her children and a keen desire to get ahead of the Jones's. Where she differed was in the way she seemed to look on violent crime as the natural path down which her boys had had to go in order to achieve the status and success she'd always wanted for herself and for her family.

I understood Vi Kray a little better after meeting other members of the family. Reg was keen for me to see his aunt, Vi's younger sister, Auntie May, who lived next door at number 176. But Auntie May was not at home so, nothing daunted, he opened the front door of the next house down the street.

The small front room was empty. 'It's Reg,' he shouted, opening the door to the room beyond. There in the tiny back parlour of the house, with a coal fire blazing in an iron grate, sat Violet's parents, the Twins' maternal grandparents, Jimmie 'the Southpaw Cannonball' Lee, and his wife. The atmosphere was like the lair of some hibernating animal.

Cannonball was tiny, and had washed-out pale blue eyes, abundant grey-black hair, and a face as gnarled and knotted as an ancient olive. He was ninety-two, but still had an air of wonderful wickedness about him. He rose from his armchair by the fire as we entered, and, recognising Reg, grinned toothlessly and started sparring.

Blocking a sharp right jab from the old pugilist, Reg introduced us. 'Grandad, show John your famous left,' he shouted.

Cannonball was deaf, but started going through the crab-like motions of an old-style boxer, very fast, with shoulders hunched, fists mottled brown and purple and the knuckles of his left hand swollen with arthritis after eighty years of punching.

If the desire for fame can be inherited, much of the Twins' passion for celebrity must have come from Cannonball. I could see that he was a natural showman; having been in his time a boxer, juggler, street performer and impromptu poet, he had become something of an East End character. He still had all his wits about him, which he must have needed in order to survive and even prosper in the pitiless wilderness of the old East End.

His wife was a large silent woman and Cannonball did the talking, as I imagine he always had. His was a tale of extraordinary survival. He told me how the name Lee was Romany. His mother was Irish, but his father, John Quicher Lee, was also 'part Yiddish'. His father had worked as a butcher, taken to the bottle, attempted to kill his wife and all their children in a drunken frenzy, and died in a lunatic asylum. This fearful story explained why Cannonball had been a strict teetotaller all his life.

Despite his size, he had been a famous boxer in his day – 'all my strength was in my left hand, which was why I was known as the Southpaw Cannonball'. Weighing just nine stone, he fought professionally as a featherweight and used to take on all comers of all weights at five pounds a time. He said he never lost a fight. As well as boxing, he'd tried everything he could think of to make a living, working in the market, running a haulage business 'with 23 wagons till we went bust in the Depression', and then somehow supporting the family by performing on the old East End music halls. He could recite poetry of his own composition and walk across upended bottles, and had learned 'from a big black fellow on Mile End Waste' how to lick a white-hot poker. This became his *pièce de resistance*. 'You're safe enough as long as the poker's white-hot. If it's just red-hot you lose your tongue.'

Apart from his extraordinary toughness, what came over most of all was the iron-clad Victorian morality with which old Cannonball seemed to rule his family: no alcohol was ever permitted in the house, the women were kept firmly in their places, and always and whatever happened, Cannonball's word was law.

Along with the Twins' obsession with celebrity, I imagine that much of their inborn love of violence and fighting must have come from Cannonball as well, for the old man was clearly quite a scrapper.

'There were a lot of street fights in the old days, and because of who I was, people seemed to want to have a go at me. One night in Whitechapel, Mike Thomson came for me with a brick. I told him, "if you want to have a go, have a go, but let's fight clean," and up came the old left, straight from the shoulder and landed crack on the bridge of his nose. That took care of 'im. Same with Peter Ellis. He came for me one night, down in the Cut. The police didn't dare go to the Cut at night in them days, so it was safe enough for a fight. I only 'ad to 'it 'im once and, as usual, once was enough.'

It seems that his reputation as a streetfighter made Cannonball a local hero, so when the Twins began fighting in the streets of Bethnal Green themselves, no one was going to criticise them for following in Grandad's footsteps. All the same, I was puzzled by the way this tough old martinet who, as I soon discovered, like some cockney Mr Barratt of Wimpole Street, had disowned his daughter for marrying beneath her, could be so proud of his two grandsons for being such successful criminals.

* * *

Violet explained the saga of her marriage when I returned to Vallance Road that afternoon.

'We was all like devoted as a family. There was us three sisters, Rosie, May an' me, an' my brother, Johnnie, who kept a caff across the road in Vallance Road. Everyone used to know us and they used to call Vallance Road 'Lee Street'. I'd say as we was very well looked after as children. Always. Me mum'd see to that. An' we always lived very close together.

'The only trouble was my dad. He was terrible strict. Us girls all had to be in by nine o'clock, every night. I used to like life. Always have. And I was the one who couldn't get home on time. I used to go all up Mare Street to the dance halls and I never could seem to get home on time, no matter how hard I tried. As my dad worked in the market, he had to be up early, and I can remember creeping up the stairs so's not to wake him up.'

She smiled at the memory of what had happened.

'Sounds daft, but that's why I got married at seventeen. That's what I put it down to. Me bein' young and silly, an' him so strict, I thought I'd do anything to get out.' Having met her formidable father, I could understand how at seventeen pretty Violet had accepted the advances of dapper Charles Kray.

'Course he disowned me completely. No proper wedding, nor anything like that, an' he wouldn't even come to the register office in the Kingsland Road. We got married on 6 March 1927.

'I had my first nine months later. We called him Charlie after Mr Kray and after he was born there was a sort of reconciliation in the family, although my dad still wouldn't talk to my husband.'

I was keen to meet the object of Canonball's dislike, but

Charles Kray proved elusive. I eventually tracked him down, a few days later: Violet arranged a meeting in a Lyons teashop in Bishopsgate. He was almost as much of a surprise as Violet. He was wearing shiny winkle-pickers and a very bright blue suit for the occasion. What struck me from the start was how much of him there was in both the Twins, particularly in Reg – a canniness combined with the vein of permanent suspicion, a faintly servile manner in the presence of what he would have termed 'his betters', dark agate eyes, which Reg – but curiously not Ron – seemed to have inherited.

Once he started talking I realised that Charles Kray was a clever man in his way, who, like his hated father-in-law, had earned a lot of money by his wits. But there the resemblance ended. Charles was not a fighter but a drinker and a gambler. Had he not been, he could have made a fortune, and as he said regretfully on numerous occasions, 'I'd have moved the family out of Bethnal Green to a nice house in Gidea Park. Then none of the trouble would have started.'

He told me that he was born in 1906 in Stene Street, Haggerston, and I was fascinated that the Twins had another battling grandad on his side of the family. 'My father was a tough old boy, very good-looking, but wild. Same type as Ronnie. He was known as "Mad Jimmy Kray".

'When I left school I started off with a barrow like him, going to Covent Garden market early in the morning and buying aspidistras to sell to the Italians in Clerkenwell and Bloomsbury. But there was no money in aspidistras, so I got into wardrobe dealing and saw there was good money in second-hand clothes, if you looked the part and knew how to handle people properly. I put the old man on to it as well, and told him he'd have to wear a collar and tie instead of the white stook [stock] he'd worn round his neck all his life. Then around 1930 I moved into buying old gold as well as old clothes. It could bring you in a lot if you had your wits about you.

'How much? That's as may be. We'd go off to the country for a fortnight at a time in a clapped-out van I'd bought. Sometimes we'd get as far as Dorset and even Somerset, and we could make up to forty or fifty quid a week. You'd take your scales – we called 'em "jumpers" – they'd weigh up to four ounces. And you'd knock on a door and say, "Excuse me, madam, but I just wondered if by any chance you have any old gold or silver."

'The first time they'd always say no. And you'd have to say, "It doesn't matter at all, madam, but it so happens I'll be passing back this way in half an hour." A bloody lie, of course, but you gotta tell a few lies in life. That's business. When you came back you'd be surprised how often they'd have found you something. I used to sell to Abe Sokolok in Black Lion Yard Whitechapel on Sunday mornings, him being Yiddish. And most weeks I'd come back from him with thirty or forty quid for the gold alone. Before the war I can tell you that was real money.'

Charlie refused anything to eat, and sat sipping tea with evident distaste.

'I've always been free,' he mused. 'That's how I like it. I don't believe in workin' for a guvnor. That's a mug's game. Of course, most of what I made I lost, gambling and drinking, but at least I had the enjoyment of it, which was something.'

He told me of how when the Second World War came he was called up, served three weeks in a barracks at Devizes, then deserted and returned to the wardrobe business. Fifteen months later he was caught in Cambridge Heath Road, served nine months in the Artillery, and was sent to the depot at Hounslow with the promise of a posting as a batman. 'At the last minute I found out it was a drafting depot. I said to myself, "I came here to play the game, not to be sent off somewhere daft abroad." So I went on the trot again and took the train back to Whitechapel and that was that. For the next twenty-three years I was a deserter, though I still earned a living from the wardrobe business.'

For the Twins this not only meant they had a father who was rarely at home, but also one who was on the run from the police, living much of the time under a false name in the East End underworld. Since Charlie clearly had a taste for low life, this must have suited him.

'Funny thing, the crime business,' he remarked. 'I was brought up with most of the famous villains in the old East End. Knew 'em all in my time, 'specially when I was on the trot. Me being a gambler and playin' dice and cards, I used to go to the Spreadeagle in Shoreditch, where I met the likes of Dodger Mullins, Jimmy Murrell, Arthur Treserden and Harry Mellership. Villains all of 'em. But I couldn't see anything in it. Say you get caught for doin' a grand and get ten years for it, I ask you, what does it represent? How much a week?'

He grinned.

'Too much like hard work for me. Course, if it was necessary to 'ave a go, I'd stand up for myself an' 'ave a go, but I didn't enjoy fightin' for the sake of it. That was something that I never could get home to the Twins, not to neither of 'em. I rucked 'em and rucked 'em when they was young but it never seemed to do no good. An' anyhow after he's fifteen I don't think there's much you can do to hold a boy back if that's the way he's inclined.'

He paused and lit a cigarette.

'That's why I think you really 'ave to be born that way. I wasn't, but the Twins was.'

The marriage of Charles and Violet Kray was a long and

unhappy one that would last until Violet's death in 1982. Much later it struck me that in a strange way this pair of parents represented two clear forces that had always been in opposition in the old East End and were at odds within the Twins' natures, as an inheritance from deep within the old East End itself.

Charlie was really a creature from the past, with his deep involvement in the Cockney low life that dated back to the time of Dickens, while Violet embodied the typical East Ender's desire to escape from the surrounding misery and poverty and 'make themself somebody'.

The Twins both embodied and suffered from this divided inheritance, as we shall see, with their career as criminals combining their mother's craving for respectability and success with their father's love of low life, violent crime and easy money. Violet represented the Twins' constant urge for celebrity and acceptance, Charlie their deep nostalgia for the past. Ron in particular had a lifelong fascination with the legendary villains, pugilists and violent heroes of the old East End that was clearly something he had picked up from his father.

To understand this legacy fully one must understand more about the world they came from.

During the nineteenth century there was nowhere in the whole of Britain where the poverty that followed in the wake of the Industrial Revolution created a culture of such unique deprivation as in the East End of London. By the time Queen Victoria came to the throne, a string of once-picturesque Thameside villages like Stepney and Whitechapel and Bethnal Green had become the dumping ground for the richest city in the world.

Beyond London Docks was where most of the activities took place which the city did not wish to see, smell or be aware of – the tanneries and breweries and sweat shops and the dwellings of the poorest of the poor. This was where the penniless migrants from abroad were forced to settle – French Huguenots escaping from religious persecution, Irish refugees from the potato famine and Jews from the pogroms of Eastern Europe. There was virtually no law, no sanitation and no control. After travelling the world the American writer Jack London said in his book *The People of the Abyss* that 'no more dreary spectacle can be found on this earth than the whole of that "awful east".'

Its population lived off the city that rejected them. Those who could earned starvation wages in the docks or by sewing shirts or making matches. Those who couldn't turned to crime or prostitution; violence was endemic and inevitable. What morality there was centred on survival, loyalty to the family and the tribe, and deep suspicion of the world outside; all combined in an ethos that united these excluded people. This ethos produced in the old East Enders many of the attitudes the Twins would come to exemplify. Combined with their overriding sense of tribal solidarity was a contempt for 'middle-class morality'. True East Enders would never 'grass' to the police. They were loyal to each other, and they lived by a code of conduct all their own.

But there was another important fact about this whole benighted area, which set it totally apart from the other deprived areas in the country. Westwards up the Bethnal Green Road, past Tubby Issacs's famous whelk stall and Bishopsgate, was the Bank of England, the Stock Exchange and the richest financial centre in the world. Being so close, neither the east nor west could ever really manage to escape the other.

The East End resented and despised the rich world up the road, while for the West End and the City, and indeed for much of respectable, middle-class England, 'the awful East' was a nightmare and, for just a few, a burden on their consciences. Because of its proximity, respectable Londoners were wary and sometimes frightened of this dangerous part of London, where violence could erupt at any time – as it did in the period of near starvation in the 1860s when 'a mob' of 20,000 East Enders marched through the City to Trafalgar Square to demand a living wage. (They didn't get it.)

Even more threatening in its way was the fact that the mysterious East End had become synonymous with evil and depravity. This was encapsulated in fiction: in Dickens's novels, Bill Sykes and Fagin would always be reminders of the brutality and wickedness of East End crime, while Limehouse was where the wicked Fu Manchu had his stronghold, and where Sherlock Holmes would come to smoke his opium. At a more gruesome level, not in fiction but in reality, there was the disembowelling and murder of six prostitutes in Whitechapel and Bethnal Green, which turned the anonymous killer, 'Jack the Ripper', into an East End character who would live for ever.

For the Krays, born into this culture and all its associations, the old East End was above all a lawless area where their own myths would one day flourish. In a way this made it like the American Wild West, where the criminal outlaw stood alone, and where all that counted was his grit, his ruthlessness and ultimately his willingness to kill.

FIVE

'Twins is Special'

Twins who closely resemble each other in childhood
and early youth, and are reared under not very dissimilar
conditions, either grow unalike through the development
of natural characteristics which had lain dormant at first,
or else they continue their lives, keeping time like two
watches, hardly to be thrown out of accord except by
some physical jar.

Sir Francis Galton, 1875

'Oh, they was lovely. Everybody loved the Twins. When
they was tiny, I knitted them white woolly hats, an' when I
pushed 'em out together in their pram down the Kingsland
Road, they looked just like a pair of little bunny rabbits.'

I imagine Hitler's mother might have talked like this
about young Adolf, but Vi Kray's Twins would be her
bunny rabbits to the day she died. Her absolute devotion
to them both was obvious, but it took me a while to
understand how closely this was linked to the fact that they
were twins. I remember asking her once about their elder
brother, Charlie, as a child.

'Oh, Charlie was a lovely little boy. Real lovely. Never
no trouble and good as gold. But the Twins was different.
Twins is special.'

This was tough on Charlie, who would suffer just because
the Twins were 'special' all his life; so, in their different
ways, would all the members of the family. But for Violet,
her new babies, by the very fact of being twins, became the
centre of her life from the moment they were born.

It was only when she talked about her early unhappy

years of marriage that I understood the bleakness of the life
that she had landed herself in by marrying the elusive Mr
Kray. Not only was she suddenly cut off from the love and
the security, however strict, of her parents and her sisters,
but even after the birth of Charlie, she was still living
cheek-by-jowl with her in-laws in their tiny house in
Hoxton. She was seeing her mother, but Cannonball was
still rejecting her, although a sort of reconciliation
followed Charlie's birth. Then in 1933 the twins were
born. 'While I was expecting I used to go to a sort of
nursing place in the Kingsland Road and the night before
they was born they examined me an' said, "I think you
could be 'aving twins," just like that. I s'pose I was a bit
took aback at the time, but when they was born the Twins
was so lovely. Everybody spoiled 'em, even my dad. With
the Twins somehow you couldn't 'elp yourself.' Only with
their birth was Violet able to feel truly reunited with her
family, which made the Twins additionally important.

'My Dad just loved the Twins,' she said. 'In his eyes
nothing they could do was wrong.' It was, of course, the
same for her. In the last resort the twins were hers, and
quite unlike any other children she had ever known. Violet
was the only one who really understood them and, I
suspect, apart from each other, the only person that they
ever really loved.

By then her sisters, Rose and May, had married, and
moved close to their parents' house in Vallance Road, and
her brother John had followed. When the Twins were
born, Charles agreed to move to number 178, and Violet
was back at the centre of her family.

When she was pushing the Twins out in their shiny pram
down the Kingsland Road, Violet felt special too. She
could even see herself in the glamorous film-star role that
she and her sisters used to dream about before they married.

The Twins became her comfort, and her compensation for the disappointments in her marriage. And as the Twins grew, she instinctively taught herself that whatever happened, she would never blame them or reject them. During those first days when I was staying in the Blackwall Buildings and used to chat with her over endless cups of tea in Vallance Road, I would come away wondering if Vi Kray was extremely stupid or really rather wicked. In the end I decided she was neither, but that her dependence on the Twins was embedded deep within her, and had been there from the moment of their birth.

But this was only the beginning of the story. From what Violet told me and from what I discovered later, I believe that early in their childhood, something happened that transformed the whole relationship between the Twins themselves.

I clearly remember one of our early conversations when Violet told me what occurred. I had been sitting with her in the parlour when she lit a cigarette and turned down the television, as she sometimes did to emphasise what she was saying. She began by telling me how the Twins had fallen ill shortly after their third birthday. Until then, thanks to her devoted care (and to be fair, to Charles Kray's money) young Charlie and the Twins, compared with most Bethnal Green children in the thirties, were growing up strong and healthy. She could afford to feed them well, and took trouble over what they ate – 'I always made them drink greens water for the vitamins, an' my mum would call in most days with a piece of cheese or a bit of fish for the Twins from the market.'

Despite the dilapidated state of number 178, they didn't lack for coal for heating either, 'so I could always keep them warm and cosy'. But early in 1937, there was an outbreak of measles and diphtheria in the district, two illnesses that were still a scourge of children in the thirties. One morning Ron and Reg awoke with a raging temperature.

'The doctor told me it was only measles and that being as they was such healthy babies, the Twins would soon be on the mend,' Violet said. 'But next morning they was worse, Ronnie especially. As soon as I saw my Ronnie's nose-holes movin' in and out I knew it was the diphtheria.'

Diphtheria is a highly infectious bacterial infection of the throat which, as well as sometimes causing death by suffocation in young children, can produce neurotoxins that cause damage to the brain and nervous system. Since the war, it has been almost eradicated in Britain by immunisation, but in the thirties it could prove a killer for young children, particularly in poor, overcrowded neighbourhoods like Bethnal Green.

Fearing the effect on the remaining twin if one of them died, the doctor sent them to separate isolation hospitals. It was the first time they had been apart since they were born. Reg gave little sign of missing Ron, and quickly started to recover. But Ron was more seriously affected and for nearly three months was critically ill. Charles Kray was soon off again on his travels buying old gold, leaving Violet as usual with the burdens of the family and naturally beside herself with worry.

'I wasn't allowed near either of my babies. All I could do was peep in at them through a window at the end of the ward. Reggie weren't too bad, but it broke my heart to look at little Ronnie.'

Soon Reg was well and back playing with his friends in Vallance Road, but for nearly three months Ron remained desperately ill in the children's ward of Homerton Isolation Hospital. It was then that gentle Violet decided to assert herself.

'I could see my Ronnie was frettin' for his Reggie and for me, and that he wouldn't get no better if we left him there.' So she insisted on bringing Ron home. The fact that the doctors didn't try to stop her suggests that by then they'd given up on him and thought he'd probably die anyway. Not so Violet. Back in Vallance Road she nursed him devotedly by day, and kept him in her bed at night. Slowly, slowly he recovered. As she put it, 'All 'e really needed was me an' his Reggie.'

'It was his mother saved his life,' said old Charles. 'If it 'adn't been for 'er and what she done for 'im, Ron'd 'ave been a gonner.'

When Ron finally did recover, and was once more playing in the street with Reg, the Twins appeared more inseparable than ever. Outwardly it looked as if nothing had changed, but something had. Something had shifted in the balance of their interlocked relationship with each other.

Before I got to know the Krays I knew next to nothing on the subject of twins, apart from the fact that they fall into two distinct categories. When two separate eggs are fertilised in the womb, the offspring, though born as twins, are not identical in their genetic make-up. Such twins are called dizygotic. A second group of twins are those formed when a single fertilised egg cell divides into two at an early stage of development. Since each resultant twin had the same complement of chromosomes and genes, they are genetically identical and are called monozygotic. Ron and Reg were monozygotic, and therefore genetically speaking they were exact carbon copies of each other. There were uncanny similarities between Ron and Reg in looks, physique and overall appearance, which lasted until well into their early twenties.

I learned that in certain cases identical twins not only

look alike but can act and think alike as well. Sometimes they seem telepathic and can apparently share each others' thoughts. There have been frequent accounts of the effect of such genetic links between identical twins – the way in which abilities, tastes, occupations, even sexuality are governed by their shared genetic destiny.

This has led to much involved research, which started in the 1850s when Sir Francis Galton used his observations on the behaviour of identical twins to reinforce his views on the crucial factors of heredity, which formed the basis of his highly controversial theories on the subject of what he called 'eugenics', aimed at encouraging what he thought to be the best and strongest genetic strains in society. But what interested me were theories on criminal identical twins and I found the most dramatic findings in Lange's classic study on the subject *Crime as Destiny*, published in Leipzig in 1930. By methodical detective work, Lange had discovered a number of cases of identical twins who had been separated at birth, and where one had subsequently become a known criminal. When he investigated, he often discovered that the separated twin brother, although brought up apart in completely different circumstances, had also turned to crime. More extraordinary still, Lange's separated criminal twins appeared to commit roughly the same sort of crime. A con man living in Hamburg would turn out to have an unsuspected twin brother in Dresden with convictions for deception; a violent criminal in Berlin proved to have an identical twin living in another part of Germany with a similar tendency to crimes of violence. He came to the conclusion that there was a strong genetic correlation between identical twins who turned to crime. If one was a criminal, the other tended to be as well. Lange's work became largely discredited when it was used to back up Nazi theories on the need for so-called 'racial purity', later in the thirties; and I think I originally placed too much importance on Lange's work and its application to the Twins when I wrote about his book in *The Profession of Violence*. Lange took a very small and carefully selected sample, and subsequent research suggests that he exaggerated what he saw as the overwhelming role of heredity in criminal behaviour.

With the Kray Twins too, it is clear that heredity must have played at least some part in making them what they were. For instance, the Twins had a lot of fighting genes to draw on with a pair of extremely violent grandparents in the family – Mad Jimmy Kray and the still 'madder' and more violent alcoholic maternal great-grandfather, John Quicher Lee. They may have also inherited an element of mental instability from their forebears. If they did, because they were genetically similar, the Twins would have shared this too. But I am now convinced that with the Kray Twins, the genetic make-up that they shared is only part of the story. Something else is needed to explain what linked their lives so indissolubly, and disastrously, together.

It was from Dr Tomroi Sharma, a neurologist at London's Maudsley Hospital for Nervous Illnesses, who specialises in twins, that I first discovered the existence of a rare group of identical twins, in one of whom their genetic similarities have become distorted, either by damage in the womb or by subsequent trauma. If this damage is serious enough to throw the balance of their twinship out of kilter, such twins are known as 'discordant identicals'. Since we know that Ron himself became a paranoid schizophrenic who was twice certified insane, while Reg was apparently 'normal', it seems that the Kray Twins qualify as discordant identicals on the basis of Ron's mental instability.

Neurologists are still trying to discover what causes schizophrenia. One view is that it originates with damage to the frontal cortex of the brain. This is possible, but research is now inclining to the view that schizophrenia more frequently begins with a recurring hormone imbalance in the brain's extremely subtle chemistry. Damage to the brain can occur in the womb or at birth, but as far as I was able to discover after Ron's death, the pathologist who performed the autopsy on him found no evidence of any physical damage to his brain to account for his mental condition. Besides, the apparently normal and healthy nature of both Twins during their first three years of life makes it more than likely that Ron's lifelong schizophrenia originated with that prolonged and nearly fatal battle with diphtheria when he was three and a half years old. Acute diptheria is known to sometimes cause damage to the central nervous system.

These effects would not necessarily have shown at first, but as he grew, whatever mental damage Ron had suffered would have become increasingly obvious to those around him, as in fact it did.

One must understand that, certainly to start with, Reg was completely sane. Everything that Violet and members of the family told me suggests that he recovered from diphtheria unscathed. But Ron did not. By the time he went to school, Violet could see that 'her Ronnie' was noticeably slower, shyer and more dependent on her than he had been before his illness. He was also moodier, less co-ordinated and clumsier than his twin. Reg seemed altogether brighter, quicker in his responses, spoke better and made friends more easily than Ron. But because of his weaknesses, Ron had a constant need for Reg, just as Reg felt a deep responsibility to look after Ron. This meant that while they were growing up and becoming increasingly 'discordant', so they became more and more closely locked together. This helped to form a pattern they would follow for the rest of their lives.

Violet, far from detecting anything remotely wrong or worrying in what was happening, regarded the Twins' dependence on each other as rather touching and she seems to have encouraged them to live their lives entirely as one. She continued to dress them identically and treat them like one person. 'Twins,' she used to call them. 'Twins', and very rarely, 'Ron' or 'Reg'.

What research there has been on discordant identical twins suggests that this condition usually ends in disaster or collapse for both of them; it is rare for discordant twins to lead happy and successful lives. Certainly none of the fairly widespread research that has been conducted on the lives of criminal identicals has unearthed a single case of discordant identical twins becoming successful big-time criminals – with the one exception of the Krays. It is this that makes the case of the Kray Twins totally unique. More than this, the way in which their criminal career as discordant identical twins would lead them both through violence, on to wealth, murder and celebrity sets them in a class apart from any other famous criminals in history. From what I was told by Violet and by members of the family, I have tried to piece together how this happened.

During their early years of childhood, although the Twins *looked* similar, Ron always seemed to be the one who was most at risk, and he would do anything for Violet's attention and affection – sulk, scream, indulge in tantrums, throw his arms around her. Violet, in her soft, indulgent way, would always make allowances for his bad behaviour. As she said, 'It was as if he was making up for all the love and care he'd missed so much in hospital.' Ronnie would respond accordingly, and no sooner had Violet forgiven him than he would smother her with childish affection. This became something of a set routine. But throughout his childish tantrums, there was one thing Ronnie clearly couldn't cope with – the thought that, in spite of all the love she gave him, Violet really loved his twin brother more.

Ron's jealousy of Reg was almost pathological. The Twins' cousin, Billy Wilshire, told me that, while they were still toddlers, Ronnie had already started watching Reg to make sure that he never came off best in anything they did – and Reg started watching Ronnie in return. Billy told me how they used to watch each other 'like two young hawks', and how he had actually witnessed Ron count out the peas on his and Reg's plates, then throw a scene because Reg had been given half a dozen more than him.

Although he loved Reg, Ron would resort to anything to undermine his twin's advantages in Violet's eyes. Sometimes a sneer would be enough, and calling him 'Mummy's little darling'. When this failed he could always get his brother blamed for something. For with the perceptiveness of the disadvantaged, Ron had an instinct for involving Reg in trouble. Almost from the moment they could walk, it was obvious that the Twins were fighters and by the age of five or six, they were picking up a local reputation as exceptionally wicked little boys. Theirs was a tough neighbourhood, but they would take on other boys twice their size and as long as they were together they feared no one. Since they were twins, they were conspicuous, and they attracted trouble. Violet said that because they were twins 'others used to pick on them'. Others told me that 'as little kids they already had the devil in them. They used to fight and make mischief and smash things up for the hell of it.'

Although it was usually Ron who would start the trouble, Reg, as he told me several times, 'was no little angel', and needed no encouragement to join his brother in a fight. As Ron knew quite well, Reg would always be there with him when the scrapping started, and would always back him up. One thing that Reg could never bear was his brother's taunt of cowardice.

I began to understand how the pattern started which repeated throughout their lives. It was as if they were always trying to correct the imbalance in their linked emotions caused by the fatal flaw that threatened to divide them. As a result, the lives they shared became a sort of battlefield between good and evil. Time and again, people told me, 'Well, of course, the Twins were really one person', but it was one person with a fatally divided nature. Certainly to begin with, the part that was Reg was sane and attractive and creative, desiring nothing more than the admiration and success that Violet represented. Since they were one, Ron shared in all his twin's ambitions, but continually his damaged nature stopped him from attaining them. It was then that the jealousy began, the conflicts started, and if Ron found himself unable to match Reg by being good, he would end up by compelling Reg to equal him in being evil.

It was a frightening equation, and since they were one person, there was no escape. Each knew the other too well and observed the other far too closely for that to be a possibility. When it became impossible to reach a truce between their 'discordant' but 'identical' twin natures, civil war would start between them, and they would fight each other like demons.

Their cousin Billy Wilshire told me that he had never seen a pair of brothers fight each other like the Twins, and no one could ever stop them, not even Violet. 'I used to think they'd kill each other, fighting with no holds barred, and screaming obscenities at each other.' Ten minutes later, when they'd had enough, everything was over and forgotten and the Twins were inseparable as ever.

They were also very strange. Whenever I thought about them, I was haunted by the words of old Charles Kray: 'To me they'll always be a mystery, the Twins. I've never understood 'em. There's not another two in the country like 'em. I try to think why things have turned out as they have, an' for the life of me I can't.'

SIX

Ron's Madness

The most dangerous word in any tongue is the word for brother. It's inflammatory.

Tennessee Williams, *Camino Real*

During my penitential days in Blackwall Buildings I was as mystified as their father was about the Twins, particularly with the contrasting stories I was picking up about them. Violet, of course, would always sing their praises, and her view was generally backed by the chorus of approval I heard from the senior citizens of crime, to whom the Twins were still introducing me. 'Lovely boys, the Twins. Do anything to help anyone in trouble. Always count on their support for any good cause going,' was the usual gist of what I heard. In their case, I knew that these ancient fans had been carefully primed by the Twins over what they told me, and I wondered why the Twins bothered – if they were so powerful, why were they so anxious to be liked, and why, for that matter, did they so clearly long to be considered local heroes?

But I also realised that some of the good reports about the Twins were almost certainly genuine. For along with blatant old flatterers, such as Sammy Lederman, there was another group of people who had known them well and who, clearly without prior instruction, bore witness to the most unlikely virtues in the Twins during childhood and early adolescence.

First of these was burly William Evans, the headmaster

of nearby Daneford School, who had taught them twenty years before. A former rugby player from Newport, Monmouthshire, who had spent his teaching life in Bethnal Green, he started by complaining, when I met him, that schoolmastering was not what it used to be in the old days – 'otherwise I'd not be taking early retirement at the end of this year at the age of sixty-one.'

'Mind you,' he continued, 'Bethnal Green was a very poor, rough area indeed when the Twins were boys, and there was a lot of local crime. But the Twins were both marvellous boys, and never the slightest trouble if you knew how to handle them. They were fighters but not bullies, and if they had to be punished they'd take it like gents. If there was anything needing to be done at school, like a sporting gala or something of the sort, they'd be utterly co-operative. Believe me, kids round here really were better in those days, and the Krays were part of a good bunch. Boys seem different now, softer, and a lot less humorous. It's all part of the search to be middle-class at all costs, which is even reaching Bethnal Green. I suppose it's a good thing, but shall we say it makes life a lot less interesting.'

Some months later, when I was trying to discover more about Reg's fated marriage, I stumbled on someone else who had known the Twins as children and backed up their old teacher's glowing testimonial. This was their one-time local vicar, Father Hetherington. Although he tended to agree with Mr Evans – 'They were very kind boys and they'd do anything for me apart from come to church' – he also had a more sophisticated view of their psychology.

By the time I met him the Twins had been arrested, and were on remand, accused of murder. I asked him how he thought, as a priest, that such kind boys could have turned out to be so violent and apparently evil.

He shook his head. 'I don't believe the Twins were evil. What they were was completely and utterly amoral, and for various reasons even as children they had built themselves a fantasy world with certain very definite rules of its own. The key to it was that they divided up the world into honest people they respected and blackguards who they didn't. If you were in the first category, they'd treat you with courtesy, consideration and often much kindness. But if you were in the second, then the Good Lord help you. For in that case they believed they had a perfect right to deal with you entirely as they saw fit. This doesn't excuse whatever they may have done, but I think it makes some of their behaviour more comprehensible.'

I was discovering that everything about the Twins seemed marked with the same strange mixture, 'good' and 'evil', with everything about them apparently balanced by its opposite. Even in Vallance Road, there were the two opposed worlds of their father and their mother, with old Charlie on the run as a deserter, living and drinking with his East End villains, and Violet somehow maintaining herself as the model of respectability while accepting their criminal behaviour. The same dichotomy seems to have been present in the way the Twins first became involved in violence.

There was no mystery over how their violent behaviour started. With their genetic inheritance, background and physique, it was inevitable that the Twins should have both been drawn to boxing long before adolescence. In Bethnal Green, organised boxing used to be regarded as a serious youth activity, which took boys off the streets, built up their characters and channelled their aggression. At the nearby Repton Boys' Club, Teddy Berry's father, Harry 'Kid' Berry, who once fought as a professional, used to run the Midget's Club for schoolboy boxers, which the Twins attended. By the age of nine or ten, they were already beating boys considerably beyond their age. Boxing had long been seen as a path to fame from the poverty of the old East End, and by their early teens the Twins were highly motivated fighters, as was their elder brother Charlie, who was a stylish boxer on his own account. But the great white hope of the family was Reg.

Kid Berry told me, 'Reg was a natural boxer who was born to be a champion. It was like he had all the experience of an old fighter there in his two hands before he even started, and I never had to tell him anything twice. He was an artist in the ring, and he could – and should – have been a champion.

'Ron was different. Where Reg was a boxer, Ron was a fighter. Ron would never say no to taking on anyone, even if he was twice his size. To stop him, you'd have had to kill him.'

By their mid-teens, both the Twins seemed poised upon careers as successful boxers, and were soon to turn professional. But then something happened that put an end to their careers, almost before they started. No one could tell me what it was, but from what I gathered, it seemed that boxing started to upset the balance in their all-encompassing relationship as twins. As boxers, the differences between them became all too obvious. Unlike Ron, Reg would never be defeated in the ring, but it was clear that if he did make a successful career as a professional, the Twins' paths would start to diverge and Ron might well have lost him. But before this could happen, Reg simply gave up boxing.

Boxing always had a constant rival for the Twins' attention from a very different sort of fighting with a more powerful appeal – the traditional East End gang fights and no-holds-barred encounters in the streets. Here ruthlessness was seen as next to manliness. The Twins were hardly likely to forget that their grandfathers, Mad Jimmy Kray and Cannonball Lee, had been celebrated streetfighters, and while they were starting their careers as boxers they were already building up a gang around them.

Apart from the enhanced excitement in the streets, there was an important difference for the Twins between violence in the boxing ring and in the streets. In the ring, it was Reg who was the champion, but in a brawl the roles would be reversed, with Ron completely in his element. In a street fight, the mental instability that was already starting to affect him placed him at an advantage over Reg. Several people told me how as soon as Ron was in a fight he would be taken over by a sort of madness which, coupled with a total lack of fear or feeling, even hardened men found scary.

The Twins' success in gang fights was also due to the simple fact that as twins they looked so alike. There undoubtedly *is* something quite uncanny about two separate human beings who look totally identical, particularly when you're in a fight with them. In his researches into identical twins, Dr Sharma has discovered that because the human eye is not accustomed to seeing double versions of the same person, people can at first be baffled and made to feel uneasy by identical twins. This is something most identical twins take advantage of when they switch places and play tricks on others. There is also evidence that when united, twins seem to generate what is known as synergy, an enhanced joint power between them.

This must have been the reason for the Twins' unbeaten record in their early local fights. I never heard of any other gang seriously harming them, for not only did they think as one and fight as one, but once Reg's blood was up, and his twin brother was beside him, he would start sharing Ron's non-caring madness and be just as dangerous.

By their late teens, gang violence was fast becoming a key factor in the Kray Twins' lives. It not only kept the pair of them united, but placed Ron at an advantage over Reg. Ron's latent paranoia made him fearless, fearsome and virtually invulnerable. This meant that in the context of the constant see-saw of emotions going on between them, violence was placing the retarded Ron in the dominant position over his brighter and more co-ordinated twin brother, Reg.

At sixteen the Twins were acknowledged by the other boys in Bethnal Green as the wickedest young tearaways around. This gave them both prestige as natural leaders, but only the toughest boys would follow them. When it came to fighting, nothing could restrain them. No rules, principles or pity held them back, and they fought so viciously that no other gang around could beat them. As Father Hetherington remarked, for anyone they disapproved of, it was a case of 'May the Good Lord help them.'

As well as their fists they used whatever came to hand that would inflict the greatest damage – bicycle chains, iron bars and broken bottles. Reg was also developing what he called his 'cigarette punch'. With his left hand he'd offer somebody a cigarette, and just as his victim was putting it in his mouth, his right fist would sock him on the side of the chin. This took timing and a lot of practice, but once he'd perfected it, Reg could usually count on his cigarette punch to break the jaw of any unsuspecting enemy.

Ron specialised in simpler forms of violence, and at sixteen was already working on techniques for cutting an opponent in the face. Experience had taught him that if properly sharpened, a large sheath knife produced better results than the traditional cut-throat razor. At sixteen the Twins also bought their first revolver which they hid beneath the floorboards in their bedroom.

One important point about the Twins that is often over-looked is that their violence, like their loyalty to each other, was never in any way affected by sexual relationships with women. At this stage, both the Twins were homosexual. They shared each others' boys and it was even rumoured that they were physically in love with one another.

It was around this time, early in 1950, that the fighting moved from Bethnal Green to the streets and clubs of Hackney and started becoming serious. The police were expecting someone to be killed. Following one battle in the street, a sixteen-year-old Hackney boy was still alive when the ambulance men arrived and picked him from the gutter. Although he had been kicked all over, his nose broken, and his face and neck ripped with bicycle chains, he refused to talk to the police in hospital. But the police had other witnesses, including a nineteen-year-old local secretary and an insurance salesman, both of whom identified the Twins as the assailants. In the end the boy reluctantly confirmed this.

The Twins appeared to be in dire trouble and the case was referred to the Old Bailey. But when it came to trial there was mysteriously no case against them. The key witnesses had suddenly forgotten what they'd seen, and the victim could no longer remember who had hit him. This meant that the prosecution had no alternative but to drop the charges.

But the case was more important to the Twins than it appeared, and taught them some important lessons for the future. Number one was that the so-called 'first commandment' of the old East End, 'Thou shalt not grass to the police', still held and could be effectively enforced. (Someone had apparently told the secretary that if she spoke in court against the Krays, she might find a razor 'put across her face'.) And number two was that they needn't fear the power of the law, since even a trial at the Old Bailey could be fixed, once they put their minds to it.

One thing that could not be fixed was National Service in the army, and in March 1953, the eighteen-year-old Twins were ordered to report to the Royal Fusiliers at the Tower of London.

In many ways the army should have suited them. Not for nothing was the house in Vallance Road known as 'Fort Vallance'. Ron was already organising his followers on military lines, and liked being called 'the Colonel'. It's even possible that their sort of wild violence might have won them death or glory on the battlefield. But in 1953, there were no British battlefields and the Twins followed the example of their father, who was still legally classified as a deserter. Before they could be forced into a uniform, one of the Twins hit the squad corporal on the jaw, and soon they were on the bus back to Bethnal Green, where they joined their father 'on the trot'.

Unlike smart old Charlie, they were fairly rapidly recaptured and their entire army service was spent either in further efforts to escape or in various military detention centres, ending up with a nine-month stretch in the notorious army 'Glasshouse' at Shepton Mallet.

'The Mallet' was the Kray Twins' university. They found it perfectly congenial, and spent their time there toughening up, defying the system, and discussing crime and criminal techniques with some of the liveliest up-and-coming young evildoers in the country, whom they met among their fellow prisoners. By now the army had taught them that the 'straight' world was emphatically not for them. After being 'ignominiously dismissed from the Service' early in 1954, the Twins would henceforth be single-mindedly united in the pursuit of crime and violence.

59

As Ron said to me on one occasion, a life of crime and violence 'was better than doing some stinking job in the market, which was the only work I could have got'. It was also more exciting and more profitable. Professor Dick Hobbs, the authority on East End crime, has written that crime, in this period, was still 'integral to East End culture'. This meant that there was no criticism or sense of shame attached to their new career when the Twins adopted it. The traditional rackets of the old East End were waiting for them – fraud, protection, dealing in stolen goods, enforcement and extortion. But the Twins stock-in-trade was always violence and the threat of violence. Violence could be marketed like any other commodity. Reg did the marketing.

Reg often explained to me how 'villains' were what he liked to call 'the aristocracy of crime', the praetorian guard of the underworld, whose presence kept lesser criminals in order. A less romantic view of successful East End 'villains' like the Krays was expressed to me by a former professional criminal himself, the writer John McVicar. They were, he said, 'thieves' ponces, who made their living out of crimes they couldn't do themselves'.

Certainly, neither Twin could have burgled a house or robbed a bank, and still less picked a pocket or a safe to save his life. Such menial tasks were best left to the 'workers', and there was never any shortage of them. The Twins took their percentage from criminals like these through violence or the fear of violence. Also Reg already had a knack for working out 'the business'. Even before the Twins had 'joined' the army, the older generation of self-styled 'lords of the underworld' – successful London racketeers such as Jack Spot Comer and Billie Hill – were in tentative alliance with them and offering them a little 'business' on their own account – 'minding' some bookies' pitches at the races, or 'looking after' a few illicit gambling clubs or dubious bars within what was nominally 'their territory'. The notorious property racketeer of Notting Hill, Peter Rachman, also used the Twins – in fact usually their name and their chosen henchmen – to 'put the frighteners on' his more difficult tenants. Spot once described the twins as 'tasty, very tasty' and their reputation as the most vicious up-and-coming gang in London was already offering them both power and money. Ron enjoyed the power, Reg the money.

As the fights continued and the blood and money flowed, it seemed, for the Twins at least, a most satisfactory arrangement, up until the beginning of November 1956. The Twins had just turned twenty-three when something happened that almost tore the fabric of their dangerous relationship apart – with enduring consequences for both of them.

By now the Twins were effectively 'in command' of most of the criminal East End. They were sharp, they were feared and they were smart enough to know more or less exactly what was going on throughout their part of London. Since nobody could beat them in a stand-up fight, they were invulnerable and feared. They were making their money from protection and their percentages from any rackets going. But Ron had homicidal tendencies that seemed to be getting out of hand. With increasing regularity, he would become obsessed with the idea of killing someone.

Up to a point this was good for business. A willingness to kill is the ultimate test of seriousness for any commercial gangster, but there is always an element of bluff about it. While the threat to kill is part of every gangster's stock-in-trade, actual murder can be bad for business, bringing trouble, the police and even a shut-down of operations in the form of imprisonment in its wake. Reg understood this perfectly, and was something of a virtuoso at the art of parleying the threat of murder into profit. Ron was more of a purist in such matters. He loved the whole idea of mayhem on its own account. He thought more of murder than of money.

I'm still not sure how far Reg was aware of this, and to what extent he shared his brother's homicidal fantasies. It seems that, unlike Ron, Reg was not fundamentally homicidal and, as the violence began to escalate, much of his time and energy were spent trying to restrain his brother and, when he couldn't achieve this, they went into what he called 'clearing up' afterwards. This could mean anything from squaring witnesses to arranging swift, impromptu medical treatment from the 'villains' doctor', old Doc Blasker, and even paying for a little incidental damage. In the very last resort, it might even mean bribing the police.

Certainly by early 1956, Ron's violence was making Reg busier than ever, as Ron increasingly indulged in violence for the fun of it. There was absolutely no need for him to have stormed into the showroom of the car dealer the Twins were currently 'protecting', all-but-shooting an unhappy customer's leg off. Reg had to spend much time and money in arranging compensation for the injured customer, squaring the police and keeping the case out of court.

But trouble wasn't over. Come August, the Colonel was once more on the warpath, leading his forces into battle with a rival gang at a local pub, the Britannia. As was increasingly happening by now, the enemy fled, rather than face the Krays, but they left behind a boy called Martin. Although Martin was really not involved, the Colonel had a grudge against him, and he set about him out of sheer frustration. Reg stopped him from actually killing him, but he was so badly hurt that he refused all Reg's subsequent efforts at negotiation. The case went to the Old Bailey, and thanks to the pleading of the expensive lawyer Reg had hired to represent him, Ron was very lucky to get off with a two-year sentence. This meant that for the first time since they were sent to those separate isolation hospitals when they had diphtheria at the age of three, the Twins were parted.

At first they both appeared completely unaffected. 'Don't do the crime, if you can't serve the time' is one of the basic rules of villainy, and when Ron was consigned to the notoriously tough Wandsworth Prison, he seemed to take it in his stride. Here he was among a group of serious fellow East End criminals, many of whom were friends already. These included a mentally subnormal but immensely strong, good-looking would-be villain called Frank Mitchell. It is sometimes said that he and Ron were lovers. Ron certainly admired his physique and, since Mitchell feared that his mental state might upset his chances of parole, Ron promised to do all he could to help him after his own release.

Then in 1958, when Ron had served more than a year in Wandsworth, he was moved to the more relaxed regime of Camp Hill Prison on the Isle of Wight. He hated it. He missed Mitchell and his hardened fellow criminals, and he missed the tough regime at Wandsworth. He became nervous and reclusive. He began staring obsessively at his face in the mirror, convinced that it was changing and that he was going off his head. Shortly after this he went berserk in the recreation hall, floored several fellow inmates who tried to reason with him, and bawled out the governor. This was immediately followed by a devastating nervous breakdown.

It seems unbelievable that anyone as tough and violent

as Ron could have started weeping uncontrollably, banging his head against the wall and cowering in his cell, convinced that the prison authorities would kill him. The prison governor was so concerned about him that he had him transferred to Winchester Prison, which had a psychiatric unit. Briefly Ron calmed down. Then he heard from Reg that their Auntie Rose had died of cancer.

Battling Auntie Rose, Violet's youngest sister, was Ron's favourite aunt. Like him, she would fight anyone who crossed her or annoyed her, regardless of their size or sex. In a straight encounter, she once fought, and beat, two women who upset her. But a long and painful battle with leukaemia was her last fight. Ron was distraught with grief on hearing she had died and his condition worsened. He became so violent that the warders had to force him into a straitjacket for his own protection. The prison medical officer certified him insane, and since his condition was so serious, he was sent from prison for specialist treatment at Long Grove Mental Hospital, a former lunatic asylum outside Epsom in Surrey.

Reg talked a lot to me about this period, which seemed to have deeply affected him as well. 'After Auntie Rose died, I knew that something was happening to my brother before anybody told me.' From what he told me, it seemed as if he had undergone some sort of near-breakdown too, and although he soon recovered, whenever he thought of Ron he became miserable and uneasy. He said, 'I was tortured by the thought I couldn't help my brother when he really needed me.'

Violet, too, was beside herself with worry, and as usual in a crisis, her husband, who was still on the run from the police, was not around to support her. For unbelievably, although it was more than twenty years by then since he first went on the run from the army, he was still officially a deserter, and the police had been keeping Fort Vallance under surveillance in the hope of catching him. One of the policemen, whom Violet recognised and particularly disliked, knocked on the door late one night to inform her about Ron. When she told me about this, it was one of the few times I ever saw her really angry.

'Imagine what it's like to have a copper you hate coming round in the middle of the night to tell you that your son's been certified insane,' she said. 'Just imagine.'

Reg was also bitter, blaming the prison authorities for giving Ron a nervous breakdown in the first place through the way they had treated him. 'All the same,' he said, 'I knew I had to pull myself together. Someone had to earn some money.'

He was, in fact, doing this extremely well already, for he had been demonstrating something of his father's business acumen and cunning, which he may have picked up from him during brief periods as a teenager when the old man took him with him gold-buying 'on the knocker'. Although, like Ron, Reg was perfectly prepared to 'thump' his father on occasions, he never really shared Ron's deep dislike for him, and in certain ways Reg was not unlike him. Without the goading presence of his twin beside him, Reg had been increasingly avoiding violence and concentrating on the business side of crime. The rackets became better organised, and he started to display an aptitude for con tricks, small-time scams and protection rackets with the local East End gambling clubs called 'spielers'.

As profits rose, the violence decreased, and Reg embarked on his first straight business venture, opening a club of his own in Walthamstow where, as he put it, 'East Enders could bring their girlfriends and enjoy a drink together.' But to demonstrate that the Twins were still united, Reg put their entwined initials over the door, and called the club the Double R.

There was a lot going for the Double R. By the mid-fifties the East End was just coming into fashion. As a young journalist I remember drinking in pubs like the Grapes in Narrow Street, and eating salt beef at Blooms', Chinese food at the Old Friends in Limehouse and white-bait on the balcony of the Prospect of Whitby. Joan Littlewood had started her experimental theatre barely a mile away from Vallance Road at the Theatre Royal in Stratford East. And the sentimentalising of cockney culture had begun with films such as Wolf Mankowitz's tear-jerking *Kid for Two Farthings*, starring the East End's own 'blonde bombshell', Diana Dors.

Even royalty found itself a private perch in this new East End, when the young photographer Tony Armstrong-Jones bought himself a tiny flat in Narrow Street, two doors away from another friend of the Twins, the gay writer and journalist Daniel Farson. From the bedroom windows of the flat there were romantic views across the Thames towards the Isle of Dogs. Nobody in the press knew he lived there, and the future Lord Snowdon used it as a secret hideaway in which to woo and win his future bride, Princess Margaret.

The Double R shared in the growing popularity of the area, and became known as an 'in' place on the East End circuit for visitors from 'up West'. It also started to develop something of the atmosphere of those New York clubs and bars from the days of Prohibition, where stars came to fraternise with gangsters. Diana Dors was an early patron of the Double R and became a friend of Reg's. So did the popular singer Lita Rosa, and the musician Victor Spinelli, along with celebrities such as Jackie Collins, Sybil Burton and the young cockney starlet Barbara Windsor.

Today it's hard to appreciate the extent of the young Reg Kray's success at the Double R. He somehow matched the period, and possessed the knack of mixing just the right amount of charm and cockney brashness with a barely stated hint of crime and violence. I once asked him how he did it, and he replied, 'I don't know why, but the upper classes always seem to think that the idea of crime is rather sexy.'

Perhaps they simply found Reg sexy, for he was good-looking in those days, and was already dressing the part of a movie gangster. He had persuaded his local tailor, Woods of Kingsland Road, to make him a dark blue, double-breasted suit, copied from his favourite movie star, George Raft. Violet was particularly pleased. She liked to see her Reg dress smartly, with his highly polished, slightly pointed shoes, his tightly knotted dark silk tie and spotless white shirt. She still did all his washing and ironing for him, and if it's true, as he told me, that during his time at the Double R he sometimes changed his shirt three times a day, she must have had her work cut out.

Ron, meanwhile, was still in a locked ward in Long Grove Mental Hospital, under close supervision by trained nurses night and day.

He talked to me quite openly about this period how he wasn't quite sure who he really was, and how he sat all day huddled round a radiator. 'The radiator seemed the only friend I had because it was warm.' He felt utterly alone and in his isolation 'funny things used to come and go through my mind'. He became obsessed with the idea that one of his fellow patients was a dog, and that if he could only guess his name he could call him and he'd wag his tail and come and jump into his lap. 'Then at last I'd have a friend, but I could never guess his name.'

While he was in this state, he couldn't recognise anyone, not even Violet or Reg when they came to visit. He was suicidal, and from time to time 'I used to think I had to kill myself to stop someone else doing it first.' Before the nurses could restrain him, he smashed his fist through a window, cutting his wrist and hand severely.

His medical reports described him as 'a simple man of low intelligence, poorly in touch with the world outside'. There was no mention on the report of his criminal case history, but he was described as 'unstable and in fear of bodily change', showing 'signs of verbigeration and marked thought blocking'. 'Verbigeration' is a psychologist's term which, according to the Oxford Dictionary, means 'to go on repeating the same word or phrase in a meaningless fashion, as a symptom of mental disease'.

Although Ron was clearly mentally extremely sick, the doctors at Long Grove were able to relieve the more alarming symptoms of his breakdown by placing him on a powerful new sedative called Stematol. Stematol was one of a new generation of tranquillizers that were then revolutionising the treatment of the mentally sick. It helped damp down the patient's wilder neurotic symptoms, without doping him completely, and in Ron's case it seemed to work. Although even the doctors were none too sure of the real nature of his illness, he responded to his medication. Soon he believed that he was cured, and since he was still being kept in a locked ward, he began to feel deserted and increasingly jealous of his well-dressed, obviously successful twin brother when he came to visit. He was transferred to an unlocked ward, and started getting anxious to be 'decertified' by the doctors and declared sane enough to return to prison to complete his sentence. But the doctors urged caution and, despite his pleading, told him he must wait a few weeks longer.

There were apparently some stormy meetings in the Long Grove visitors' room, with Violet insisting that of course her Ronnie was 'perfectly all right'. Reg thought the same and would return home feeling guilty. Afterwards the family would endlessly discuss what should be done. Violet was the one who seems to have been the driving force. Even when I talked to her, she would never admit that there was anything seriously wrong with Ron. She even told me that his breakdown was 'just Ronnie acting up a bit, as he often did when he got the hump. He was just trying to kid the authorities into letting him have a change of scene'. She was convinced that 'he couldn't just be left to rot in a loonie bin'. Something must be done.

Since I first described what happened in *The Profession of Violence*, the story of Ron's escape from Long Grove has become part of the legend of the Twins and been endlessly repeated.

It is something both of them were proud of, since it showed them in their favourite role as twins united to outwit the authorities. The story tells how the family told Ron to wear the same blue suit, white shirt and dark red tie that Reg would be wearing when he came to visit him, how Ron pretended to be Reg when he told the nurse he was just going to the kitchen to collect their tea, and how he walked out to a waiting car outside instead. Ten minutes later, Reg innocently asked the nurse where his brother was.

'He went off to get the tea,' the nurse replied.

'Are you sure?' said Reg. 'I can't hang around all day. I've got to be getting back to London.'

'Back to London? Don't be silly, Ron,' the nurse replied.

'Who're you calling Ron? I'm Reg. Here's my driving licence to prove it. It was Ron went out to get the tea. You'd better find out where he is.'

It seemed a splendid caper, worthy of the sort of daring wartime colonel Ron secretly longed to be. (He once told me that his two greatest heroes were Gordon of Khartoum and Lawrence of Arabia.) But as usual with the Twins, the reality was not as carefree as it seemed. The problem wasn't getting Ron out of Long Grove, but what to do with him afterwards.

Since all the members of the family believed by now that Ron had 'got over his spot of nervous trouble', as Violet put it, the plan was to keep him quietly out of sight until he could get to a private psychiatrist who would examine him and declare him sane. He would then give himself up, use the psychiatrist's letter to get himself 'decertified', and return to prison to serve out the remaining six months of his sentence.

Reg had already found him the ideal hiding place with an old friend of theirs – Geoff Allan, the con man, property speculator, arsonist and squire of Gedding Hall, where I had met him. At this stage in his career, Geoff had yet to purchase his stately home, but he already owned a farmhouse near the village of Hadleigh. This was in the part of Suffolk where the Twins had been sent as wartime evacuees. They even knew the stretch of woodland Geoff had bought beside his farm, where he kept a caravan. The people from the village rarely went there. What better hiding place for Ron?

There was just one problem, which no one had foreseen. Ron wasn't cured. In fact he wasn't, strictly speaking, sane. At Long Grove his condition had been stabilised by careful nursing and by Stematol. Now that he had neither, he almost immediately started to relapse. The Stematol had not cured him, for the simple reason that there was no cure for his condition. He needed the regular and carefully adjusted medication they had given him at Long Grove.

Without it he could become terrified again. When terrified, he was perfectly prepared to murder anyone who threatened him.

I was always puzzled by the true nature of Ron's paranoia, and later had a chance to talk to Dr Lewis Klein, the resident psychiatrist at Long Grove who had treated him. Dr Klein is a gentle, quiet-spoken man, and I could understand at once why Ron had trusted him. He told me how he prescribed him Stematol, which had proved most effective. It was because of drugs like Stematol that Long Grove Mental Hospital was no longer full of the untreatable lunatics and madmen of the past. But like most psychiatrists, Dr Klein became cagey when I asked him to be more precise about the actual nature of Ron's illness.

He defined his breakdown as 'a fairly classic case of a paranoid episode, which had probably been building up over many years', and said that he 'gathered that he'd suffered from serious diphtheria as a child', and thought that this 'might well account for the metabolic changes which are frequently associated with schizophrenia'. When I asked him about Ron's fears about his changed appearance, he said that this too was quite possible. 'Schizophrenics often do bloat and their features sometimes coarsen, exactly as Ron's did, supporting the theory that schizophrenia is part of a physical disease affecting the metabolic balance of the body.'

In spite of this, Dr Klein refused to speculate on the extent and nature of Ron Kray's mental illness. Rather to my surprise, he said that Ron's satisfactory response to Stematol made him think that he was not much more than 'mildly schizophrenic', and that provided he continued to take Stematol as prescribed, 'he could live a relatively normal life'.

One thing puzzled me. Dr Klein confirmed the text-book theory that schizophrenics are usually 'the least dangerous of all the mentally sick, and the least likely to indulge in violence'. They can be dangerous to themselves, but not to others, since they are liable to depression and 'tend to have a low sex-drive and a low energy quotient in general'. Clearly none of this applied to Ron, and I discovered later that almost all the clinical experience of Dr Klein and his fellow psychologists at Long Grove was with everyday patients and that they rarely came into contact with mentally disturbed violent criminals. This meant that they had little experience of a rare and mysterious form of schizophrenia that can afflict the most unpredictable and dangerous group of violent criminals – a form that is known as paranoid schizophrenia.

According to Meyer-Gross, Roth and Slater's standard work on clinical psychiatry, although this condition was first described by Kraeplin in the 1890s, paranoid schizo-phrenics can be difficult to identify with certainty. Sigmund Freud, who was fascinated by the subject, believed that 'there was a strong homosexual element in paranoid schizophrenia'. This is as maybe, although it would certainly have applied to Ron. However, most of the text-book symptoms for the condition also fitted in with what I already knew about him, or would learn in the months ahead.

Unlike the sad, unassertive, undersexed ordinary schizo-phrenics, true paranoid schizophrenics often harbour illusions of grandeur and omnipotence. They sometimes hear inner voices. They can be cold to the point of sadism in the face of human suffering, then switch abruptly to outbursts of enormous emotion. According to Meyer-Gross, Roth and Slater, in chronic cases, 'more often than not all efforts to modify the situation fail, and the patient continues in a vicious circle of ill-advised aggressiveness, self-protection, misinterpretation, spread of delusional ideas and increased watchfulness'. What is described as the 'flattening of emotional reaction' coupled with the 'rapid fluctuation of emotions' can lead the paranoid schizophrenic away from any genuine feeling for others, in favour of 'primitive emotions of fear, rage, hilarity and eroticism'. They often have strong feelings of fatalism, and of 'direction by some other being'. The authors end this section of their book with a note of warning which I must admit I found alarming. 'This quality of personality contributes to the make-up of society's most ruthless, dangerous and incorrigible criminals.'

Without jumping to conclusions, it seemed clear that Ron was a text-book case of a highly dangerous paranoid schizophrenic.

Once I had learned this, it began to make the conclusion to the tale of Ron's escape from Long Grove most alarming. Predictably, when he was left alone in Geoff Allan's caravan, his mental state rapidly deteriorated. Since Reg couldn't stay with him, he arranged for a member of the Firm to come and keep him company; he even found him boys to keep him happy. But nothing made much difference.

In the end Reg collected Ron from Suffolk and drove him back to London to consult the Firm's tried and trusted 'medical adviser', old Doc Blasker, the 'villains' doctor', who had a surgery in Dockland. Reg had relied upon the doctor so often in the past, for removing bullets, setting bones or sewing up slashed faces, that he knew he could rely on him implicitly. Knowing Ron already, Doc Blasker understood the problem. The doctor realised at once that only Stematol could stabilise his condition, and although such drugs were strictly regulated, even on prescription, he was able to obtain it for him. Thanks to Stematol, and Doc

Blasker's regular advice, Ron's mental condition was once more stablised. Soon he appeared sane enough to visit a well-known Harley Street psychiatrist under another name and obtain a letter to the effect that his state of mind was 'normal'. Once he had this, the family was able to persuade him to give himself up to the police, so that he could be officially decertified by the prison medical authorities, return to prison and complete his sentence, which had barely six months more to run. Then he would be free at last.

Which is exactly what occurred. The only trouble was that once Ron was back inside, the prison medical officers consulted none of the psychiatrists at Long Grove for advice. Now that Ron was theoretically sane and fit to complete his sentence, he was not eligible for medication. So he never got it. When he was finally released from Wandsworth early in 1959 he was in a state of such acute anxiety that Reg had to comfort him and hurry him to a waiting car. He was kept in a secret flat, given Stematol by Doc Blasker, and guarded night and day to make sure he didn't kill himself – or someone else. Then slowly, over the next few months, Ron gradually 'recovered' and, to all intents and purposes, appeared to be his old self again.

Since Doc Blasker had played such a key part in what Ron liked to call 'my recovery', Ron was anxious that I should see him, and gave me the address of his surgery in Millwall.

I remember driving one wet December evening from Limehouse down the lifeless canyon of West Ferry Road, with its endless gaol-style walls built at the turn of the century to stop pilfering from the docks and warehouses, cutting one off completely from all sight or contact with the river. This was a very different East End from Bethnal Green, and the doctor's house, in Manchester Grove, was a neglected small suburban house in a cul-de-sac. A broken front gate was hanging on its hinges, and the privet hedge had been left uncut so long that it had become a thicket almost obscuring the house from the road. No one answered when I knocked on the front door, but I saw a light on round the side of the house and banged on the back door. An upstairs window opened, and a voice shouted, 'Come in. Come on up, whoever you are, come up.'

Doc Blasker was a bouncy little man with a bright pink face, a prominent broken nose and pale, unblinking eyes. He welcomed me into the most untidy surgery I've ever seen, littered with surgical instruments, unemptied ashtrays and back numbers of the *Sporting Times*. I imagined that the large examination couch, covered in black American cloth, must have seen some extraordinary impromptu surgery in its time. But the really disturbing thing about Doc Blasker was that, as if we were in some strange medical comedy, he seemed unable to stop laughing. As what he told me was anything but funny, I put this down to nerves.

'Ronnie Kray? A tragedy, my dear sir. A tragedy but then, what is life if not a tragedy?'

He chuckled to himself as if relishing a private joke, and his face lit up.

'You don't believe me? Only the day before yesterday I had to attend a post mortem on a poor chap who'd been a patient of mine for several years. Top civil servant no less. Cancer. Discovered just like that, three weeks earlier, and before that we'd been laughing and joking together just as the two of us are doing here today. Nice, intelligent man, he was, and in the prime of life, and yet there we were, just a few weeks later, cutting up bits of his liver like cat's meat.'

Even this elicited a laugh, as if the idea of someone's liver as food for the cat was another of life's unexpected little jokes. He made an evident effort to look serious.

75

'You must excuse me, sir. We were talking about Ronnie. Well, I suppose the truth is that even now he is technically insane, although you'd not necessarily notice it when you talk to him. He's got an inborn mental instability, and he knows it and he fights against it, but it will never change. All I was able to do when he was on the run was prescribe drugs to help preserve his stability. You will appreciate my problem, as his medical adviser, sir. Please be tactful when you come to write your book.'

I said I would, and kept my promise. I asked him how he came to know the Twins.

'I first met the Twins when they were boys, boxing at the Repton Club. I was the club's official doctor, and looked after all the family. Both Twins were intensely mother-fixated, but I had no idea of his mental condition until after his escape from Long Grove. Reg contacted me first, then I saw Ron regularly and gave him the tablets which more or less stabilised his condition. He always made a point of not phoning me in case his phone was tapped. He said that he didn't want to drag me into it, but that was not the point. You see, he was like a diabetic or hyperthyroid – he couldn't live without his tablets. He told me that he'd tried to do so, but whenever he did, his naturally aggressive nature became unbearable, even for him. He'd tell me how he'd see a man sitting opposite him in a café who he knew was minding his own business, but he'd get the idea that he was staring at him, and suddenly he'd want to kill him. Kill him. Well, I ask you. What could I do, except get the poor fellow his tablets?'

The thought of giving someone pills to stop him killing someone else seemed to strike Doc Blasker as so humorous that he was once again beside himself with laughter.

'He was afraid, you see, that to get the Stematol he absolutely needed, he'd have to submit to further psychiatric examination by qualified psychologists who'd find out who he was and end up by sending him back to Long Grove. So I got the tablets for him.'

'Without a prescription?'

He giggled. 'But of course. I didn't want the poor boy rearrested. So I used to buy the drugs for him myself. I usually paid 27/6 for twenty-five tablets. They'd give me thirty bob, and I'd keep the change. That's all they paid me.'

'Didn't it worry you?'

'Worry?' He chuckled. 'I suppose it did. Well, they were my patients. Always had been, and I liked them. Always polite. And after all, it wasn't as if they asked me to murder anyone.'

He had a wart on the side of his nose and I found myself watching it as he paused and seemed to be making an effort to control his hilarity.

'Once I'd got him stabilised on Stematol, Ron started going from psychiatrist to psychiatrist, most of them in Harley Street. He called himself John Lee. He was desperate, you see, to get himself some sort of a cure. And I knew that there really was no cure. When he was really down he started to imbibe because he wanted to get away from it all. He wanted to escape.'

'Imbibe?'

'Drink, sir. Drink. My God, I'll say he did. As much as anyone I've known. Alcohol was the only thing that gave him relief, you see. And I think it was primarily the drink which produced further physical change in him around this time. I'd warn him. Dear me, yes, I'd warn him. But I ask you, what's the use of the warnings from an old man like me to a tough young man like Ronnie Kray? "Ronnie, dear boy," I'd say, "you may be made of iron, but no man on earth can take the punishment you're inflicting on yourself. If you continue drinking like this you'll end up murdering your constitution."

'Which of course is exactly what he was doing. Really he should have been off alcohol altogether. It's terribly dangerous taking such quantities of alcohol with a drug as strong as Stematol. And I'd say, "Ronnie, the sands are running out for you." You see, alcohol mixed with a drug like Stematol affecting the central nervous system can have frightening oblique effects. I think even he used to feel scared at times. That was when he came to me. But when I told him what he was doing to himself, he'd always shake his head and say, "Ah well, none of us wants to live for ever, do we doctor?"'

'And is he still dangerous?'

The question started Doc Blasker off on a final fit of silent laughter.

'My dear sir, what a question. What a question. Ask him yourself.'

SEVEN

Meet the Firm

Bars and cemeteries are full of best friends.
Arturo Perez-Réverte, *The Dumas Club*

I was back in Rome just before Christmas. It was perfect
winter weather in that golden city. Each morning from the
windows of the flat I watched the sun appear above the
pines on the Gianiculum and glint upon the river. When I
think of Rome this is how I remember it, but with my
marriage over I no longer felt that I belonged there, and I
realised that I was becoming obsessed by the Krays. I was
even missing the squalor of the Blackwall Buildings.
Nothing had been settled with Frank Taylor, who seemed
to have disappeared for the holidays, but by the beginning
of the new year, 1968, I was back in London.

Blackwall Buildings was a useful base from which to
work, but as a place in which to live it left me a touch too
vulnerable for comfort. So I found myself a flat in familiar,
middle-class Richmond, hired a car and rang Charlie Kray
to tell him I was back in England.

That Friday night, just after nine, I was doing something
I'd never done before: driving from the West End of
London to the East, down the Clerkenwell Road, turning
right into Shoreditch High Street, then left again into the
ghetto-like tunnel of Cheshire Street and on to Vallance
Road. After Rome, I was struck by the strangeness of this

city that I thought I knew so well. It was as if, within the space of twenty minutes, I had driven through a frontier between two separate countries. It is different today, with merchant bankers living in Hackney, and Spitalfields gentrified past recognition; but in the sixties, less than twenty minutes from the opulent great squares of Belgravia, somewhere towards the end of Shoreditch High Street, Eastern Europe started – dead houses, furtive figures scurrying in shawls and the occasional police car nosing past, its blue lights flashing over hostile territory.

One thing that hadn't changed in my absence was the Blackwall Buildings. The rain was falling just as it was falling when I left, and there was still the cloyingly collusive smell of rotting garbage, with the same dead condoms and used Tampax lying in the courtyard. Once I had struggled with the door and switched on the light, I could see that my stuff was where I left it – along with my Olivetti portable, my old tweed jacket on the chair and, since this was the sixties, my framed print of Chairman Mao by Andy Warhol on the wall. I had left them as hostages to my return; with the Krays around to protect them, no one had ventured to molest them. In a strange way I felt that I was home.

I drove to the Old Horns, where Lil was still hammering at her piano, and Ron was drinking pale ale, surrounded by his old familiar cronies.

''Ullo, John. You're back,' was all he said.

Before I left, he'd said that now that I had met his family, he wanted to introduce me to more members of the Firm. This, one by one, he duly did. During those wet dark winter evenings, I think I met everyone who would later figure at the Twins' trial at the Old Bailey one year later, either as murderers, accessories to murder or betrayers.

The trial, of course, was still to come, and meeting these cheery characters, gathered in such apparent amity around the Krays during these beery January evenings, it would have been appalling to have entertained such evil thoughts about them. Particularly as none of them struck me as looking or behaving very much like my idea of real gangsters. Not that I was all that clear on the subject, but even to my untrained eye, few of these characters seemed remotely serious as would-be villains. However, one thing, I realised, united them: all of them, without exception, were quietly in awe and terror of the Twins.

After what I had been learning before I left for Rome about the Twins' psychology, this seemed sensible, but it also made the Twins themselves more puzzling than ever. Everyone seemed to be taking it for granted that they were big-time gangsters, kings of the underworld, criminals of unrivalled influence and power. But could these really be the people I had met amid the gangsterous splendours of Gedding Hall, the same characters Frank Taylor had insisted ruled the London underworld on terms of equality with the US Mafia? If they really were, what were they doing in this clapped-out boozer, drinking bottled beer and getting sentimental over hunch-backed Lil at her iron piano? And why was Reg Kray ending up maundering and incoherent every night, and drinking like a maniac?

Even the relationship between the Twins was unpredictable. The tensions between them were volatile, and at times they could be as edgy and as bitter with each other as any evil-tempered old Cockney married couple. On the second or third night after my return I remember a raging argument over whether I should or shouldn't meet the former 'lord of the underworld', Billie Hill.

Over the years I'd heard much of Billie Hill, the so-called 'grey eminence' of London crime, who 'ruled' the London crime scene immediately after the Second World War and who, after supplanting his chief rival, the jovial, dark-spectacled Jack 'Spot' Comer, had upped sticks and disappeared abroad with a large, ill-gotten fortune. After Hill had apparently 'advised' and used the Twins when they were young, the Krays were generally assumed to have 'taken over' in his place.

Reg still seemed fond of him. In the final, death-bed interview he gave to Aubrey Powell for BBC television thirty-five years later, Reg was still referring to the old gangster as 'my mentor', as if he was some revered and much beloved professor. This was ridiculous, but it confirmed my hunch that as far as Reg was concerned, Hill had represented something that he longed for all his life. My theory is that for Reg Kray, Billie Hill was the great example of that will-o'-the-wisp who haunts the mind of every big-time criminal, the guy who makes crime pay, cleans up and gets away while he's still young enough to enjoy life and invest the takings. This was probably why Reg was so eager I should meet him – just as it may have been why Ron disliked him.

That evening was one of the few occasions when I saw Reg get the better of his brother in an argument. Just as I was leaving, he gave me a page torn from a notebook with an address scrawled in bright blue biro in his dreadful writing. 'This is where Bill lives,' he muttered. 'He's expecting you at ten tomorrow.'

I managed to decipher the address – 4 Windsor Court, Moscow Road, Bayswater – and when I reached Moscow Road next morning, I recognised Windsor Court immediately. It was an anonymous red-brick mansion block, opposite the Greek Orthodox cathedral, four doors along from where I once interviewed Dame Edith Sitwell, who was living there with her companion, Helen Rootham, writing her poetry in noble poverty.

Only King Billie would have found a flat with Dame

Edith as a neighbour for his London *pied à terre*; and only a former burglar, which he also was, would have considered it necessary to install such cumbrous security as faced me now – an entryphone, a rarity in 1968, not one but two brand new Chubb locks fitted to the solid oak front door, and a spyhole through which I realised that I was being carefully observed before the door was opened.

Billie was a shortish man in his mid-fifties, smoother and better-looking than I had expected, with large expensive spectacles and longish grey hair carefully brushed back in a way that would have looked better on a younger man; he was softly spoken with no noticeable accent. Reg had told me that he was in London on a flying visit from Morocco, where he kept an apartment. I discovered later that he also had a house in southern Spain, and was a founder member of what was later known as the 'Costa del Crime'.

If he reminded me of anyone it was of one of the top tycoons I used to interview for the business pages of the *Sunday Times*; he could have been a successful chairman in retirement who still enjoyed the use of the company flat. It was that sort of apartment, and could not have been more different from the tattered cosiness of Vallance Road. Heavy, dusty-coral-coloured velvet curtains were still pulled in the middle of the morning, and there was a device that made the light from the big Italian chandeliers gently rise and fall as we were talking, giving me the feeling that we were not in London but in some far-off corner of civilisation where the electricity supply was not to be relied on.

I liked Billie Hill, but then I liked everybody in those days, and what struck me increasingly throughout our meeting was how totally different he was from either of the Twins. This extended to the long scar running down one side of his nose – the faces of the Twins were ominously free of scars.

Scarred or not, he had all the signs of a man very much at ease with his success. The Twins would have been wearing suits and ties for an interview, but Bill's expensive white Swiss nylon shirt was open at the neck. He'd kept his figure. He was wearing soft, dark blue, Moroccan-leather slippers on his bare feet, and on his wrist the slimmest of gold watches, in contrast with Ron's great eighteen-carat, knuckle-dusting Rolex.

In fact this really was your Mr Big, a very serious old-time criminal indeed, who'd risen through the ranks, learning his lessons on the way and landing a fortune at the end of it. And soon, like any self-made big-time businessman, he was talking rather proudly, as they all do in the end, about himself. He started with his origins which, as he made a point of reminding me, were considerably poorer and tougher than the Twins'.

'I was born in St Pancras in 1915. My parents were Irish immigrants and my mother was a good Catholic who produced twenty-three children. As kids we were starving and I suppose you could say I was rebelling against it all. The first thing I ever did against the law was to raid the stalls in Farringdon Road for fruit to eat, and for books, which I'd sell on again for a few pennies. Then I was sent to Borstal. When I ran away in 1928 and was recaptured I was given nine months' imprisonment and a flogging. As I was thirteen, they said I was too young for the 'cat-o-nine-tails', so they gave me twelve strokes with the birch instead. Of course, even the birch tears you to pieces, but once you've had it you feel you've really overcome something. You're tougher, and from then on I knew that nothing on God's earth could stop me.'

On the sideboard behind him I noticed three framed photographs, one of a long hacienda-style house with a swimming pool, another of a big white open Cadillac, the third of a pretty dark-haired woman in a white bikini.

He talked of his career, proudly explaining that whereas the Krays were strong-arm men and racketeers from the beginning, he originally learned his trade as an expert thief.

'In all I've been sentenced to twenty-three years in prison and served seventeen of them. Although I was probably the best screwsman [safeblower] in the business, I didn't keep a penny of anything I earned until 1947, when I got into the rackets too. It happened by accident. I was living in Camden Town with my brother; he was a thief like me, and the Whites, who had the gang that used to run the races, tried to put the squeeze on us, asking for a share of what we took. We decided to stop this from the start, so we faced them, and they gave in. But we knew that from then on we were up against them, and would need all the help that we could get to beat them.

'One of the advantages of spending so long in prison is that you end up knowing a lot of criminals, some of whom are desperate men. They joined me, not only for the money, but because they knew me and were loyal. Soon we had taken over the Whites' position at the races, and I was letting pitches to the bookmakers at five pounds a time. It was a natural progression into gambling, where the real money was. As boss of my own gang I could declare myself into anything I wanted; during the four years before gambling became legal, I was running thirteen gambling clubs, including two in Belgravia. After the Betting and Gaming Act it was more profitable to concentrate on two – one in Green Street, Mayfair, and the other in Virginia Water.'

'And that was all?' I said.

For the first time since I arrived, Billie laughed, and shook his head.

'All? I'm not one to boast, but you know I laid the pattern for modern big-time crime in Britain. I'm not saying that I organised the quarter-of-a-million-pound mailbag job or the KLM gold robbery at Hatton Garden. They've been attributed to me, and people can attribute what they like as far as I'm concerned. I worked out all the possibilities of entering straight business too. I had a fancy goods business and several restaurants, and I went into demolition in a big way. Bought up buildings where they stood. At one time I owned the old Earls Court Exhibition Building, and the Rothschild mansion just along from Apsley House.'

He confirmed that he'd stepped down in favour of the Twins, but still kept 'certain interests' which they were 'looking after' for him. He had a soft spot for his club in Green Street, along with some unspecified 'bits of business', which they also did for him in London. It was then I realised that he wasn't quite the sweet old pussycat he seemed. One of the Firm assured me later that he'd recently given Ron an American police Smith and Wesson .38 revolver.

But the more I talked to Billie Hill, the more I realised that his was a different world from anything the Krays could possibly aspire to. Like the big businessman he had become, he talked about the friends he had in Monte Carlo and Marbella and the south of France. He liked good food and good hotels. He said he'd started serious reading; his favourite book was Zola's *Germinal*. Somehow I couldn't see the Twins enjoying Zola, or reaching this sort of status in a thousand years – or being particularly happy if they did.

Another difference from the Twins was his total lack of their sort of togetherness and involvement with the world they came from.

When I asked if he was ever lonely, he shrugged.

'It's something you get used to in my sort of life. I've cut myself off from my old friends, and I can't say I regret it. A few months back I returned to King's Cross and met some people I grew up with. They're old men now, and more or less worn out, though they're only in their fifties.'

He was guarded when I asked about the Twins. There was clearly much he could have said but didn't. 'It's tougher for them today than it was for me. There's more competition. They need to do certain things I never had to do.'

One thing about them seemed to puzzle him.

'Why do they have so many people round them? I keep telling them they soak up all the money and they're just not necessary.'

I was beginning to ask myself the same question.

Much has been written on the fearsome nature of the Krays' notorious Firm but, as I look back on them all, they strike me as a very odd bunch indeed. They included quite a following of old-timers, dead-beats and unworthy causes, who enjoyed their hospitality and could be called upon for help when necessary. But at the heart of the Firm was a core of between twelve and fifteen serious villains who were on the payroll.

Without exception, they were very kind to me, and there were some whose company and conversation I genuinely enjoyed. Clearly all of them were capable of varying degrees of villainy – they could drink a lot, talked big, looked nasty, and I've no doubt that if it came to it, most of them could, as they say, 'take care of themselves' in a bar fight or a punch-up, use a knife, hurt anyone they had to and, if hurt themselves, take their punishment without complaining or grassing to the police.

But there was also something slightly pathetic about them, and to be absolutely truthful, I thought them not quite up to scratch for a gang attached to such notorious criminals as the Krays. These were rather threadbare gangsters. None of them drove a decent car, or dressed particularly well, or threw his money around; as I soon discovered, this wasn't meanness, but because there wasn't much to throw. And if they drank a lot, it was because the Twins were generally paying. When I met their women, I noticed that there was not a sexy gangsters' moll among them.

Ron's closest confidant and current favourite was a close relation, his cousin Ronald Hart, who played the part of ADC to Ronnie's Colonel. He was still in his mid-twenties, tall and rather vapidly good-looking. He had spent two years with the merchant navy, followed by a period in Soho as a pimp living off 'immoral earnings'. I asked him why he joined the Firm.

'The Twins have always been my heroes. Since I was a kid I wanted to be like them, you know, different from ordinary people.'

The Krays had certainly made him that: not many 'ordinary people' become accessories to murder. Although I didn't know it yet, barely three months earlier, the Twins had involved Ronald Hart in Jack McVitie's murder.

Because of this, and because he was a member of the family, which meant a lot to the Twins, he was in a favoured situation, and was one of the few members of the Firm who was doing well from the protection rackets. Once he showed me a list of clubs and spielers from which he collected money every week. Although most if this went to the Twins, he must also have been picking up a fairly hefty weekly income for himself.

He made one remark that intrigued me, repeating as it did the criticism made by Billie Hill. 'The Twins don't really need us. They're doin' us a favour lettin' us be with them.'

This wasn't strictly true; it was obvious that the Twins required a constant group of threatening-looking characters around them who would do their bidding. This was part of the power game they were playing, and I gradually discovered that the members of the Firm were also the supporting cast for the great ongoing drama which the Twins were living. Each member of the Firm appeared to have his own distinctive role to play within it. Apart from the real old-timers, who were always there, there were also a number of close friends who had known them for years, such as Dickie Morgan and Checker Berry, both of whom had grown up with them in Bethnal Green.

I got on particularly well with Dickie, a genuine original who had been with them in the army. With his long pale face and broken nose, he was a comedian who specialised in gangster humour and he could make Ron laugh even on his blackest days.

Checker was another old-time friend, who ran several of the Twins' clubs for them. His brother, Teddy Berry, was the landlord of the Old Horns, who had been the victim of one of Ron's little paranoid 'mistakes' a few years earlier. After being shot in error during one of Ron's suspicious rages he had been obliged to have a leg amputated. Reg had been, as usual, most apologetic. I never discovered what, if anything, Teddy had received in compensation, but it seems that being made landlord of the Kray Twins' favourite pub was in the nature of a reward for having kept his mouth shut. It may even have been Ron's way of saying sorry.

I had discovered more about discreet Little Tom, a.k.a. Tommy Cowley. He too had known the Twins for years, and was a small-time thief and con man who had run various clubs and fraudulent businesses on their behalf. He was currently holding down a job as a debt collector and enforcer with a double-glazing millionaire, who was an old client of the Twins and whom they could always 'touch' for the odd few thousand.

Then there were the professional 'heavies' of the Firm, such as 'Big Albert' Donoghue, a deceptively quiet Irishman who played his part in the Twins' strange carnival of violence along with an even bigger character, huge, lumbering 'Scotch Pat' Connolly, who was always brooding on the fact that his wife had left him. Now that he had no personal commitments, his only consolation seemed to be his total involvement with the Twins, for whom it seemed he would do absolutely anything.

The Firm's two really tough guys also happened to be Scots: 'Scotch Jack' Dickson, a former Royal Marine commando, and silent Ian Barrie. Both of them were former safeblowers from the Gorbals, who had migrated south in search of a softer life and easier money than they could find in Glasgow. They had both been serious professionals, and the Twins increasingly relied on them to do their dirty work and act as their private bodyguards.

They were very different from the Firm's most recent recruits, two brothers of Cypriot extraction, Chris and Tony Lambrianou, both of whom had been small-time tearaways and petty thieves. They had been attracted by the 'glamour' of the Twins and were flattered to have been included in their gang – which turned out to be extremely bad luck for both of them.

I had also discovered more about Big Tom, the giant who had driven me in silence from the Ritz to Gedding Hall. His real name was Tommy Brown and he was a professional all-in wrestler. Although not a full-time member of the Firm, he worked on a casual basis for the Krays, chiefly when prestige was needed, besides doing his share of 'minding' and 'enforcing' as required. In fact, though, his wife, 'Blonde Doris', was more important to the Twins, and particularly to Ron, as they both believed that she was psychic. They had appointed her their 'spiritual adviser' and personal astrologer, and wanted me to meet her.

Doris was a majestic woman, like a very big blonde female Buddha. At the time, I remember wondering how she and her enormous husband fitted into their tiny flat above a betting shop in Walthamstow. Like most of the members of the Firm, Little Tom, who was highly superstitious, was wary of her. 'Be careful what you say to her. Doris is a witch and she can read your thoughts,' were his final words of warning as he dropped me off outside her flat.

In fact I've met few people less witch-like than Doris Brown, but it seemed that she played a role in that whole weird set-up around the Twins as the Firm's collective psychic mother.

According to Little Tom, she had once told Ron that he was the reincarnation of Genghis Khan or Attila the Hun – he wasn't quite sure which. Doris denied this when I asked her. I noticed that she kept a crystal ball beside her box of chocolates on her coffee table and wondered if she used it. What was certain, though, for she told me, was that she encouraged Ron during moments of depression by reminding him about his psychic powers and sense of destiny.

'Ronald has a very strong spirit guide protecting him,' she said. 'It's stronger than that of anyone I've ever met, except my own father, who was strongly clairvoyant too. When Ronald consults me, his spirit guide can clash with mine and give me an instant headache.

'When he first started hearing voices from his spirit

guide, they used to upset him, but he accepts them now, and he's that much stronger as a result. He doesn't want to know the future, but nor does he feel regret for whatever has happened in the past. His sort never do. His spirit guide always tells him what to do, so that no one can ever harm him. Sometimes he consults me when he's confused, but I always tell him, "Ronald, let your spirit guide take over."'

'And Reg?' I asked her.

'Reginald shares the same spirit guide, of course, seeing as they're twins and so one person. But he won't accept his guidance like Ronald. I only wish he would – then I could help him. You know, of course, that Reginald is passing through a difficult time at present. He can't find himself. But thank goodness he has Ronald and his spirit guide beside him. They'll look after him.'

Watching the Twins surrounded by members of the Firm, I was reminded of the famous remark about the Beatles: 'When John Lennon laughs, everyone around him laughs.' When the Twins were in a good mood, it would have been hard to find a more enthusiastic band of brothers, and the Firm seemed less like gangsters than ageing groupies around a pair of pop stars. I learned another strange thing about the Twins: that their role as criminals was tied up with their overwhelming passion for celebrity. But it took the arrival of David Bailey on the scene one evening to make me realise how seriously the Twins took the whole culture of celebrity.

Ron had casually informed me that he had invited Bailey to take the photographs for 'our book', but as yet I hadn't realised Bailey's importance to the cult that was already growing up around them. From what I remembered of Bailey from my days in journalism, I thought it unlikely that I'd be meeting him again in Bethnal Green, but next evening, sure enough, what should greet my eyes but the improbable figure of the most fashionable photographer in London snapping away at the Twins with his Hasselblad in the saloon bar of The Old Horns.

Bailey was in unusually amiable mode that evening, and as a souvenir of this curious occasion one of the Firm took a picture of the two of us together, looking like a pair of trainee gangsters in between Checker Berry and his brother Teddy. As good as his word, during the next month or so, Bailey took a number of pictures of the Twins in their parents' flat, including several with Ron in the serpentine embrace of Read, his favourite python. Someone had told Ron that in those days, Harrods still guaranteed to supply their customers with anything they wanted, from a mutton pie to an elephant, so he ordered himself a pair of pythons by telephone from the Harrods pet department. When they arrived, he named them Read and Butler after two Scotland Yard detectives who had tried – and failed – to catch the Twins in the past.

Bailey's visit brought the Twins another celebrated ally in their quest for fame. It was probably inevitable that trouble would develop between Frank Taylor at McGraw-Hill and the Twins over their contribution to my book, and particularly over the terms for the great film on themselves and their career, which increasingly obsessed them. Reg mentioned this to Bailey, who suggested that his own representative, David Puttnam, might act for them and sort things out. Puttnam was interested, met the Twins, and seems to have got on particularly well with Reg.

Even so, I was surprised to hear that he really was representing the Twins in their dealings with McGraw-Hill and with my own agent, Deborah Rogers, today the *doyenne* of London literary agents. From then on, David

Puttnam, together with David Bailey, came to have a particular importance for the Twins as unlikely role models in their unrelenting obsession with celebrity.

As lively young working-class Londoners themselves, both Bailey and Puttnam were characters the Twins could easily relate to. Bailey was born at Leytonstone – Puttnam, from north London, was the son of a press photographer. Still barely in their late twenties, and having overcome the barriers of geography and class, both were already enormously successful. Bailey slept with starlets, drove a pale blue Rolls, and was one of the most highly paid fashion photographers in the country. Puttnam drove a more stylish old Mercedes coupe, had dated one of the Supremes and as well as Bailey represented several of the most important up-and-coming photographers of the sixties.

It was this that really made them so much more appealing to the Twins, and particularly to Ron, than a reclusive old crimino-capitalist-in-exile like Billie Hill. And one can see that, unlike Billie Hill, the two Davids came complete with all the trappings of youth and glamour and success. All the same, there was something quite uncanny in the way these East End gangsters had first picked on the most fashionable photographer in London to take their photographs, and had now persuaded a future Oscar-winning film producer, who would end up in the House of Lords, to handle their story and the film rights.

With Billie Hill safely in retirement, and the Richardsons and their gang in prison, the time when I was getting to know them should have been the moment for the Twins to consolidate their criminal and business interests, as Hill had done, and quietly and calmly make their fortunes. London was growing richer by the minute, and the Twins had no effective competition.

But, as Billie Hill had hinted, none of this was happening.

When they acted together, the Twins had surprisingly little in the way of organising power. In the past they had always had 'advisers' who directed them towards activities where they could use their name to underwrite lucrative financial rackets, large-scale frauds, protection and the gangster's sure-fire moneymaker, gambling. In their day both Billie Hill and the property racketeer Peter Rachman had acted as the Twins' 'advisers', together with a string of dodgy businessmen who'd tried to use their services. Much the most important of the Twins' discreet advisers had been a silver-tongued con man by the name of Leslie Payne, but he had broken with the Twins sometime before, and they always spoke of him with venom.

Now the advisers were gone, and most of the lucrative rackets of the past were drying up. Widespread extortion continued in the name of Kray, but the more I tried to learn about the actual organisation of the Firm, the more I realised that there really wasn't any, in the sense of the complex gangland structures of the Italian and American Mafia. As Billie Hill had hinted, the Firm was really just the Twins themselves, surrounded by a motley crew of would-be gangsters, hangers-on and boozing partners, who would use their name to 'nip' or grab or terrorise anything they could from pubs, clubs or lesser criminals. Such characters were backed by nothing remotely resembling the organisation and cast-iron discipline of the Mafia.

But with the Firm, this wasn't really necessary since its members served an altogether different purpose. Because the Twins believed that a real gangster had to have his gangs, they were partly there for ceremonial and social purposes, as part of the Twins' public entourage to guarantee 'respect'. As I discovered later, they also had a role as the supporting cast for the crazy schemes and acts of violence dictated by the Twins' imaginations, which were getting wilder all the time. This meant they had to hold themselves in readiness for the Twins' setpiece battles, fights and woundings – and, when the need arose, for their killings.

Apart from straightforward fear of the Twins, what really held the Firm together was not the money, nor the free booze, nor, as Ron Hart claimed, the spirit of adventure, but one thing only: by now the Twins had carefully involved each member of the Firm in their own dark secret and by doing so they genuinely believed they held them in their power for ever.

By late January, 1969, the police had reached the firm conclusion that the Kray Twins had murdered Jack 'the Hat' McVitie as well as the gangster George Cornell, and probably several others.

Amongst the Firm I had been hearing discreet references to 'so-and-so who's been taken care of' and bodies cemented into motorways. I remember an evening talking to Dickie Morgan when, not for the first time, McVitie's name was mentioned.

What was so special about him, I inquired naively.

'He was someone who should have known better. Took too many liberties with the Twins, an' look what happened,' said Dickie.

'What did?'

Clenching his right fist, he stuck out his index finger.

'Pow!' he said, and started laughing.

A few days later I heard of the death of George Cornell in more detail when Ron instructed Ronnie Hart to take me to the Blind Beggar, where Cornell was killed. Looking back, it seems a weird experience. As he sat drinking at the bar, Hart made it fairly clear that he knew exactly what had happened with Cornell and as he described in graphic detail how he died with a single bullet through the brain, the Blind Beggar suddenly struck me as the most repellent pub in London. Without actually telling me that Ron had pulled the trigger, he made it obvious that he had, and the more I talked to other members of the Firm, the clearer it became that not only did they all know about the Twins' killings, but that in one way or another most of them were implicated.

I realised something else: that the Twins wanted me to know about the killings too, provided that they never had to tell me personally. And I realised that, far from being furtive or ashamed about these murders, they were already seeing them as crucial episodes in what they were starting to refer to as 'our legend'.

EIGHT

'Crims and Toffs'

There are born victims, born to have their throats cut,
as the cut-throats are born to be hanged. You can see it
in their faces.

Aldous Huxley, *Point Counterpoint*

Quite early on, while I was still struggling to understand
the Twins, one of the most engaging characters I met was
Bobby Buckley. He was immensely charming, and charm
was rare around the Twins. He was said to be the love of
Ron's life, and when Ron introduced us he remarked, 'If I
could 'ave done it legal, I'd 'ave married 'im.'

We were in the Old Horns yet again, surrounded by
members of the Firm, but Bobby was the only one who
laughed – apart from me. In the circumstances, I found the
sudden high-camp turn in the conversation rather funny.

'What makes you think I'd ever have accepted you?'
Bobby answered. He shrugged and turned to me, nodding
in Ron's direction. 'He always carries on like that. You'd
think at his age he'd know better.'

Ron smiled back at him indulgently, while the rest of the
gangsters looked on, stony-faced.

'Careful, son,' said Ron, 'or I might 'ave to smack your
bottom.'

This sort of banter from Ron happened only when
Bobby was around, and one could see at once why he was
fond of him. Bobby was in his mid-twenties, but looked
younger. His family was Irish, which was probably where

his charm came from. He was very small, with bright black eyes, and had a face of extraordinary sweetness, and a sprightly manner, making him look like a young jockey who had put on weight. His constant affability marked him out at once from all the would-be villains, chancers, fantasists and possible murderers around the Twins, who clearly disapproved of him but wouldn't dare to say so.

'He's no more than a male prostitute,' Little Tom confided later when we were alone. Criminals can be uncomfortably judgemental, to the point of stuffiness on matters sexual. In fact Bobby used to work as a croupier in clubs the Twins controlled and several people told me he was one of the very best in London, sometimes picking up £500 a night from the tables. He had recently married a girl called Monica. Like him, she was very small and charming. Surprisingly, Ron liked her, and called her his daughter. Both died in the early seventies from overdosing drugs.

I was sad to hear about their deaths, as by then I'd grown to like them, and I owed a lot to Bobby when I came to write *The Profession of Violence*. He was bright and without his help I'd have missed much about the Twins. It was he who filled me in about the gambling scene in London at the time, and in particular about Esmeralda's Barn, the club the Twins had owned in Wilton Place, Knightsbridge, where he used to work.

The Betting and Gaming Act of 1961 was one of three crucial pieces of sixties legislation without which the Krays could never have raised their heads above the slough of long-forgotten cockney criminals (the other two being the legalising of sex between same-sex consenting adults in July 1967 and, more important still for them as things turned out, the abolition of capital punishment for murder at the end of 1965).

Like so much well-intentioned social legislation, the Gaming Act, which was seen as a way of driving the gangster out of gambling, achieved the opposite. Just as Prohibition turned twenties America into a paradise for gangsters, so the Gaming Act turned early sixties London into an Eldorado for rich racketeers like Billie Hill and up-and-coming villains like the Krays. With gambling legalised, a rash of clubs erupted throughout the capital. Many were run by criminals. Those that weren't soon would be, or would come under criminal protection. This new growth industry was particularly vulnerable to the threat of violence; and in those days wherever violence was needed, the Krays had a way of suddenly appearing.

One such place was Esmeralda's Barn in Wilton Place, just down the road from Harrods in the very heart of the affluent, 'swinging' London of the early sixties.

Esmeralda's Barn had motored through the feeble fifties enjoying a sedate existence on the débutante circuit, with low lights, smoochy dancing, overpriced and fairly lousy food, and a resident singer called Cy Grant, who helped to give the place its reputation. But by the sixties this was becoming slightly *passé*. There was a different clientele around and ownership of Esmeralda's Barn had slipped into the hands of a businessman called Stefan de Faye, author of a book entitled *Profitable Bar Management*. Knowing that the Gaming Act was coming, and anxious to benefit from the more relaxed attitude that the law was already showing to gambling, early in 1960, de Faye put his theories into practice and turned Esmeralda's into a gambling club.

It was supposedly via Peter Rachman, who was trying to keep in with the Twins, that news of this reached the sharp-eared fraudsman Leslie Payne, then a new friend of theirs. In that wonderfully relaxed con man's way of his, he was soon talking to de Faye and suggesting that possibly the Kray Twins would be more at home than Stefan in a place like this, since they could guarantee immunity from the sort of trouble that had such a way of following such clubs around, and was so very bad for business. So reasonable and so persuasive was Leslie Payne that soon afterwards the Twins took over Esmeralda's Barn, leaving Stefan de Faye with a cheque for £1000 for his interest in the club, and one of life's lessons in unprofitable bar management.

According to Bobby Buckley, another of Leslie Payne's bright ideas was inviting Mowbray Henry Gordon Howard on to the board of Esmeralda's Barn. Mowbray was an unsuccessful gambler, a would-be womaniser, a bankrupt and a drunk. He was also 6th Earl of Effingham, direct descendant in the junior line from the man who commanded the English fleet that destroyed the Armada, and one of the premier peers of England. Grateful for anything to supplement the £13-a-day attendance allowance he was being given by a grateful government for tottering into the House of Lords when it was sitting, he happily accepted £10 a week to place his name beside that of Ronald and Reginald Kray on the fresh headed paper that was being printed for the new directors of Esmeralda's Barn.

I met Leslie Payne later on in my researches. A tall, fair-haired man in a light-weight dark blue suit and casually tied, white-spotted blue bowtie, he was so plausible and so stylishly dishonest that I took him for an Old Etonian. He was, in fact, the son of a failed solicitor turned vet, and after serving as an infantry sergeant in the Second World War, and fighting at Cassino, he had graduated from selling Hoovers to a crooked used-car business in the Commercial Road, from which he moved on to large-scale fraud in general. In criminal circles he was known as 'the man with the briefcase' or 'Payne the Brain' and he first became involved with the Twins when he and his partner, an accountant called Freddie Gore, were running an extremely profitable series of so-called 'long-firm frauds' in various parts of London. The idea of the long-firm fraud was simple – buying goods on credit, selling them off as fast as possible below cost price, and disappearing before the creditors caught up with you. When things went wrong, as they often did, it was always useful to be backed by someone in the underworld with a known reputation for violence. That was how Payne had come to meet the Twins in 1959. He told me, 'When it came to organised violence the Kray Twins were the very best in London.'

As specialists in violence, the Twins were living through interesting times. The new casinos and gambling clubs of the early sixties, with their high profits and newly rich middle-class clients, were more vulnerable to violence than the undercover clubs of the past. Rather than risk having their customers upset, these clubs would buy peace at almost any price. Reg had a knack of ensuring that the price was right. There was rarely any need for actual violence. The name of Kray had a way of convincing people, and some clients genuinely came to him, asking for protection.

Payne's long-firm frauds were another source of profit for the Twins. He always had several going simultaneously, and he told me that in 1962, the Twins received more than £100,000 between them as their share of profit from this source alone. But the most lucrative developments were now coming from abroad as foreign syndicates became interested in the profits to be made from London gambling. These foreign interests included top French and German syndicates, and by far the most important for the Twins, representatives of the US Mafia. Like the multinational businessmen they were, the American Mafia had sent their representatives to London to check out the criminal potential in Europe's latest boom town – particularly for large-scale gambling 'junkets' of high-rolling gamblers from the United States, who could be flown in by specially chartered flights from California, Las Vegas and New York.

This was criminal big business on a major scale, with the Mafia milking every level of the operation. But it needed careful handling – only the best hotels, the richest, best-run gambling clubs, attractive women, reliable restaurants for their well-heeled clients, and above all, no trouble, cither from the law or from uncouth local criminals. During negotiations with the Twins, these foreign emissaries always took it for granted that smoothly organised protection on the American pattern operated in London – an assumption Reg was more than willing to agree with. During 1962, discussions started with various influential Americans, most of them introduced to Reg by Leslie Payne. Encouraging reports about the Twins were getting back to Las Vegas and New York.

In comparison with such criminal big business, Esmeralda's Barn was little more than a sideline for the Twins, but it proved to be of great importance to their lives. At first, Reg was predictably keen on the idea of becoming involved in it, while Ron supposedly was not. As they donned their smart tuxedos and started mingling with the varied clientele of this club, which they had almost casually acquired, it should have been the point when Reg achieved the social and personal success he'd always wanted. He'd crossed the Rubicon from east to west and here at last he was in his element – he was the acceptable face of sixties gangsterdom in person, smart, smooth, attractive to a certain sort of woman, and so obsessionally concerned with celebrities that he was on the verge of becoming one himself.

So this should have been the moment when, backed by his 'name', and his growing involvement in organised crime, Reg could have resumed his favourite role of celebrity club owner, (which he had so enjoyed at the Double R, which had been closed in 1959 soon after Ron's release from prison). At Esmeralda's Barn he could reappear, not unlike his hero George Raft, in the role of the elegant, rough-diamond celebrity gangster proprietor.

But it didn't work like that, for several reasons. First, the truth was that, despite his presentable appearance at the Double R, when seen against the backdrop of sophisticated early sixties Chelsea, Reg in presentable gangster mode was something of a bore. In the second place, Reg's business and social life was rudely interrupted at the end of 1960, when his appeal against an earlier conviction for demanding money with menaces was rejected, and he was unceremoniously bundled back to prison to serve out the last six months of an interrupted sentence. But by far the most important factor in the Krays' control of Esmeralda's Barn was a sad fact that straight people tend to overlook when mingling with gangsters: criminals are by definition crooked, and the Twins were congenitally incapable of running anything without milking it unmercifully.

To nobody's surprise, no one on the staff at Esmeralda's Barn felt like personally complaining when, while Reg was still in prison, Ron began treating the cash till as his private moneybox, offering fellow criminals and favoured punters endless credit, and putting the squeeze on wealthy clients. Soon the Twins' smart, non-crooked partner, Alf Mancini, who had been brought in to reorganise the gambling, decided he had had enough, cut his losses and went off to start his own successful club in Curzon Street. When the

Twins decided to replace him with their Uncle Alf, the days of Esmeralda's Barn were numbered. By early 1963, the tax man was knocking on the door; the bailiffs followed, the doors were locked, the Twins departed. But although it seemed as if the Twins' involvement in the Barn had ended in disaster, it was of great importance in their growing role as criminal celebrities. It also started a dangerous development in the relationship between the Twins themselves.

During those early days of 1960 when the Krays arrived at Esmeralda's Barn, there was one character its gilded clientele were either scared or fascinated by. This was not the mumbling, sometimes kindly Reg, but the brooding figure of his brother, Ron, who was emerging from the shadows of the madhouse as a figure capable of arousing fear and speculation.

Criminals and monsters were in vogue in early sixties London. There was even a reviving cult around the memory of Aleister Crowley, the self-proclaimed diabolist, black magician and 'Great Beast 666'. I remember Ian Fleming being fascinated by this tedious old fraud and using him as the model for his sado-masochistic villain, Chiffre, in his first James Bond thriller, *Casino Royale*. But where Crowley's reputation had been built on fantasy, Ron was real.

Ron was Aleister Crowley with a knife and an uppercut and a genuine capacity to kill. Crowley was a joke, Ron was not; and from his base at Esmeralda's Barn, Ron was becoming swinging London's first genuine monster in residence. Who could tell how true the stories being told about him really were, but for anyone who'd seen him in the flesh, such tales possessed a chilling credibility, quite lacking in the fantasies of the Great Beast 666. One oft-repeated tale related how Ron had recently met six would-be gangsters in a club in Windmill Street, Soho, chopped off the leader's trigger finger with a machete, then departed, taking the finger with him and locking the door behind him. Another one that went the rounds was of how he had blasted off some over-sexed gangster's testicles with a shotgun, while others told of how he had branded one villain on the cheek with a red-hot poker, and went berserk with another in the men's room of a roadhouse on the Kingston bypass and effectively removed his face. Ron was getting increasingly talked about as fresh stories were added to the list, but these stories rarely included Reg.

As potential celebrity material, Ron possessed two advantages over brother Reg. By now the physical and mental changes Dr Klein had noticed were affecting his physiognomy and one of Ron's most bankable assets as a villain was a capacity to look like a murderer several years before he murdered anyone. It was a gradual process, but physically as well as emotionally, Ron was still changing and appearing like what he was – a highly dangerous paranoid schizophrenic. At this stage, Reg had no more than latent, inherited schizophrenic tendencies, and was still relatively normal. The Twins' passport photos taken in 1960 show them as virtually identical, but since then Ron's schizophrenia had advanced. His eyes were bulging faintly now. The voice had begun to flatten and the neck to thicken. One of the regular punters at Esmeralda's Barn, the painter Francis Bacon, once told me that Ronnie had the most frightening face he'd ever seen, which, coming from the creator of those screaming popes and tortured victims, is quite a testimonial.

Along with his appearance and his growing reputation, Ron had one further way of winning friends and influencing people, which had an unexpected impact on an influential group in swinging early sixties London – his homosexuality.

As his cousin Billie Wilshire once told me, Ron's homosexuality had been a source of deep embarrassment and shame to him throughout his adolescence. (Smarter and more socially adept, Reg had less difficulty in hiding his sexual inclinations at this period.) So it came as something of a revelation when Ron discovered that in this new liberated society not only was he readily accepted for what he was, but that his status as a homosexual opened up for him an apparently classless world which he could never previously have dreamed of entering. In the basement under Esmeralda's Barn was the Cellar Club, run by a woman called Ginette, which, although technically for lesbians, was in fact a free and easy meeting place for those of almost every sexual inclination. Ginette and Ron became acquainted, and with friends like her, he began discovering that, far from being shameful, being gay was fun and self-fulfilling. At her club and in the Barn itself, he was also meeting others who, instead of attempting to disguise their sexuality, were flaunting it and clearly enjoying themselves.

Ron himself was far too square to have been sexually outrageous in manner. 'I'm not queer, I'm 'omosexual,' he once solemnly informed me. Some of his new gay acquaintances treated him simply as a friend, but others saw him as a source not just of high camp gossip but of something more – for teenage boys, for the company of criminals, and for rough-trade sex with the constant threat of serious violence. This was to offer Ron a role of some importance for the future, but it is hard to see this role developing as it did without the active help of one of the most extraordinary characters in sixties London.

It was Bobby Buckley who first told me that I ought to

contact an elusive character called David Litvinoff. He said that Litvinoff had been one of Ron's most important associates in the days of Esmeralda's Barn, but by the beginning of 1968, whenever I tried the telephone number Bobby gave me, I could never reach him. In fact there was a simple reason for my failure. Sometime earlier, someone had broken into Litvinoff's flat on the fifth floor of a block in Kensington High Street, stripped him, shaved his head, cut his mouth from ear to ear and beaten him up so badly that he had lost consciousness. He was then tied upside down in a chair propped on the sill of his open window, and came to some hours later with the noise of CND marchers singing as they passed along the street below.

The Krays were blamed, particularly as Ron had fallen out with the accident-prone Litvinoff by then and in a previous encounter had smashed his nose in a club in Earls Court. But the shaving and cutting incident had in fact been ordered and paid for by an influential former Chelsea friend of Litvinoff's whom he had seriously offended – so seriously that he wanted him taught a lesson he would not forget. The law of libel still protects this friend's identity. However, the Krays, far from denying any involvement in the business, were perfectly happy to accept responsibility. Litvinoff went on the run, and by the time I was trying to locate him in January 1968, he was moving from one un-disclosed address to another. But although his long love affair with the Krays had ended badly, fate decreed that David Litvinoff would play an extraordinary part in fixing the image of the Krays for ever in the *Zeitgeist* of the London of the 1960s.

Recently an eight-by-ten-inch portrait of an anonymous man entitled *Man in a Headscarf* by Lucian Freud was sold at auction for £1 million. It was in fact a portrait of David Litvinoff and was originally entitled *The Procurer*, which was one of the sitter's many roles in life; it was painted long before his troubles had caught up with him, before his nose was smashed by Ronnie Kray and his mouth sliced open, leaving him with a sinister perpetual grin. In his time Litvinoff had been a boxer, a con man, a part-time villain, a full-time social parasite, a practical joker and a gambler. But he was one thing above all others – he was that genuine rarity, a compulsive and mesmerising talker.

The son of poor Russian Jewish immigrants in Whitechapel – his mother spoke little but Russian to the day she died – Litvinoff came from a gifted family. His half-brother Emmanuel is a novelist and poet of distinction; while another brother, Barnet Litvinoff, a respected figure in the ranks of British Jewry, was the friend and official biographer of Ben Gurion.

Inheriting his share of family intelligence, and entirely self-taught and self-invented, Litvinoff became another of those sixties emigrés from the old East End to the land of opportunity in the West; these included David Bailey and his fellow-photographer Terence Donovan, the actor Terence Stamp and the playwright Harold Pinter. Litvinoff's flow of conversation clearly was remarkable. One of his friends, the so-called 'uncrowned king of Chelsea' at the time, was the good-looking young art dealer, set designer and social star Christopher Gibbs, who rated him 'one of the truly great chat-merchants of our time. His flow of words,' says Gibbs, 'could be positively lyrical.' So was his apparent knowledge of every subject under the sun, on which he could effortlessly hold forth at a moment's notice. His niece Vida, herself a novelist, goes so far as to rate him 'a sort of genius', but, she is quick to add, 'a genius with a fatal flaw'.

Instead of doing anything as dull as working for a living, Litvinoff preferred to be what Vida called 'the court jester to the rich, smart Chelsea set of the sixties'. His friends were not necessarily rich. Some were famous artists. As well as Lucian Freud he knew Francis Bacon, and the influential gallery owner Robert Fraser. Another friend he sponged off quite unmercifully was a famous society painter, who had a house at the end of Cheyne Walk, with Christopher Gibbs, Mick Jagger and J. Paul Getty Jr. as close neighbours. This painter also rented a large studio above the old Pheasantry Club in the King's Road, Chelsea, where the royal portrait painter Pietro Annigoni had his studio. It was here that Litvinoff, who was often there, met one of Annigoni's pupils, a rich, talented, but still indecisive young Scot called Donald Cammell (scion of the Scottish shipbuilders Cammell Laird), who at this stage in life had set his heart on becoming a society portrait painter like the maestro Annigoni.

Part of Litvinoff's attraction to the whole Chelsea set was a sort of satanic virtuosity as a practical joker. He was emphatically no gentle japer. His jokes were rarely kind, but nor was a society that could appreciate his uncomfortable talents. Usually his jokes were at the expense of someone weaker or more vulnerable than himself, gaining him a reputation as the most outrageous man in London.

One story about him that did the rounds is of how he was at a family party when a young mother with a baby asked him to look after her child as it sat on its potty while she took a telephone call in the room next door. The story goes that Litvinoff got someone else to mind the infant while he went to the lavatory with the pot, used it generously himself and replaced the child upon the steaming offering, which reduced the mother to hysterics when she returned and saw what her baby had produced.

Another story about Litvinoff from the early sixties is of how he was present at a party when a celebrated Chelsea drunk passed out in the bathroom and ended up lying unconscious in the empty bathtub. Seeing him lying there, Litvinoff rushed to the kitchen, where he'd seen some fresh chickens' livers in the refrigerator, which he tipped down the drunken partygoer's shirt front. Then he woke him. 'For God's sake,' shouted Litvinoff, 'Wake up! Wake up! Someone call a doctor. You've just sicked up your lungs.'

All Litvinoff's jokes seem to have had the same sort of faintly sadistic and surreal quality and presumably brought a touch of the unthinkable to the lives of the bored and wealthy. Like the fat boy in *The Pickwick Papers*, his stock-in-trade was to 'make your flesh creep'. During the time he got to know Ron Kray at Esmeralda's Barn, he played a part in teaching him to do the same.

In fact what sealed the relationship between Litvinoff and Ron was not a shared interest in boys and violence but Litvinoff's disastrous love of gambling. Having built up gaming debts at the Barn which he could not possibly repay, he was growing nervous at the thought of what would happen if he didn't. Following a short discussion, Ron set his mind at rest. Litvinoff owned the tail lease on a flat in Ashburn Gardens, just off the Gloucester Road in smartest Kensington. After a word with Uncle Alf, the debts were forgotten in exchange for the lease. Ron moved in with Bobby Buckley, and Litvinoff stayed on. For an extraordinary period early in 1962, all three of them lived at this smart address just off the Cromwell Road, getting up to God knows what together.

In the free and easy world of early sixties Chelsea, there was a new freedom among homosexuals with a taste for rough trade, boys and violence. In the days of Oscar Wilde, West End 'toffs' who were so inclined came east for sex, and enjoyed the sailors of Limehouse and the male brothels of Wapping; but this was kept hidden, as it always had to be. Homosexuality was not just 'the love that dare not speak its name'; its practice was hounded by the law, and all involved knew better than to overstep the boundaries of class as well as of propriety. In the 1960s, however, this was changing and homosexuality was giving Ron a passport between the two quite separate worlds he was now inhabiting. A wider, richer, and remarkably influential society was ready to welcome him and indeed to use him.

Litvinoff was at the centre of one of many extraordinary networks that London has always specialised in. He had been remarkably successful himself in making the difficult transition between the East End where he was born to a social world where everyone who was anyone seemed to know each other. In those days Chelsea was something like a club. Ronnie could never hope to join this club himself, but with Litvinoff to help him he could do something more remarkable.

Litvinoff, having trained as a boxer, sometimes liked to act the villain himself. With his secret love of violence, it isn't hard to understand the satisfaction that he must have felt at being able to count the most dangerous gangster in London as his flatmate and his friend. But for Ronnie, friendship with Litvinoff could bestow still greater benefits. The social world of Litvinoff was the world of celebrity and success, which Ron, like Reg, had always dreamed of entering. Now, as well as acting as Ron's guide between the two distinct worlds of the East End and the smartest area of swinging London, Litvinoff became a compulsive publicist on his behalf. He was becoming obsessive about the Krays, and it was enough for him to talk about them, as he often did, for his horror tales and skilful imitations of the Twins, and particularly of Ron, to become setpieces in his after-dinner Chelsea repertoire. Soon he was holding the smartest dinner tables spellbound with first-hand despatches from the front line of East End violent crime. This explains how Ron, who met hardly any of Litvinoff's smart friends, was rapidly becoming known by all of them.

One of the very few who actually met the Twins, although only very briefly, was Christopher Gibbs, who remembers an evening when a car drew up beside him in the Earls Court Road. In it was Litvinoff, with two dark-suited characters.

'Christopher,' he said, 'I'd like you to meet the Kray Twins.' They all shook hands, and that, it seems, was that.

Here, for the first time, one discerns the true uniqueness of the Twins as criminals. No other London criminals, be they villains, con men, murderers or thieves, possessed a fraction of their weird appeal. None could produce that instant *frisson* at the very mention of their name, none got talked about in such a way or inspired their very special sense of dread. For that matter, no other criminals moved so effortlessly between the so-called 'café society' of the West and the roughest, toughest parts of Bethnal Green.

Although later decades would make the sixties seem almost innocent and touchingly naive in comparison, at the time some of its inhabitants seemed to have attained the ultimate in sex, in drugs, in pop music and in unrestrained behaviour. In such a world it was inevitable that there should have been an honoured place for the ultimate in violent crime; and in Chelsea at any rate, Ron was already becoming the sixties' ultimate criminal celebrity.

In 1963 when the Barn closed and the lease expired on the flat in Kensington, Reg was still living in Vallance Road and Ron followed him back to the East End. He said that he missed living there, and that East Enders were 'more genuine' than any other Londoners, but unlike Reg he had no intention of returning to the family. After Ashburn Gardens he wanted his independence to continue, so he rented a modern first-floor flat in Cedra Court in Cazenove Road in Walthamstow. On the face of it, this was an unlikely place for Ron – most of the residents of Cedra Court were highly respectable, middle-class Jewish families; but it did give him what he wanted. He was back in the East End, but he had kept his freedom and his independence. And here he could be anonymous. He could have his boys, meet his criminal friends and continue to cater for the special tastes of his West End clientele. The move to Cedra Court began a whole new chapter in his life.

Walking into his flat was like entering the home of a crazy sultan in a rundown kasbah. Along with the flower-patterned carpets and the garish vases he had a passion for, there were Indian and Persian rugs hanging on the walls, and between them a life-sized painting of a naked boy in a heavily gilded frame, which he had bought in the market for £100. In the bedroom there was a big four-poster, and mirrors on the ceiling and the walls, and his suits hung from a rail that he had 'borrowed' from a bankrupt dress shop. He proudly told me that he had thirty-seven hand-made suits, most of them from Savile Row. He also boasted that he bought his shirts by the dozen from Turnbull and Asser in Jermyn Street, but since he could not be bothered with furniture, he kept them in laundry baskets.

It was this casual atmosphere that made the flat appear not so much a home as a living space where he could camp with his possessions round him, drink with his lovers and his friends, sleep with his boys, organise sex shows and orgies for the West End rough trade, and, for the first time in his life, feel free and be entirely himself.

There was also a curiously domesticated side to life at Cedra Court, especially when Bobby Buckley lived there. One of the waitresses from Esmeralda's Barn, called Lorraine, acted as a housekeeper. Not only did she cook and occasionally clean for Ron, but according to one member of the Firm she had another role. 'When he couldn't find a boy to spend the night with, Ron would say, "OK, Lorraine, go an' 'ave a bath," and he'd make do with her.'

For although Ron's abiding passion was for boys, he never slept alone if he could help it. According to Bobby Buckley, if this occasionally meant sleeping with someone like Lorraine it was probably less for sex than because Ron was frightened of the dark. He was also terrified of mice.

Sunday afternoons always found Ron 'at home' to close friends and attendant boys, all gathered round the big television, drinking nothing stronger than endless cups of tea. The room was dominated by his zoo-size aquarium of tropical fish. (It says a lot about what was happening to the Firm that the most important task of one of its members, the diminutive gangster Billie Exley, was to keep the glass clean, check the water twice a day and ensure that the fish were fed.)

Early in 1964, both Twins became involved in the most elaborate of Leslie Payne's adventures – an ambitious scheme, in concert with a British construction company and the Nigerian government, to build a brand-new township at Enugu in what is now Biafra. Inevitably the project failed, but not before both the Twins had enjoyed a VIP visit to Enugu, where a minister from the Nigerian government treated them as important, rich celebrities. Africa made an unforgettable impression on both the Twins, and particularly on Ron. One of his most treasured possessions in the flat was a four-foot-high ebony elephant with genuine ivory tusks which he had brought back from Enugu.

When he was at home, Ron liked to play the potentate, ordering his minions to look after him. He looked the part and held forth upon a range of subjects that obsessed him – the animals he'd buy, the tame bear he wanted, together with parrots, snakes, a gibbon and a chimpanzee. He could become obsessed with crazy projects. One day he decided to enlist as a mercenary in the Congo, the next to retire to the country as a priest, and a few days later to go off and work in a leper colony. 'But you know,' he said. 'I've always thought I'll end up as vicar. A lot of 'omosexuals do.'

I suppose that he felt safe in Cedra Court and, feeling safe, he could relax for once and be surprisingly easy-going. He enjoyed taunting Bobby Buckley, and whenever Bobby became petulant or bored, Ron would smile with those curiously dull black eyes behind the rimless spectacles and say, 'Now, don't go getting cross wiv your old dad.' On one occasion Lorraine left a basket full of his freshly laundered shirts near the gas fire; when they caught fire, she was terrified that he would kill her. But when he discovered it, all he said was, 'That was a silly thing to do, Lorraine, my dear,' and never mentioned it again.

The emergence of Ron from the closet in the early sixties, coupled with his growing notoriety, started to tilt the balance, yet again, in the ever volatile relationship between the Twins.

Although in their late teens Ron's violence had made him the dominant twin, since Ron first went to prison and was certified insane, Reg had been effectively in charge, and the coarsening of Ron's appearance had made Reg appear the more intelligent and more attractive of the two.

At the time the Twins themselves played up to this with a calculated soft-twin, hard-twin act. Reg was the approachable one, the twin everybody liked, while Ron was the one who gave everyone the shivers. Always brighter than Ron, Reg was the 'live wire' with whom the crooked businessmen made their agreements. Reg was the one who started clubs like the Double R and the Kentucky, which gave him the chance to meet the celebrities he loved. Reg had always been the one who dressed well, creating the Krays' own version of early gangster chic, modelling himself consciously on George Raft and the early Humphrey Bogart.

But by the time Ron moved to Cedra Court in 1963, Reg's superiority over Ron was on the wane. Thanks to Doc Blasker's prescriptions and advice, Ron's more alarming episodes of paranoia were more or less controlled, and his personality was emerging from his breakdown with a force and power that it had never had before. As a full-blown but erratically controlled paranoid schizophrenic, he was becoming stronger and more forceful than his identical twin brother. Within the relationship in which they were permanently locked, the 'mad' twin had become the dominant one.

Soon he was even copying Reg's choice and style of tailoring the sharp, dark blue suits beautifully tailored for them by Woods of Kingsland Road. And gradually, within the extremity-obsessed, sensation-seeking, weirdo-loving, high-camp world of swinging London, it was lumbering Ron, not sharp-eyed Reg, who was emerging as the real 'character'.

The three years from 1960 to 1963, during which the Twins exploited and finally destroyed Esmeralda's Barn, were also the flush years for them both. Life would never be so good to them again. It was also in the London of the early sixties, free at last from the busy tongues and ever-watchful eyes of friends and enemies in Vallance Road, that Ron Kray's freakish personality reached its violent flowering.

NINE

The Peer and the Gangster

In the size of the lie there is always contained a certain factor of credibility, since the great mass of the people will more easily fall victim to a great lie than a small one.
Adolf Hitler

Talking to Ron Kray reminded me of a silly joke my children used to ask around this time: 'How do porcupines make love?' The answer: 'Carefully.'

Much the same applies to getting information out of someone you are starting to suspect to be a murderer. A tough-guy biographer such as Norman Mailer would probably have reached the point by now where he was confident enough to say, 'Well, Ron, just why did you kill that louse, Cornell?' Or 'Where the fuck is the body of Frank Mitchell?' Instead, remembering the porcupines, I played safe, and let Ron talk about himself, which he enjoyed when in the mood. But I noticed that beneath the talk, he was always wary. So I became wary too, asking general questions about his friends and childhood, which meant that most of his reminiscences related to ancient East End villains and boxers he had known as a boy, usually followed by anecdotes about the rich and famous.

I particularly remember an evening with him towards the end of February 1968 in the unlikely venue of the Gallipoli Turkish Club near Liverpool Street station. God knows why he liked this dreary spot, steeped as it was in the authentic Turkish gloom of a bar in downtown Ankara.

I know he was getting money from the owner, and he may have liked the faintly oriental air about the place.

It was an odd evening from the start. Ron had put on weight since I first saw him at Gedding Hall, just five months previously, and that evening he was sweating so profusely that several times he had to remove his spectacles and clean them with his handkerchief. He had brought along Fat Steph, one of his criminal old-timers, to join us for a drink. Fat Steph was a big man, but he was not a talker nor, apart from having an ability to pack away unlimited quantities of brown ale, was he a life enhancer – any more than was the fourth member of our group that evening, good-looking Ronnie Hart, whom Ron had brought along as his bodyguard, but who seemed taciturn and jumpy throughout our meeting. Adding one final touch of the bizarre to the occasion, an aging belly-dancer was performing to dirge-like Turkish music in a pale blue spotlight while the few early evening drinkers totally ignored her.

Ron was in his gangster-as-philosopher mode and started holding forth on life in general. He was a great one for aphorisms. 'Better a has-been than a never-was' was one of his favourites.

Then, as he often did, he went on to talk about celebrities he'd known. Most of these were boxers such as Joe Louis and Sonny Liston, and to change the subject I asked if he'd known any politicians. At first he was rather cagey, but he mentioned the journalist and left-wing Labour MP Tom Driberg. He wouldn't tell me how he knew him but said that he was a friend, and muttered something about having met him in the House of Lords. This sounded so unlikely that I was genuinely interested.

'When did you go there?' I asked.

'I've been there several times. I've had dinner there. I'd rather like to be a lord myself. I think I might enjoy it.

You'd be surprised at how many lords I know,' he continued. 'I've had dinner there with Lord Effingham. And
with Lord Shinwell. He was a nice man. And I had dinner
there with Boothby.'

'With who?' I asked, hardly able to believe what I was
hearing.

'With Lord Boothby. Afterwards he took me to White's
club for a drink, and I met Judge Cohen. He was a nice
man, too. We had a very interesting conversation.' It was
then that I remembered Vi Kray once mentioning that
Boothby had visited Vallance Road, but I hadn't believed
her.

'So you really know Lord Boothby?'

''Course I do. Know him very well,' he said.

I think my interest was arousing his suspicions. The
belly-dancer was coming to the end of her gyrations, and
as the music rose to a climax and she sent one final tremor
through her undulating flesh, Ron changed the subject.

But he had said enough. If what he said was true, the
implications were astounding. For apart from the sheer
improbability of Baron Boothby of Rattray Head entertain-
ing Ronald Kray in the dining room of the House of Lords,
before taking him on to such an upper-class bastion as
White's club in St James's, I knew that anything apart from
three short, carefully specified business meetings between
Ron Kray and Lord Boothby legally had never occurred.

If any other meetings had occurred, something quite
extraordinary had been going on.

I was particularly aware of this because, a few days earlier,
I'd been working in the cuttings library at the *Sunday
Times*, going through the press references to the Krays. By
far the most extensive of these concerned the Boothby libel
case in the early summer of 1964, which hinged entirely

upon an alleged 'relationship' between the famous baron and 'the king of the underworld', who was later revealed to have been Ron Kray.

This case had been the first occasion when the Twins, and Ron in particular, had really made it big in the media. Even four years later, while I reread the story as it unfolded in those yellowing press cuttings, it struck me as distinctly odd. It had all started with a front-page story in the *Sunday Mirror* of 12 July 1964, headlined 'PEER AND THE GANGSTER', alleging that Scotland Yard was about to make arrests in a sensational case involving a 'relationship' between 'a peer who is a household name and a homosexual thug at the head of the London underworld'.

No one was named. But references in the foreign press, which rapidly picked up on the story, made it clear that the peer was in fact Lord Boothby. Thanks to television, Boothby was probably the best-known politician in the country. In his day he had been a close friend and ally of Winston Churchill, and at one time was his parliamentary private secretary. Until Churchill sacked him, he had also been a minister in his wartime government. For many years he had been the lover of the wife of another prime minister, Harold Macmillan, from whom he had begged and finally obtained a peerage.

The *Sunday Mirror* confirmed the fact that the peer in the 12 July article was in fact Lord Boothby by sticking to its story on the following Sunday, 19 July. At this stage Ron was still being referred to as 'a homosexual thug' and 'king of the underworld'. By now it seemed as if a major scandal was about to burst upon Westminster, but the Metropolitan Police Commissioner, Sir Joseph Simpson, had damped down these exciting speculations, denying all knowledge of an investigation of a member of the House of Lords, and that any arrests were contemplated. Then the formidable

Arnold (later to be Lord) Goodman came on the scene as Lord Boothby's legal adviser, and the *Sunday Mirror* 'scoop' of the year collapsed like a punctured bouncy castle.

The pin that burst it was a letter from Lord Boothby that was prominently published in *The Times* on 4 August 1964, in which he declared his total innocence of all the *Sunday Mirror* charges. He stated emphatically that he was not, repeat not, homosexual and that, far from having had 'a relationship' with Ronald Kray, he barely knew him. He made it clear that he had met him on just three occasions earlier that year at his office in his flat in Eaton Place, to discuss a business proposition Ronald Kray had put to him. (The 'proposition' turned out to have been to head the Nigerian building scheme in which the Twins were involved through Leslie Payne.) Boothby had finally declined. And that, it seemed, was all there was to all the rumours and the innuendos. Lord Boothby's letter seemed to settle the case and put an end to Fleet Street's unpleasant suspicions.

For by now the reporting staff of the *Sunday Mirror* had been unable to produce any evidence to substantiate the allegations, and, backed by Lord Boothby's assertions in *The Times*, the formidable Goodman rapidly obtained a £40,000 settlement from the *Sunday Mirror*'s proprietors, the International Printing Corporation. In those days this was a fairly massive settlement, well over half a million pounds in today's inflated currency, but Goodman argued that it was more than justified, considering the seriousness of the allegations, and in lieu of the much heavier libel damages and legal costs his noble client would have been awarded had the case ever gone to court. As they say, one saw his point.

But if the truth was *not* as Lord Boothby had stated in his letter to *The Times*, and if in fact he had known Ron Kray well enough to have taken him to White's club after dining at the House of Lords, what of that massive libel settlement? What of Arnold Goodman's sudden intervention? More important still, I wondered, what was Lord Boothby up to, taking a character like Ron Kray to his club and for dinner at the House of Lords in the first place? What had been going on?

As the world discovered a very long time afterwards, many people in unusually high places had been asking much the same questions on that second Sunday in July 1964, when they opened that morning's *Sunday Mirror*. But the full extent of shock and horror the article caused among what *The Times* still called 'top people' was not revealed until 1 January 1995 when, under the so-called 'thirty-year rule', a batch of Cabinet papers from 1964 was placed in the Public Records Office.

These included classified reports by Sir Timothy Bligh, Private Secretary to the then Prime Minister, Sir Alec Douglas-Home, which revealed that one week later, on the morning of Sunday, 19 July 1964, the Prime Minister had called a hurried breakfast meeting at Chequers, his official country residence in Buckinghamshire, which was attended by two key members of his Cabinet: the Lord Chancellor, Lord Dilhorne, and the Home Secretary, Henry Brooke.

Sir Alec, supposedly the acme of P.G. Wodehouse-like unflappability and cool, was involved in something out of character. He and his two Cabinet colleagues were in fact verging on a state of panic. For with the *Sunday Mirror* sticking to its story, if anyone could appreciate the danger of these accusations for his fragile government, it was the Prime Minister.

In the first place he knew more than most about Bob Boothby. Both men came from much the same Scottish upper-class society, both had served many years as

Conservative MPs and both moved in the inner circles of the political establishment. He also knew the devastating effect of a serious sexual scandal on a government. The year before just such a scandal, involving the Minister of War, John Profumo, the rich Lord Astor and the call girl Christine Keeler, had led to the resignation of Harold Macmillan, the near destruction of the Conservative government, and Sir Alec's own improbable succession to the post of Prime Minister.

So one can understand the state of rare alarm of these three distinguished members of the Cabinet over the coffee and the toast and marmalade on that peaceful summer morning in Buckinghamshire. One thing and one alone was on their minds – that thanks to the peccadilloes of 'dear old Bob', history might well be going to repeat itself unless they did something very quickly to prevent it. As the Prime Minister's official papers show, their anxious discussions covered 'the growing tide of rumours about the involvement of members of both Houses of Parliament in protection rackets and homosexual activities'. For in grim addition to the story in the *Sunday Mirror*, the Prime Minister had just privately received yet further evidence, from his Parliamentary Chief Whip, Martin Redmayne, of Lord Boothby's mounting indiscretions. According to a secret note Sir Timothy Bligh had made on 19 July, two Conservative MPs, Brigadier Terence Clarke and Barnaby Drayson, had informed Redmayne that 'Lord Boothby and Tom Driberg had been importuning males at a dog track and were involved with gangs of thugs who go to dog tracks to dispose of their money.'

As a result of all of this, Sir Alec convened an urgent meeting of members of the Cabinet, law officers and 'Tory chiefs' on 21 July to decide on how to avert political disaster. To begin with, Henry Brooke was able to offer them some crumbs of comfort, having discussed Lord Boothby with the heads of MI5 and Scotland Yard. MI5 confirmed that there was no evidence of Russian influence in the case. Sir Joseph Simpson was as emollient as ever: as the country's senior policeman, he assured the Home Secretary that, 'While it was known that the Kray Twins were involved in protection rackets, the problem was in general less serious in London at the present time than it used to be.'

Apart from being nonsense, this was cold comfort for the Tory hierarchy, who by now had read the Chief Whip's report about the sightings of Boothby with Tom Driberg at the dog track. The Home Secretary had asked Lord Boothby outright about these accusations, which he had vehemently denied, but Sir Peter Rawlinson, the hard-boiled and hard-headed Solicitor General, probably expressed the general feeling of the Tory leadership when he said that he didn't find Lord Boothby's denial of his links with the Krays 'in the least bit plausible'. On which sombre note the meeting ended. The Home Secretary promised to discuss the matter further with Sir Joseph Simpson. As for the other members of the government, all they could do was keep their fingers crossed in the face of what must have seemed like inevitable disaster. But help was coming from an unexpected quarter.

To understand the extraordinary sequence of events that saved the government, Lord Boothby and also the Krays in July 1964, one must go back to the moment where the *Sunday Mirror*'s 'Peer and the Gangster' story started. This was on Thursday, 9 July, when one of the most seasoned crime reporters of his day, the lugubrious, cynical but usually extremely well-informed old journalist Norman Lucas, paid one of his regular visits to his friends in Scotland Yard. Lucas, an ex-policeman, was an old-school crime reporter who made the most of the freemasonry between police and crime reporters. And like most old-school crime reporters, Norman took great care to protect – and cultivate – his sources.

One of these was Chief Inspector John E. Cummings, the head of C11, the fledgling intelligence section at the Yard. When I met him later, Cummings told me that he and his detectives had been keeping the Twins and their henchmen under observation since the beginning of the year, in preparation for a full-scale police offensive against them. They had information on a range of their activities, including the large-scale frauds, the woundings and shootings, and their protection rackets. They had also been observing Ron meeting boys, in the company of several well-known personalities, in pubs and clubs in the East End, and also entering and leaving the flat at Cedra Court in their company. The most famous and recognisable of the personalities that the police had seen around the Krays was Lord Boothby.

Apart from improbable but harmless social occasions such as Lord Boothby's dinner with Ron Kray and a fair-haired boy with a pair of known criminals at Ron's favourite restaurant, the Society (now the nightclub Tramp) in Jermyn Street, together with the dinner Ron had mentioned at the House of Lords, there had been other sightings. Brigadier Clarke and Barnaby Drayson had apparently been right: Lord Boothby and his friend Tom Driberg had been in the habit of frequenting White City dog track, which was also a favourite venue for the Krays and their followers.

By the afternoon of 9 July when Norman Lucas visited Scotland Yard, C11's work was apparently complete, John Cummings had prepared his report and a full-scale offensive by Scotland Yard against the Krays was set to follow.

I never did discover who showed C11's report to Norman Lucas. Cummings denied doing so and I'm fairly certain that he didn't, if only because it was not in his interests to have done so, even for a fairly hefty payment. As it was, the whole episode caused him endless trouble and may well have stymied his promotion. And although I asked Norman outright several times for the identity of the leaker, he had no intention of being one himself. I imagine that he must have had some other member of Scotland Yard on his payroll who, recognising a red-hot story, saw his chance of earning some easy money from the press and took it.

As so often happened with the Twins, something quite unexpected now occurred which saved them. The key to it was the fact that a bitter feud was coming to the boil in the Holborn offices of the International Printing Corporation (IPC) between the great crusading popular journalist of his day, the Mirror Group's editor-in-chief Hugh Cudlipp, and the corporation's chairman, Cecil Harmsworth King, the very rich and half-crazed nephew of the totally crazed godfather of modern journalism.

Both were hugely ambitious – and both were locked in combat, not simply for control of IPC and Mirror Newspapers, but also for the basket of assorted goodies – prestige, titles, enhanced self-importance – that they were hoping for from the next Labour government, which they were counting on being elected in the imminent general election. They had reached that melancholy age where such things matter, and each had set his beady eye upon a peerage.

With much at stake behind the scenes in the offices of Mirror Newspapers, one understands the eagerness with which Cecil Harmsworth King seized on Norman Lucas's story. And here chance intervened again. Hugh Cudlipp was on a sailing holiday off the coast of France, and bad weather was delaying his return, leaving Cecil Harmsworth King in charge of the *Sunday Mirror*, and ultimately responsible for producing that Sunday's paper in Cudlipp's absence. Cecil saw his chance and took it.

Norman Lucas told me later of the excitement in the *Sunday Mirror* offices on that Saturday evening when Cecil Harmsworth King read the story he had written. 'Cecil was absolutely cock-a-hoop, and was determined to make the very most of it,' he said, 'and he swiftly did so'. For not only would a dramatic front-page scandal on the front page of the *Sunday Mirror* upstage Cudlipp with the sort of story he'd have loved, but King was apparently convinced that a full-blown criminal and sexual scandal involving a Conservative politician as prominent as Boothby on the eve of the election could be a death blow to Tory hopes. If this resulted in Labour getting back to power, the new Prime Minister, Harold Wilson, would be in debt to Cecil Harmsworth King for ever.

But no sooner was the story published on 12 July than reality started to abort the dreamchild of Cecil Harmsworth King. For not only did the Prime Minister, Sir Alec Douglas-Hume, make desperate efforts to defuse the story, but the Leader of the Opposition, Harold Wilson, looked Cecil's gift horse in the mouth and sensed trouble. His instincts were against making political capital out of sexual scandal and he guessed that he could win the election without descending to the gutter and resorting to unseemly scandal. This was one of those rare occasions when the deepest feelings of the Leader of the Opposition and Prime Minister coincided.

But whereas the Prime Minister and his Home Secretary, Henry Brooke, seemed unable to do anything to scotch the rumours, and before the impending scandal caused serious damage to the government, the Labour opposition proved itself more effective. Within days of the first *Sunday Mirror* article, several influential members of the Labour hierarchy had suddenly appeared with succour for Lord Boothby.

The first of these was a Lithuanian timber millionaire called Harold Kissin (later to become Lord Kissin). A close personal friend of Harold Wilson's and member of his so-called 'Hampstead circle', he was a born political insider with many friends in politics including inevitably Lord Boothby. Soon after the appearance of the *Sunday Mirror* article, he called at Boothby's flat at number 1 Eaton Place and, as he told me later 'found Bob in a dreadful state'.

Boothby felt that his old party had deserted him, and he had no one to turn to. According to Kissin, he was actually contemplating suicide. Kissin suggested bringing in another of his friends, Harold Wilson's favourite solicitor, his 'Mr Fixit', Arnold Goodman, who agreed to help. Goodman in turn suggested using the distinguished Labour barrister Gerald Gardiner, Harold Wilson's choice as Lord Chancellor if Labour were elected.

Gardiner asked Boothby on his honour if there was any truth in the allegations. 'Not a scrap,' replied Lord Boothby. 'You have my word on it.' And Gerald Gardiner, unlike Sir Peter Rawlinson, believed him.

Later I discovered that by now Lord Boothby also had two even more potent figures from the Labour hierachy on his side.

In the autumn of 1968, when I had the chance to interview him, Lord Boothby told me that on the Sunday of 12 July 1964, when the story broke, he been been enjoying a short holiday in the spa town of Vichy in France, with his old friend Sir Colin Coote, editor of the *Daily Telegraph*.

The two of them had read that morning's *Sunday Mirror* and speculated in all innocence on who the mysterious peer could be. Next morning back in his flat at Eaton Place, he rang an old friend with good insider press connections, to ask him who it was.

'I'm sorry, Bob,' the friend replied 'It's you.'

'But who was this friend?' I asked.

I remember a long pause before he gave an answer.

'It was my old friend, Tom,' he said. 'Tom Driberg.'

During the same interview I also had a chance to ask Lord Boothby why Harold Kissin called on him that afternoon and suggested the services of Arnold Goodman. Was it simply kindness and coincidence? He laughed that famous deep brown laugh of his, and said in fact it wasn't a coincidence.

'Who was behind it then?' I asked.

'The little man,' he said.

'What little man?' I asked naively.

More deep laughter. 'Use your imagination, my dear fellow. Harold Wilson.'

Although I'd heard that Harold Wilson had an unexpected streak of kindness in his nature, it was stretching the bounds of naivety to suppose that at a time like this, with a general election in the offing, kindness to Bob Boothby would have been his real concern, any more than that Arnold Goodman had been brought in to save Lord Boothby from suicide. I realised Arnold Goodman had a more important agenda: to ensure that Cecil Harmsworth King's unwanted story went away for ever, leaving Labour free to go ahead and win the next election. In addition to this, if Harold Wilson had genuinely been intent on saving anybody's reputation it would almost certainly not have been Bob Boothby's, but more likely that of his own extremely vulnerable MP Tom Driberg, whose friendship with Ron Kray seems to have landed him in another of those sexual 'scrapes' for which he was all too famous.

Since one of the conditions of the £40,000 settlement Goodman negotiated with the proprietors of the *Sunday Mirror* on behalf of Boothby was a confidentiality clause imposed on everyone involved, nobody explained how Arnold did it. But for a legal negotiator of the calibre of Arnold Goodman, it can't have been too difficult, when almost everyone involved now wished for one thing only – to kill the story. Sir Joseph Simpson's denial that any arrests were contemplated had already made it clear that as head of Scotland Yard, he at least had no intention of becoming caught up in any scandal that involved important politicians. Similarly, back at the *Mirror* building, Hugh Cudlipp was hardly likely to support his rival Cecil Harmsworth King over sensational allegations against Lord Boothby that he couldn't prove. On the contrary, it would have been in Cudlipp's deepest interests to have urged the board of IPC to settle and force King to apologise to Boothby as soon as possible. And whatever the suspicions of Conservative politicians such as Sir Peter Rawlinson and Martin Redmayne, not to mention the Prime Minister, that Boothby's denials of involvement with the Krays were 'not in the least bit plausible', it was not in their interests either to drag on with a squalid case about an aging peer who should have known better.

So one can understand the sheer relief throughout the Establishment on 6 August when it was announced that Arnold Goodman had obtained his speedy settlement. But there remained just one small problem which no one liked to mention. For once in his crazy life the unfortunate Cecil Harmsworth King just happened to have been right.

At Cedra Court Ron could not help noticing a good-looking, fair-haired boy in his mid-twenties living in the same block as him. Soon he had got to know him. His name was Leslie Holt. He was the son of a Shoreditch dustman, but as Ron found out, he made his living as a cat burglar. He was small with an elfin, Tommy Steele-like cockney charm, and in the time-honoured way of the London underworld, he also earned money from servicing older rich homosexual men from the upper classes. Among Leslie Holt's lovers was Lord Boothby.

During the autumn of 1963, Ron had got to know Lord Boothby through Leslie Holt, who had inevitably become Ron's lover too; and, just as inevitably, Ron had introduced Lord Boothby to the gay rough-trade network he had established with David Litvinoff in the early days at Esmeralda's Barn. From what one knows of Boothby, this can't have been difficult, particularly as another politician, Boothby's 'old friend Tom', Tom Driberg, had already been introduced to Ron Kray's sexual circus through another mutual gangland friend of the Krays, a good-looking, highly dangerous, gay gangster known as 'Mad Teddy Smith'.

As far as one can gather, there was nothing particularly startling in what they all got up to. The pattern was established many years before when male members of the upper classes ventured East in search of the pleasures of illicit sex. Apart from blue movies, the pleasures seem to have been much the same as ever – willing adolescent boys, rough-trade sex and recherché sex shows for a favoured few at Cedra Court. All this was very much to Boothby's taste. From the end of 1963, when his friendship with Ron began in earnest, he became such a familiar sight in parts of the East End that in the Firm he was commonly referred to as 'the Queen Mother'. At Cedra Court the shows were evidently tailored to Lord Boothby's taste in the bizarre.

According to one member of the Firm to whom I spoke

later, Boothby objected to Ron's insistence on swapping boys with him, and when this happened, 'would sulk throughout the entire evening'. What he apparently enjoyed was lying under a glass-topped table 'watching his boys excreting on the glass'. He 'also used to stick strings of beads up his rear and liked to sit naked with "crackers" – things like curling tongs women use for curling their hair – gripping the flesh of his stomach'.

If it suited Ron to organise such happenings in private, I suppose they didn't matter very much as long they were what the clients wanted. But Lord Boothby and Tom Driberg weren't ordinary clients. They were well-known politicians who must have understood that, if nothing else, the opportunities for blackmail they were offering known criminals through such behaviour were enormous. And now, thanks to the *Sunday Mirror* and the subsequent involvement of the entire government and opposition, Lord Boothby's antics had gone way beyond the realms of ordinary blackmail.

For suddenly, by trying to prevent a public scandal, the whole Establishment was effectively in collusion with Lord Boothby, Tom Driberg and the Kray Twins in their efforts to suppress the truth of what had happened. Cecil Harmsworth King had even had to apologise not just to Boothby but to Ron as well, on behalf of Mirror Newspapers. And now that the case was dead and buried, no politician was going to revive it. Even politicians who had previously campaigned against the threat of organised crime and protection rackets in London suddenly fell silent.

The press fell silent too. For as well as humiliating King, and getting Lord Boothby a bonus of £40,000 for buggery, Arnold Goodman had inserted a confidentiality clause in his settlement with Mirror Newspapers which meant that all future discussion or reference to the case in the Mirror Group newspapers was forbidden. Since Ron had been included in King's apology, this prohibition effectively extended to the Krays as well, and other papers took the hint. In those days £40,000 was a lot of money, certainly enough to make the point that in future any paper taking on the Kray Twins did so at its peril. It is noticeable that the popular press, which early in 1964 had been demanding tough action against organised crime in London, now found other objects for its indignation.

But for the Twins' future, much the most far-reaching and important fact about the Boothby case was the effect it had on the police and particularly on Scotland Yard. Here one must remember that, unlike editors and politicians, many members of the police force had in fact had close personal experience of the Krays and knew something of the danger that they represented. In particular the members of the C11 team who had been keeping the Twins under close observation from the start of 1964 must have known that something odd was going on, particularly when they had watched Lord Boothby enjoying the company of boys and gangsters in public places.

However, policemen aren't stupid, particularly if they want promotion. And when they saw their own Commissioner repudiating an investigation being mounted against serious criminals who happened to be involved with influential politicians, they got the message. Worse still, when a well-known homosexual gangster such as Ron Kray was saved, however indirectly, through the intervention of a lawyer as powerful as Arnold Goodman, it told them all they had to know. The Krays were criminals best left alone.

So it is not surprising that no more was heard of the work of the members of C11, and that nobody I talked to later seemed to know what had happened to their report.

Nor is it surprising that at Scotland Yard the word went round that nothing was going to be done against the Krays, as long as Sir Joseph Simpson was Commissioner – which as events would prove, was right.

There was, however, one exception to Scotland Yard's dis taste for any fresh involvement with the Twins following the Boothby case. But far from showing any weakness on the Twins' behalf, it served to demonstrate the remarkable nature of their power at this moment in their extraordinary career.

It started early in January 1965 when Hew McCowan, the owner of the Hideaway Club in Soho, complained to the police that the Kray Twins had been demanding money for protection, and had had his club smashed up by their friend Mad Teddy Smith when he refused.

The case was assigned to two detectives, the highly experienced Superintendent Fred Gerard, and a newly promoted detective inspector, Leonard 'Nipper' Read. Unusually in such cases, McCowan stuck by his story and said he would give evidence against the Twins in court. On the strength of this, the Twins were both arrested, and sent on remand to Brixton Prison, to await trial at the Old Bailey.

When the trial started at the end of February, they showed their new-found strength in a most decisive way. For not only were they rich enough to retain two of the most eminent criminal barristers in the country, Paul Wrightson QC and Sir Peter Crowder QC, to defend them, but when the trial started they also had someone who was able to inform them of the names and the addresses of the members of the jury. In those days, a jury's verdict had to be unanimous, and knowing this, the Twins were able to ensure that one of the jurors was approached on their behalf. At the conclusion of the trial, this one juror's vote went in their favour. Since the jury had failed to agree, there was no alternative but a retrial.

What followed was a masterpiece in the subtle art of fixing a trial at the Old Bailey. Since the Twins wanted to be freed on bail, their first move was to try putting pressure on the government through the one member of the Establishment they knew was vulnerable – Lord Boothby. As I found out later, they had compromising letters and photographs of him in their possession, and to help them Lord Boothby did something that he must have known was unconstitutional. By tradition, Members of Parliament are not allowed to appear to criticise or interfere with the judiciary, but despite this, he rose from his seat in the House of Lords to say how unjust it was that the Twins were still in prison and to call urgently for their release on bail. Ironically, he was answered by his former barrister, Gerald Gardiner, who was now Lord Chancellor, and who indignantly ruled his question out of order.

But the Twins had also hired one of the best private detectives in London to investigate the private life of Hew McCowan, which revealed shady facts about his past, including the fact that in Scotland he had been a police informer. This was all that the Twins' clever barristers required to argue that the principal prosecution witness was not to be relied on. The judge agreed, the trial ended and the Twins were triumphantly acquitted.

The jury law was subsequently changed, but the case seems to have convinced Sir Joseph Simpson that investigations of organised crime involving the Twins must cease. Fred Gerard seems to have agreed with him, and Nipper Read was sent off on other duties, leaving the Twins to enjoy almost three years of virtual freedom from the attention of New Scotland Yard. During the three years following the Boothby case, they would become known as 'the

Untouchables', and, as we shall see, Ron would have all the freedom he required to indulge in his wildest fantasies and Reg would join him in a rampage of murder and madness.

What happened to the Establishment figures in the Boothby case now seems of little consequence. Boothby, a gambler all his life, had had the devil's luck, which for a while seemed to continue. Incredibly he almost achieved his great ambition of being made Her Britannic Majesty's Ambassador to France. Tom Driberg, Arnold Goodman, Harry Kissin and Hugh Cudlipp all ended up together on the Labour benches in the House of Lords. The future victims of the Twins were not so lucky.

TEN

The Wedding of the Year

There's nothing like marriage to spoil a perfect love.
The Princess of Cleves

By mid-March 1968 the Twins' accomplices and friends were talking to me with surprising candour of the rackets, gang fights, beatings up and even, in a roundabout way, the murders that they knew about – or didn't. But there was one area where everyone, including members of the family, would instantly clam up – whenever I mentioned Reg's marriage to twenty-two-year-old Frances Shea, in April 1965.

This made me inquisitive, which was why I took the trouble to trace Father Hetherington, who had been the priest in charge of St James the Less in Bethnal Green at the time they married. Since then Father Hetherington had retired, and I tracked him down to shabby St Barnabas Rectory in Ealing. He was fairly shabby himself by now, a big old man in a shiny, greenish black cassock. He called himself 'an old priest', and was the sort of clergyman one rarely meets today – forthright, something of a mountebank, but with a lifetime's working knowledge of the human heart. For a priest he was untypically direct.

'You want to talk about poor Frankie Shea, or Frances Kray as she became. I'm afraid there's not a great deal I can say about her.'

'But you married her,' I said.

'No, I buried her.'

'Can I ask why you didn't conduct the marriage when it took place in your church?'

'Certainly. I'd known Reg since he was a boy, but when they came and asked me to marry them, I said I couldn't. I told them that I hoped they would not go through with it.'

Why?

'Because they'd simply no idea of what marriage was about. Not merely was there was not the faintest hope of either of them finding any happiness together, but I could see them causing serious harm to one another, which of course they did.'

'And in the end she killed herself,' I said.

'In the end she killed herself.'

When I tried to press him further he would say no more about it. He made us tea in an old brown teapot. On the wall were two framed photographs of mountains, and when I asked him about them he talked of the mountain climbing he enjoyed when he was young. There were also several wedding photographs of some of the presumably happy couples that Father Hetherington *had* agreed to marry.

But while he would not elaborate on the subject of Reg's marriage, I did meet several people who were only too willing to talk, and in the end I was able to piece together most of the whole wretched story. When I came to write *The Profession of Violence*, there could be no question of including it, with Reg and the older members of both families surviving. But now that Reg is dead, there is no reason to hold back on the truth of the marriage, and its disastrous consequences, which went far beyond the death of Frances.

Father Hetherington was right of course: Reg should never

have considered marrying Frances in the first place. Reg was not a fool, and must have known enough about himself to realise that he could not make any woman happy – certainly not one as simple and unsophisticated as Frances.

She had first caught his eye as a precocious fourteen-year-old schoolgirl living with her family in Ormsby Street, just around the corner from Vallance Road. Her brother, good-looking Frank Shea, had known both the Twins. As soon as Reg began to show an interest in Frances, she virtually became his property. No other local boy would have dared to ask her out or be seen with 'Reg's girl'. And once Reg began 'courting' her in earnest, Frances became a key component in the double life that he was leading.

Since identical twins share the same genetic make-up, the fact that Reg shared Ron's homosexuality is not surprising. But lacking the confidence that had finally enabled Ron to be frank about his nature and enjoy the gay life going on around him throughout their time at Esmeralda's Barn, Reg never dared to venture from the closet.

From time to time he made tortured efforts to change – usually when he'd grown tired of his current boy and had decided to 'go straight' – by starting a romance with a local girl. Teenage Frances was usually the girl, which placed her in an unenviable position. During his 'straight' periods, Reg would take her out, make sure that he was seen around with her and shower her with gifts. She was the prettiest girl in Bethnal Green and at times like this, her role in life was to be Reg's show fiancée. On several occasions he had proudly taken her for dinner at Esmeralda's Barn, but when this happened, Ron made no secret of his deep resentment of her presence. Once there was a public shouting match between the Twins, which started when Ron told his brother that he 'ought to know better than to carry on with silly women. Don't you know women smell?'

he shouted. Members of the Firm had to hold the Twins back to prevent a battle royal ensuing.

Things were more peaceful when Reg took Frances home to Vallance Road, but even Violet, possessive as ever of her Twins, never disguised the fact that she disliked her.

'She was never good enough for my Reggie,' she told me. 'She'd just sit there, polishing her nails. She couldn't even make herself a cup of tea.'

On the other hand, Violet's sister May was fond of Frances, and Reg would end up taking her into the house next door where Auntie May would make a fuss of her.

'Reg, you're a cradle-snatcher,' Auntie May would say, giving Reg a knowing wink.

'Can you blame me with a girl like Frankie, Auntie May?' he'd answer.

He first proposed to her in 1961, when he took her on holiday to Steeple Bay in Essex, where the Twins had bought a caravan. She was just eighteen and said she felt too young for marriage, but this made little difference to Reg. He told his family and friends that they were engaged, and took her on holiday abroad, first to Barcelona, and in 1962 to Italy, where they saw *La Bohème* at La Scala opera house in Milan. When the Shea family expressed concern at what was going on, Frances apparently told her parents that Reg had never tried to make her 'do anything she shouldn't', and that he insisted on separate rooms when they went to a hotel. This seems to have reassured her father. At this point he was even saying how much he approved of Reg, who was a model of respectability in the way he treated his daughter.

'I respected Reggie as an athlete and a clean-living man. He never used bad language, even when talking to me on my own, and always had my daughter home on time. We knew he never tried anything wrong with her, but treated her like a lady. We thought that was very nice.'

Not all the Shea family, however, were so keen on pretty Frances going out with a Kray. Her brother, Frank, had been friendly with the Twins during his late teens, but the friendship ended abruptly when he claims Ron tried to rape him. He didn't dare to tell his father at the time, but apparently he reported the gist of what happened to his mother, and it was partly because of her influence on her daughter that the relationship between Reg and Frances seems to have tailed off for a while. But although at times Reg liked being seen around with other girls, he also liked keeping Frances more or less on hold. She seems to have accepted this. He always told her she was 'special', but it seems unlikely that he would have brought himself to propose to her again in February 1965 if it hadn't been for the McCowan case.

Years later when girls used to write to him in prison, Reg would sometimes fall romantically in love with them. This is what happened when Frances started writing to him while he was on remand in prison. Absence must have made his heart grow fonder, and he convinced himself that he was in love. Amid all the excitement of the Old Bailey acquittal he proposed and she accepted. By now both her parents were opposed to the idea of the marriage, and even when Frances proudly showed them the solitaire diamond engagement ring Reg had given her, they wouldn't change their minds.

But with the McCowan case behind him, Reg was on a high and determined to celebrate his freedom by marrying the girl whom the papers were already calling 'his childhood sweetheart'.

Reg being Reg, this could clearly be no ordinary wedding; it had to be 'the East End's wedding of the year'. Since Father Hetherington would not officiate, his deputy, young Father Foster, was asked to take his place, and had no objections. The wedding soon became more involved with the cult of celebrity than with living happily ever after. With her heart-shaped face and docile nature, doe-eyed Frances seemed the perfect trophy bride for an ambitious gangster, and Reg naturally didn't miss a trick when it came to publicity. There was the predictable list of famous guests – boxers like Terry Spinks and the one-time world middleweight boxing champion Ted 'Kid' Lewis, the blind pianist Lenny Peters, the East End stage director Joan Littlewood and the film star Diana Dors. But the most important guest for the Twins and their future status as celebrities was the thin young man with the long dark hair who arrived at the church in a blue velvet suit and a matching blue Rolls-Royce – the photographer David Bailey.

Although the Krays had got to know Bailey only a few weeks earlier, the rising star of London fashion photographers, whose camera recorded so much of the glamour and the glitter of the sixties, was about to play a crucial role in the lives and growing reputation of the Twins. How this happened gives an insight into the all-important changes in the way the media started to present them during the period following the Boothby scandal and the McCowan case.

Ron's inclusion in the *Sunday Mirror*'s apology to Lord Boothby, followed by Scotland Yard's failure to secure their conviction in the McCowan case, made libel-conscious editors doubly wary of even mentioning the Krays, let alone investigating them. There was one exception. In March 1965, two keen young journalists from the *Sunday Times*, Lewis Chester and Cal McCrystal, obtained an interview with the Twins and wrote a full-page article about them.

This had to be a skilful exercise in journalistic caution. With the paper's lawyers breathing down the young reporters' necks, it was impossible for them to write anything that mattered very much about the Twins – certainly no reference to gang fights, maimings, extortion, protection rackets and large-scale fraud, let alone the extraordinary examples of corruption revealed in the Boothby case.

Instead they did something which became of considerable significance in the creation of the public image of the Twins. Since they could not mention the fact that they were serious criminals, they fell back on the old standby of the hard-pressed journalist, the so-called 'colour piece', about two lively cockneys known as Ron and Reg who were part of the culture of the old East End. Here for the first time words such as 'myth' and 'legend' were applied to them. The article went on to state that ever since they were first 'discovered', like a pair of pop stars, thanks to the publicity arising from the Boothby case, 'stories of the Krays' prowess and business deals have become part of London folk-lore'. The two folk heroes were then duly described – and photographed – 'holding court in the cosy front parlour of their parents' tiny home in Vallance Road'.

The interest of the *Sunday Times* in these 'colourful' East End characters was not yet over. Francis Wyndham, kinsman of the Earl of Egremont and a feature writer on its colour magazine, was also intrigued, and wrote a polite note requesting an interview, not only to the Krays, but also to three other leading gangster families currently in business. Hardly surprisingly, none of them replied, but a few days later, Wyndham was sitting in his second-floor office at the *Sunday Times*, when the commissionaire at the front desk rang him.

'Two gentlemen here to see you, Mr Wyndham. Name of Kray.'

The Twins' latest, and most rewarding foray into the world of publicity had begun.

The friendship that followed was yet further evidence of the strange appeal of the Krays for the English upper classes – and vice versa. Wyndham became genuinely fascinated by them both. For him, as he wrote later, they were 'like characters out of Dickens'. Eager to do them justice in an article, he asked Bailey, whose work had appeared in the *Sunday Times*, to take the accompanying photographs.

As so often with the Twins, what happened next is so unlikely that one feels it could have happened with no other criminals in London, let alone a pair of highly dangerous East End gangsters. As a fashion photographer, Bailey had always been a perfectionist. Since the only place in London that could guarantee the lighting and conditions he demanded for his pictures was in the studios of *Vogue* magazine, he always used them for his fashion pictures. Now he used them for his pictures of Ron and Reg, who found themselves receiving much the same treatment that the photographer would have given models such as Twiggy or Jean Shrimpton.

So the most famous fashion photographer of the sixties came to take the most enduring portrait of the decade's most notorious murderers.

One can read what one wants to into Bailey's extraordinary double portrait of those two disturbed and most disturbing faces. But whatever else it does, Bailey's picture shows what was now occurring in the Twins' relationship, with the brooding dominating figure of Ron in the foreground, while his twin brother stands awkwardly behind him like a puppet ready to do anything, however violent, at his brother's bidding.

At the *Sunday Times* there was a feeling that the Twins had been receiving too much attention, so neither Francis Wyndham's article nor David Bailey's portrait was published in its pages. But this did not mean that they were wasted. Bailey was currently working on what he called his 'Box of Pin-ups', his definitive collection of famous faces of the sixties, which included pop stars such as the Beatles and Mick Jagger, actors such as Peter O'Toole and Michael Caine, and glamorous young females such as Jean Shrimpton and Marianne Faithfull. Rather than waste a striking image, he decided to include in it his picture of the Twins.

For Bailey, the crown prince of sixties photographers, to include his nightmare image of these two ruthless gangsters in the same collection as his box of sixties celebrities was extraordinary enough, but there was more to come when Francis Wyndham's article was used for the accompanying text on the back of the portrait. In it, he described the Twins as 'an East End legend', and compared the stories being told about them with those of American outlaws like Frank and Jesse James. 'To be with the Twins,' he added, 'is to enter the atmosphere (laconic, lavish, dangerous) of an early Bogart movie'. All this was of great importance for the Twins' expanding reputation.

They had been written about and photographed many times before, chiefly in crime reports, but never quite like this. In hailing them as 'legends', Wyndham was picking up on the Twins' most precious fantasies about themselves. As for Bailey's portrait, this virtuoso exercise in *haute couture* photography, frozen in time from the sixties, is how many people still see the Kray Twins, thirty-five years later.

Reg's marriage, three weeks after Bailey took his picture, was a fascinating mix of high life, low life and large men behaving badly – a further example of the busy social interaction that was now occurring in the sixties. It was a mix of a smart social occasion and East End thuggery. At the moment when the vows were exchanged, Bailey, the boy from Bermondsey, was behind the altar rail, with Francis Wyndham holding the flashlight for the wedding pictures of London's most notorious gangster.

The *Sunday Times* was out in force. Lewis Chester and Cal McCrystal had been invited too. Cal remembers the bridegroom's side of the church being packed with guests, while the bride's side, apart from close members of the family, was all but empty. This caused an uncomfortable atmosphere, and when the hymns began, hardly any of the congregation joined in. For years to come, Cal dined out on the story of how Ron took over the proceedings, marching up and down the aisle, shouting at the congregation, 'Sing, fuck you! Sing!'

Much the same spirit appears to have prevailed as 'the East End's wedding of the year' continued at a reception at Finsbury's Glenrae Hotel.

This was the one occasion in his life when Bailey acted as a wedding photographer. He took the wedding pictures as a wedding present to the bride and groom. In their way they were quite revealing. As usual, old Charlie Kray was nowhere in sight, but the rest of the Krays were there in force, and Violet was standing between Ron and Reg, smiling like the proudest matriarch in Bethnal Green. At the same time the bride's mother, Elsie, was standing unsmiling by her daughter, wearing a dark velvet dress. To the day he died, Reg would not forgive his mother-in-law 'for wearing black to my wedding'.

I believe that more was at stake that day than most members of the congregation can have guessed, and that when he married Frances, Reg was genuinely hoping that he could use his marriage to establish a whole new way of life. For by getting married he was making a determined effort not only to escape from his homosexuality, but also to sever the increasingly destructive bonds that linked him with his twin.

Ron had enjoyed the publicity of the Boothby business to the full – his picture on the front page of the *Express*, the apology from Cecil Harmsworth King on behalf of the *Sunday Mirror* and even the way the original article had called him a homosexual thug at the head of the London underworld. But whereas none of this troubled Ron in the least, Reg had felt worried by it. When the *Sunday Mirror* mentioned Ron's homosexuality, Reg felt that there was an implication that if Ron were gay, the chances were that he, as his identical twin brother, was probably the same.

The differing reaction of the Twins to their sexuality plays an important part in this story. Just as Reg had always tried to hide the fact that he was gay, so he tried to escape from his homosexuality, and these efforts were linked to his recurrent efforts to escape from Ron and the madness and violence of Ron's paranoid condition. When Reg asked Frances to marry him, I believe that Reg was being totally sincere in his longing for a 'normal' life with a wife and children.

Part of the tragedy that followed came from the fact that none of this was possible. Biology decreed that from the moment he was born, Reg was linked genetically to Ron. Because of who and what they were, there was no escape for either of the Twins – and now there was none for Frances.

The reality of marriage proved worse than even Father Hetherington had predicted. Reg picked Athens for their five-day honeymoon, without realising that that unalluring capital was the last place on earth to take a girl like Frances. During those five days Reg drank himself into a stupor every night. Then it was back to London and a 'luxury' flat he'd found at Lancaster Gate near Marble Arch. Away from her family and the familiar surroundings of Bethnal Green, Frances was miserable and lonely. So was Reg. Except for criminals and cockneys, they had few friends; and they had few resources. Frances had never learned to cook, but loved dancing, friends of her own age and women's magazines. Reg was nearly ten years older than his child bride, a homosexual gangster who preferred drinking gin to making love to her. Like her he missed the East End and his family. He also missed Ron. Within a month the newlyweds had abandoned the flat and were back in the East End, in a flat directly under Ron's at Cedra Court.

The problems between Reg and Frances were not exclusively sexual. They were also tied up with Reg's growing fame, wealth and longing for celebrity. His eagerness to impose on Frances the possessions and surroundings that for him spelled sophistication and success made them adopt a style of life that neither really wanted. In the cruelty and the tears that followed, one detects a sort of inescapable misery enfolding them both. One glimpses not only Frances's troubles but also the horror always lurking just below the surface in Reg's life as well.

Despite the marriage, little had really changed – except for one thing. In the past, Ron had been the one who needed looking after and who periodically couldn't cope, and Reg had looked after him. But this was no longer so. Now it was Ron who seemed to be firmly in control. He seems to have had no more fits of jealous rage, no more lapses into fear and loathing, no more shouting matches with his brother.

Frances had several girlfriends to whom she would talk when Reg wasn't at home, and from them I discovered later what happened.

Although Reg and Frances were living so close to Ron, she rarely saw him. The only times she did was when they passed each other on the stairs and he would smile at her and say, 'Evenin' Frances, my dear. Enjoyin' bein' in the family?' With increasing frequency Reg would disappear in the evening and go upstairs to be with Ron and Ron's young friends. If she went to bed alone she would be kept awake by the noise of laughter and music from the flat above. When her husband finally returned to her, he was invariably drunk. At first she risked asking him what was going on upstairs and why he was so late coming down to bed. But since he always shouted at her to mind her own fucking business, she soon gave up.

The morning after, when he had sobered up, he would be as gentle and kind with her as before, as if nothing had happened, assuring her that he loved her and seeming totally dependent on her. But once he started drinking – and since the marriage he was drinking more than ever – his character would change. He had always had a vicious temper; when he drank he became sullen at first, before lapsing into jealous rage, usually blaming Frances for the fact that they had no sex life together. With drink destroying his inhibitions, frustration and black rage came welling up from deep within him. He often threatened her with violence but never actually hit her. When almost out of control, he would threaten to kill her brother or her parents, but instead of physically hurting her he started to terrorise her. One of her friends told me how, knowing how much she hated the sight of blood, he once purposely cut his hand and dripped blood over her as she lay sleeping. Knowing how much she hated firearms, he sometimes – although this happened only when he was very drunk – threatened her with a gun.

She endured eight nightmare weeks of this at Cedra

Court; then she fled home to her mother. She told her mother that her marriage was a farce, and that the nearest her husband had come to consummating it was on one occasion when, as she put it to a friend, 'He tried taking her the other way.' She sobbed to her mother that her husband was a pervert – and her mother passed this on to others.

By talking to her parents, Frances actually made the situation worse, and members of the family were becoming fearful for their lives. Reg hated them so much that he had started threatening them. According to one account, he had Mrs Shea's Mini Minor badly scratched one night outside their house, and on several occasions he had anonymous letters sent to her husband and men she worked with at her office saying that Elsie Shea would sleep with anyone.

Although the Sheas wouldn't have Reg in the house, they couldn't stop him waiting outside to see Frances every evening. For some reason, she always waited for him and used to talk to him out of the window. It was as if she was still beneath his spell, and he wouldn't leave her either. A strange charade began that continued almost to the day she died. Each evening he arrived, and they would talk – then he would go off and get drunk and start brooding. Ron didn't help the situation.

Frances had always been highly strung, and nervous. Reg started giving her pills he got from Doc Blasker, telling her that they'd calm her nerves. Instead they made her worse, and that July, just over three months after their marriage at St James the Less, she had some sort of nervous breakdown and tried to kill herself with an overdose of Doc Blasker's drugs. Her parents found her just in time and her father called the doctor, who was able to revive her. On regaining consciousness, her first words to her father were, 'Oh, why didn't you just let me die?'

I sometimes wondered why she didn't just go – leave the East End, the Twins, her marriage and the life that was destroying her. But of course she couldn't. Reg had bewitched her. He continued to possess her, as he always had. Some thought he wished to keep her simply to destroy her, and there were people who believed that Reg had made her addicted to the amphetamines that he obtained for her from Doc Blasker and also used himself. Certainly after her first suicide attempt she seems to have lacked both the will and the wish to save herself. 'I've been defiled,' she said. 'I'm useless. What is there left for me to live for? I deserve to die.' By now she had lost her looks and those who saw her thought she was like a ghost.

But if the marriage was destroying her, there was a sort of justice in the situation: it was also destroying Reg. It was as if the two of them were locked together like a doomed couple in a Gothic novel. Just as there was no escape for her, so there was no way out for Reg either. The strain began to tell on him too. He was losing any hold he'd ever had upon his brother. In March 1966 he certainly couldn't stop Ron killing George Cornell. And in December 1966, when Ron decided that his old friend Frank Mitchell had to be released from Dartmoor, Reg went along with that as well.

Not long before Reg died, I asked him in Wayland Prison why on earth he didn't stop that whole crazy enterprise.

'You don't understand,' he answered. 'Ron was in hiding. My wife was back in hospital with her second nervous breakdown, and I was having to keep everything together.'

As events would show, he couldn't. Frank Mitchell was killed in December. And Frances had been living with her brother Frank and his wife Bubbles in their flat in Wimbourne Court. Having failed twice already, in June 1967 she succeeded in killing herself.

As Ron was still in hiding, it was Reg's adventure-seeking young cousin, Ron Hart, who did his best to look after him and console him. But for Reg there could be no consolation.

Ron Hart told me how he took Reg to the mortuary to identify his dead wife. Since he was still her lawfully wedded husband, her body now belonged entirely to him. Ron Hart said Reg made endless visits as she lay there in her coffin, and stood before her, mumbling to himself and calling her 'Frankie, my darling Frankie'.

Soon his sorrow turned to guilt, and then to bitterness and anger. His sense of responsibility for her death was too much for him to bear himself. He had to make others suffer. 'I'll get even with those bastards, even if it takes the rest of my life, because they killed her,' Hart heard him say.

Hart asked him who he meant.

'The Sheas,' he said. 'Her fucking parents. They were the ones who took her from me. They were always jealous of our happiness together, so they poisoned her mind against me.'

Since he hated the Sheas so much he never had the comfort of sharing his grief with them. All he could say about them now was, 'Bastards, fucking bastards'. All he could think of now was his longing to kill them.

He demanded all her personal belongings, down to the last lipstick, along with her solitaire diamond engagement ring. Nor would he listen for a moment to the pleas of her parents to allow them to bury their daughter as they wanted. She was a Kray, and he intended to bury her in the plot he and Ron had bought for the Kray family at Chingford Mount Cemetery.

The Sheas tried to tell him that her last wishes had been to revert to her maiden name and be buried as simple Frances Shea. But Reg would have none of it and, to make his point, he insisted that she was buried in the white satin dress she'd worn at their wedding. The Sheas had one small victory: Elsie Shea persuaded the undertaker to let her clothe her daughter's body in tights and a slip, so that as little as possible of her body would be in contact with that dress she hated so much.

Reg was always proud of the funeral he gave her. 'We had the wedding of the year, so I made sure my Frances had the funeral of the year,' he told me. There was a carpet of flowers, befitting the burial of a gangster's wife – including a five-foot-high heart made of red roses, broken by a line of white roses down the middle, representing Reg's broken heart. But for Reg the funeral settled nothing. He couldn't escape from Frances, and kept on visiting her grave, sometimes several times a day. Whenever he was there, he wept and called her 'darling Frankie', and talked endlessly about the undying nature of their love.

Ron Hart told me how on one occasion, Reg saw a robin perched beside the grave. '"That's my Frankie reincarnated as a little bird," Ron told me. Then he started talking to the robin in a strange voice. I felt embarrassed, as I'd never heard him talk like that before, so I went and stood beside the car, but I could still hear him talking. "I knew you loved me, Frankie. I always knew that you'd come back to me." When the robin flew away, he began to weep. "Come back. Come back, Frankie, don't go. I won't hurt you. You don't have to be frightened of me any more."'

Reg believed that through the robin he was now in spiritual communication with Frances, but this seemed to make him hate her parents more than ever. On her birthday, when he took flowers to her grave and found the Sheas already there with their flowers, he refused to speak to them. Although her husband tried to restrain her, Elsie Shea began to sob, and screamed at her son-in-law, 'You killed my daughter, you bastard. If you spend a thousand pounds a week on flowers it won't do any good, because we will never forgive you – and nor will Frankie.'

With that, she spat in his face, and walked away.

ELEVEN

Performance Murderers

Let's face it, the Twins were fucking murderers or they were nothing. Without those killings what would they 'ave been? Cockney hoodlums, failed gangsters, old-style East End villains. Nobodies. That's what they'd 'ave been.

A former member of the Firm

'It's easy to kill a man,' said Ron.

I should have realised the danger signs before replying as casually as I did. 'I'm sure it is,' I said.

'You think I'm jokin'.'

I saw his python, Read, uncoil itself from round his neck and glide across the carpet.

'Of course not, Ron,' I said.

'I can see you don't believe me. 'Ere, I'll show yer. You don't need a shooter or a knife. All you want's yer own bare 'ands. It's easy.'

Like the snake, Ron Kray could change from inertia to sudden movement in the twinkling of an eye, and before I could escape, his bulky arms were locked around my neck. His left hand was gripping his right elbow, while his right arm forced my head back, jamming my chin against his iron bicep.

'Can you move?' he asked.

I couldn't even shake my head. He started squeezing, and a singing noise started in my ears. The pressure seemed to be forcing my eyes from their sockets.

The arms squeezed harder. 'You'll lose consciousness with a bit more pressure ...'

My head was swimming and I realised that he was enjoying himself. His voice sounded very far away.

'A bit more pressure …' There was a pause as I struggled to escape. 'An' l'll break yer neck.'

I heard someone entering the room. It was Reg.

'Easy on, Ron,' I heard him say. 'What yer doin'? Fer Chrissake, easy on. 'E's got to write our fuckin' book.'

I realise how fortunate I was that this was the nearest I ever came to seeing Ron in homicidal mode, and like to think that he was being playful. But after this I had no illusions over what he was, and I was more than ready to believe what I was hearing of the murders that the Twins had committed.

Apart from one or possibly two killings that can never be proved against them, the Twins were directly involved in three homicides – that of George Cornell in the Blind Beggar pub in March 1966; the freeing from Dartmoor and subsequent despatch of 'the Mad Axeman', Frank Mitchell, some nine months later; and the butchering of Jack 'the Hat' McVitie in a cellar in Stoke Newington in October 1967.

Since the Twins were convicted of the Cornell and the McVitie murders and later unrepentantly confessed to both, there is no question of their guilt. Although no one was finally convicted of Frank Mitchell's murder, and the Twins denied playing a part in his death, their accomplice Freddie Foreman made a post-trial confession of the killing, both in his memoirs and on prime-time television.

What remains a mystery to this day is *why* the Twins chose to get involved in these killings. On the face of it, they had no compelling need to do so; and had they not embarked on murder, they would have been extremely difficult to catch and could have gone on piling up a fortune from their different rackets, even ending up like

Billie Hill in Spain. So why did they do it? It was a straightforward question which, for various reasons, their extremely long and costly Old Bailey trial never answered. Nor, for that matter, did the Twins themselves. But since these killings were the reason why they would have to spend the rest of their lives in prison, and came to be at the heart of their story and the legends that grew up around them, it is a question that begs an answer.

In a way the answer is simple. Given that Ron was a paranoid schizophrenic, from the moment he escaped from Long Grove Mental Hospital in 1958 and was permitted to remain at large, it was fairly certain that he would end up killing someone. The wonder is not that he killed Cornell, but that he had not killed anybody else until 1966. That this happened when it did was because of certain factors, all of which conspired to make Ron's paranoia more acute, leaving him increasingly uncontrollable, volatile and dangerous.

The first of these factors was undoubtedly the fall-out from the Boothby scandal, as the Twins' immunity from serious police attention served to heighten Ron's illusions of invulnerability. Certainly the Twins were justified in thinking they were 'special'. Theirs was a sensational achievement. They had forced the Establishment to cover up a major scandal, and then escaped scot-free from a full-scale trial at the Old Bailey. They had beaten the press, the politicians and the police. Since none of these wanted to know about them any more, the Twins were effectively free to act as and how they pleased.

For Ron this must have been clear confirmation of what his psychic adviser had told him about his spirit guide protecting him. One of the symptoms of paranoid schizophrenia is a combination of fear of persecution, along with delusions of omnipotence and grandeur – both of which, even before the McCowan case, Ron was experiencing in classic form. Now when his inner voices told him it was time to kill, he must have felt an overwhelming sense of liberation. For anyone in Ron's condition, the line between reality and fantasy is blurred, and I remembered later Doc Blasker's words about the danger of his heavy drinking when combined with mood-altering drugs like the Stematol that he relied on.

Reg's marriage, and his efforts to break free from his homosexuality and the bonds of twinship must have seemed a threat to Ron. But once the marriage had collapsed, Ron was undisputed winner in their 'discordant twin' relationship and Reg effectively abandoned any power he'd ever had to restrain his brother in his moods of madness. Certainly when Ron entered the Blind Beggar, with Ian Barrie as his bodyguard, just before five o'clock in the late afternoon of 9 March 1966, Ron hadn't even told him he was going.

Cornell, a large, powerful man, was another East End villain, who had known the Twins since they were imprisoned together, along with Charlie Richardson, in the army detention centre at Shepton Mallet. Cornell had just started drinking a pint of bitter, and clearly Ron's arrival was completely unexpected. Cornell was unarmed, and since he was not in the habit of taking unnecessary risks, he can't have been expecting trouble from the Twins – otherwise he would not have been drinking so peacefully in a pub which was almost on their doorstep.

Even when Barrie fired a shot at the ceiling that made the barmaid duck behind the bar, he made no attempt to dodge or to defend himself, but played it cool to the last. 'Well, look who's here,' were the only and indeed the final words he uttered. When Ron fired a single shot from a

German Luger automatic, he brought the weapon so close to his victim's forehead that even Ron, with his short sight and unsteady aim, could hardly miss him.

Since then, endless reasons have been put forward to explain why Ron did it. Ron's own excuse was that George Cornell was 'scum'. Then there was the idea that the murder was part of a 'war' that they'd been waging with the Richardsons. In fact there was no war, apart from a grudge against 'Mad Frank' Fraser, who'd recently beaten up Ron's old friend, Dickie Morgan, and the Richardsons had just been arrested for an 'affray' at Mr Smith's Club in Catford, which later, following a trial at the Old Bailey, earned them thirty-year sentences. This meant that any 'war' there might have been was over by the time Cornell was killed.

As a paranoid schizophrenic, Ron simply had a taste for killing people, a fact which he subsequently admitted in his 'autobiography'. 'I didn't know then, but I think now it was my mental illness, my paranoia,' he wrote. 'I just couldn't stop myself from hurting people, especially if I thought that they were slighting me or plotting against me. Also I like the feeling of guns, although I was usually happier with my fists or a knife.'

The murder of George Cornell was in fact the most cowardly of killings, which in practical gangland terms accomplished less than nothing. But in terms of Ron's obsessions, and the subsequent mythology created round the Twins, it was the most important act of his life. It sealed his fate. It involved the rest of the Firm in a disastrous escalation of violence. It made the police's attempt to get the Krays inevitable. And it formed the basis for the cult of violence which, in years to come, would blossom round the Twins.

With the killing Ron stepped unconcernedly into the

role he'd been creating for himself for years, as if acting out a scene from a gangster movie. Only recently they had been hailed in the press as the East End's own successors to Jesse James and Billy the Kid; Bailey's *Vogue* studio photograph had made them look like murderers. It was as if the photograph had been a self-fulfilling prophecy. Although they'd been beating, wounding and terrorising their victims for years, until this moment the Twins had held back from the ultimate in violence. But they both knew that real gangsters, like those played by George Raft and Humphrey Bogart, don't draw back from killing when they have to; they are prepared to 'go the limit'. The time had come for Ron to back the legend with some real-life action.

Had Ron not been a paranoid schizophrenic, this would not have been possible. Only a paranoid schizophrenic casually guns down a fellow gangster he has known for years without a word or a motive, and without showing any subsequent remorse or fear for the consequences. But because Ron was a paranoid schizophrenic who had convinced himself that he was a movie-style gangster, he fulfilled his destiny by murdering Cornell.

Everything about the murder seems to point to this. Ron was clearly in a state of paranoid excitement when he shot him. He told several people that he had an orgasm at that moment. When Barrie drove him back to the Grave Maurice pub, where Reg was waiting, he was violently sick – giving further credence to Doc Blasker's warnings of the danger for someone in his mental condition – mixing drink and drugs together – but his heightened mood continued.

Although Reg was stunned at first on hearing what Ron had done, he swiftly organised a safe house in anonymous Walthamstow, where Ron could be kept out of sight with a member of the Firm looking after him. And there he stayed, drinking himself into a stupor and listening to his favourite records of Winston Churchill's wartime speeches.

Once Ron had sobered up and come to his senses, and realised that, thanks to Reg's protection, he was still free, he was as excited as a teenager who'd stumbled on the joys of sex. He'd 'done his own' at last. Surrendering his murderer's virginity had been easy, and it made him feel good. Now that he was in the springtime of his homicidal passion, he wanted to carry on killing.

So Ron continued shooting for the fun of it, but his weaponry was erratic. Among those he wounded in a homicidal mood was George Dixon, an old villain whom both the Twins had known for years. For some reason Ron decided that he had to kill him, but when he pointed his gun at him at point-blank range and pulled the trigger, nothing happened. Apparently the gun had jammed. He laughed, took the bullet from the gun and handed it to his intended victim.

'George,' he said, 'keep it as a souvenir and think yourself lucky.'

Although this near-shooting sounds almost light-hearted, in terms of the cult now building up around the Krays, what Ron was doing was of great importance. He was starting the final act in the great on-going drama of the Twins, moving the action forward on a higher plane, and bringing excitement, drama and a heightened sense of purpose to the members of the Firm and to the Twins themselves. In particular, murder had given Ron the insouciance of power. Everyone around him was treating him with fresh respect, 'for you just could never tell with Ron'. Since no one now appeared inclined to refuse the Twins a favour, he even managed to convince himself that murder was good for business.

Reg, being his customary efficient self, put the frighteners on the witnesses, getting the message through to 'Mrs X', the barmaid (as she was always referred to by the police to protect her identity) and Patsy Quill, the barman, at the Blind Beggar that if they knew what was good for them and their families, they would 'stay loyal to their own', obey the unspoken rules of the East End and keep their mouths shut.

Since none of the locals who were in the know would wish – or dare – to 'grass' to the police, the Twins began to feel that the whole East End was behind them. East Enders were real people who were 'staunch', and who 'cared about their own', unlike the weak idiots up West who were loyal to no one.

Forget about the unarmed victim, forget his widow and his orphaned son. Cornell had known the score, the Twins told themselves. Cornell had been expendable, or as Charlie Richardson remarked later in his dry manner, 'George had been Ron's necessary sacrifice.'

At first the random and erratic nature of the murder of Cornell had appeared to threaten Ron's relationship with Reg. They had endless rows and furious arguments over what Ron had done. 'You drunken slag. You fucking idiot. Putting us all at risk,' Reg shouted. But how could Reg prevail, when in the end the murder weakened Reg, by strengthening Ron, whose dominance had been increased by his 'victory' in murdering Cornell?

The killing of Cornell also became proof of something else of great importance to the Twins – Scotland Yard's current determination to steer clear of them and not become involved in another public disaster through tangling with the Krays.

Largely for the sake of appearances, the famous detective Commander 'Tommy' Butler came to Bethnal Green, visited the scene of the crime and looked for witnesses. As by now it was an open secret throughout much of the East End, as well as at the Yard, that Ron had shot Cornell, Butler had Ron brought to an identity parade before Mrs X the barmaid. But Mrs X, still terrified for herself and for her family, proved herself a true East Ender, and, heeding Reg's warning, stayed loyal to her own. She swore on oath that among the men lined up before her, she did not recognise the murderer. And the great Commander Tommy Butler went back to Scotland Yard.

The second murder in which the Twins were involved nine months later was the killing of the so-called 'Mad Axeman', the extremely powerful but feeble-minded petty criminal Frank Mitchell. It could hardly have been more different from the first. Ron was still acting out his role as a movie gangster, but now he had a different script.

The late autumn of 1966 was a difficult time for both the Twins. Ron was involved in attempting to prove that a police detective had asked him for a bribe, but rather than appear in court as a witness for the prosecution, he went into hiding, leaving Reg to cope not only with Frances's breakdown but also with the Firm and all its business single-handed.

It was while Ron was concealed in a 'safe house' somewhere in the East End that he worked out the plot for a new role as a movie-style gangster. Instead of being just the fearless killer of Cornell, he'd be one of those much-loved figures in the Warner Brothers gang-land movies – a hard-boiled killer with a heart of gold. After the killing of Cornell, he may have also wished to reassure his fellow criminals that he could be a kindly friend too, who was more than ready to do an old comrade a good turn, who saved the oppressed and always kept his word to a buddy.

The obvious person to be a friend to was his old prison

mate Frank Mitchell, who was now a prisoner in Dartmoor. One of Ron's screen heroes, Jimmy Cagney, would have helped an old pal in need. Ron would do the same for Frank.

As he organised Frank's escape, Ron only had the best intentions, but as Dr Johnson said, 'The path to Hell is paved with good intentions.'

The Twins originally had no plan to kill their old friend, but everything went disastrously wrong, and have him killed they unquestionably did; and once again the key to their behaviour lay firmly in Ron's schizophrenic nature.

What happened shows something that one often finds in the psyche of many dangerous criminals: the volatile nature of their emotions. This was evident too in Reg's tortured relationship with Frances, with his swings between murderous threats and maudlin sentimentality. But what was typical of Ron was that even an act of kindness to a friend that ended so horribly left him with absolutely no remorse.

Being freed was actually the last thing Mitchell needed, for by now he was a trusted prisoner and the prison governor was backing his appeal for release. Nevertheless, on 12 December 1966, two members of the Firm drove to Dartmoor.

Mitchell was in a small working party on the Moor, and so freeing him was easy, and they picked him up and drove him back to London. Had Ron been sane, and had Reg not been distracted by worries over Frances, the Twins might have been practical enough to have realised that the actual freeing of Frank Mitchell from Dartmoor would not be the real problem. What no one had really thought about was what would happen next. The Twins had borrowed a basement flat in Barking where he could stay for a short time. But Mitchell was far too conspicuous to smuggle out of the country, and he was so powerful and mentally disturbed that he would not be easy to deal with if things went wrong. As soon as Mitchell had been sprung from Dartmoor, he inevitably became not only a liability but a positive danger to the Twins, and to the members of the Firm who were looking after him. Reg claimed that he even threatened to go round to Vallance Road to discuss his problems with Violet.

The only way that they could think of keeping him quiet was to find him a woman. Reg went to Churchill's Club, picked up a pretty blonde hostess called Lisa, paid her £100 in cash, and brought her back to the flat in Barking. Mitchell swiftly fell in love with her, and she kept him quiet for a few days longer.

But the Twins desperately tried to work out a way to permanently free him without incriminating themselves. Reg contacted Francis Wyndham at the *Sunday Times* and asked if he was interested in arranging an exclusive interview between Mitchell and the editor, at the same time tipping off the law. Wyndham wisely declined to get involved.

Mitchell by now was growing desperate and it was inevitable that at a certain stage the Twins' attitude towards him would change. This happened now. Frank, who only a short time before had been the best guy in the world who Ron would do anything to help, was suddenly transformed into the biggest menace to their lives and freedom, for which there was only one solution.

At 8.30 p.m. on Christmas Eve 1966, Frank Mitchell was persuaded to leave the flat and enter a van waiting in the Barking Road. He had been lured out like a trusting animal by promises from his old friends Ron and Reg that he would be taken to their lovely house in the country, where he could live with Lisa, who would join him later. Little

Lisa saw him off, kissing him goodbye. The door shut, the van drove off and Lisa heard shots. She never saw him again.

Although the Twins and their friend and ally Freddie Foreman were charged at the Old Bailey in 1969 with Mitchell's murder, they were all acquitted on the grounds of insufficient evidence. Thirty years later, Foreman took advantage of the fact that under English law no one can be tried twice for the same crime and publicly confessed to killing Mitchell with another gunman who had been waiting in the van. According to Foreman, Mitchell was so strong that it took fifteen shots to kill him. He claimed to have then disposed of Mitchell's body in the sea off Newhaven.

The black melodrama of the Twins' lives had almost reached its climax. There was now one final touch of the grotesque. Frances's death had reunited them – in violence and murder. For after her death Reg would do anything, and cared for nothing, and he increasingly relied on Ron for company and comfort. At the same time Ron, deeply back with his homicidal fantasies, couldn't resist the chance of getting 'my Reggie' back again and firmly under his control. He did so in the tried and tested way he always did when they were boys – by involving him in violence and evil. And Reg could not resist his twin brother. For Reg was essentially a broken man by now – drunken, haunted by sadistic nightmares and pursued by demons.

As with the killing of Cornell, the butchering of Jack 'the Hat' McVitie in October 1967 seems as cowardly as it was ultimately pointless. And as with Cornell, the Twins' 'reasons' for killing him were mostly dreamed up later. True, McVitie was a womaniser and a drunk, and one of the very few people who was not frightened of the Twins.

But he was also a former friend and associate, and if in a drunken moment he had foolishly made threatening remarks about them, and if, as they claimed, he had failed to keep his word when they paid him to kill their old collaborator, now turned 'traitor', Leslie 'the Brain' Payne, that was no reason to kill him.

But killing escalates by habit, and the Twins were now imposing a virtual reign of terror on those around them. Since they were now totally united and Ron's paranoia was contagious, they were effectively two paranoid schizophrenics on a rampage of homicidal violence. Every night Reg would drink himself silly and talk himself into a state of mindless violence, wounding and threatening anyone who crossed his path or annoyed him or aroused his least suspicions. Some of the members of the Firm undoubtedly led him on.

Little Tom Cowley had always been close to Reg and saw a lot of him around this time. He told me later, 'Those months after Frances died were terrible. The Twins were very gullible by now and had surrounded themselves with idiots who'd wind them up to do anything, and all the time they were acting before they even stopped to think. You see, once Reg lost his grip on himself, we were all doomed – the lot of us. And although one or two of us tried to stop things going too far, in the end there was really nothing we could do. If I'd been there, or their brother Charlie, on the night they killed McVitie, it would never have happened. Once someone said, "Send for McVitie," I'd have said, "Do me a favour and cut it out." But that lot egged them on, reporting things back to the Twins, which, knowing them, they should have had the sense not to do. And so it happened.'

Since I first described it in *The Profession of Violence*, the story of the killing of Jack McVitie has been recounted many times. How he was lured to a basement flat in Stoke Newington where the Twins and several members of the Firm were waiting; how he arrived in a happy mood, expecting a party; and how Ron urged his brother on to kill him.

From the start it was a bungled, drunken, needlessly sadistic killing. Not even an animal deserved to die as Jack McVitie died. As his gun jammed, Reg couldn't even shoot him properly – at which point one of the Firm produced a kitchen knife. Jack was strong, and didn't die easily. At one point he made a dive through the basement window, but got stuck amid the broken glass, and someone hauled him back. Someone else grabbed his arms and held him from behind, and Reg began stabbing him, first in the face, then in the stomach. According to one witness, he ended up impaling him to the floor with the knife thrust through the throat.

Apart from this making the Twins appear more frightening than ever, it's hard to see what advantage they gained from this cruel and senseless murder. Indeed, it would be for this – and in Ron's case, also for murdering Cornell – that they would end up spending the rest of their days in prison. But as the years rolled by in prison, Reg would become increasingly proud of what he'd done to Jack McVitie.

The killing would become slowly reinvented until, like some gallant battle honour, it became part of the so-called legend of the Krays.

TWELVE

Enter 'Nipper'

A human being who has exercised the right of private judgement and taken the life of another human being is not safe to exist in the community. I tell you that.

Hercule Poirot

Towards the end of March 1968, the Twins began using their parents' brand-new top-floor flat in Bunhill Row as their headquarters and sometimes slept there. I think they felt safe to be back again with Violet in this haven high above the City, particularly now that the demolition contractors were on the point of knocking down Fort Vallance. Out of interest I went to Vallance Road one evening just before they demolished it. I found the little street deserted, the houses empty, and I remember looking at the battered green front door of Fort Vallance and wondering if there was any way of obtaining it as a grim souvenir of a world that would soon be gone for ever.

I still have vivid memories of the Twins in their last few weeks of freedom in their parents' flat on the ninth floor of their high-rise block. Ron, in vest and grey baggy trousers, appeared to have expanded physically even in the few days since I saw him last. In contrast, Reg had shrunk, and was looking more than ever like his father. I was reminded of an anxious monkey in his cage, perpetually worried and unable to escape, as he chain-smoked the cigarettes that would kill him thirty-two years later.

How both the Twins had changed since I first saw them

just a few months earlier at Gedding Hall. There was something beleaguered and doomed about them now, and I had the feeling, as I often did when I was with them, that their fantasies were taking them over, and that they were acting out the last scenes of the great gangster movie of their lives that so obsessed them.

It was late afternoon. On the table by the big window with its views across London stood an empty teapot and a half-finished bottle of Gordon's gin. The sky was streaked with pale cloud, the sun was dissolving in a pool of gold behind St Paul's, and just to the right was the dome of the Law Courts with the blindfolded figure of Justice holding up her sword and scales. As the day began to die and the first lights of evening glimmered in the office blocks around us, I had a feeling of being isolated in this tiny flat high above London, with Ron as an East End Harry Lime, looking down on ant-like humanity below him from the top of his very own Ferris wheel.

If you're a big-time criminal controlling London, what better place to do it from than there? And here, away from the crammed little houses in Vallance Road and whatever they once stood for in their lives as criminals, the Twins seemed finally released from all that had bound them to their past in Bethnal Green. But however invulnerable they may have felt, they also knew by now that, somewhere in the city down below them, the police were closing in.

I know that Ron believed that they would never catch them. When I asked him of rumours I'd been hearing on the subject, he seemed as confident as ever. 'I'm not worried about the police,' he muttered. 'I suppose there must be some intelligent coppers somewhere, but I've never met one.'

But as usual Reg was fearful. 'I know that if anyone nicks us, it'll be that bugger Read,' he told me.

* * *

When I met Detective Superintendent Leonard 'Nipper' Read, shortly after the Twins were arrested, I had a feeling that I already knew him, so precisely did he seem to fit the part of the ideal detective.

He was a short, tidy man, with dark eyes and a lively face, who struck me as being both highly intelligent and intensely ambitious. Barely forty-three, he seemed to be on the threshold of a great career. Unlike the majority of successful members of the CID, he was an outsider, born in Nottingham, and he joined the police force as an escape from working in Player's Tobacco factory. He was small for a policeman, and legend has it that at five foot seven Nipper had had to take stretching exercises to reach the height required for entry to the police. Like the twins, he had been a keen and successful boxer. It was as a boxer that he earned the nickname 'Nipper', from the speed and energy of his attack. Early in the previous autumn, after twenty-two years' service, he had finally achieved his great ambition and been promoted to detective superintendent and seconded to the Murder Squad.

'Congratulations,' his new superior, Commander Ernie Millen, said to him on the morning his appointment was announced. 'I hear you're being put in charge of a new investigation on the Krays.' This was news to Nipper, and from the start he had serious doubts about his new assignment. Having tangled once already with the Twins in the McCowan case, he knew that in going back to Krayland he would meet a host of dangers and potential problems. What he can't have known was how it would also land him firmly in the middle of the jealousies and internal plots that were rife within the CID.

A subsequent police commissioner, Sir Robert Mark, called the CID of this period 'the most routinely corrupt organisation in London'. The Flying Squad was riddled with corruption, with several of its senior officers regularly receiving bribes. The head of the Vice Squad was later convicted of dealing in wholesale pornography. And as far as the Krays were concerned, it was true that, as rumoured in the Yard, the Twins would never be arrested so long as Sir Joseph Simpson remained as Metropolitan Police Commissioner. But by the summer of 1967, things were changing.

During the mid-sixties, despite its internal problems, the CID had achieved two great successes – two big, headline-grabbing trials which became part of the history of the decade: the Great Train Robbery trial at the Old Bailey in 1964 followed by the so-called 'torture trial' of the Richardson gang in 1966. Both these trials had fallen very neatly into the lap of the CID. Although there was much talk at the time of inspired detective work, the Great Train Robbers had helped to arrest themselves by leaving their fingerprints at Leatherslade Farmhouse, where they assembled following the robbery, in their hurry to share out the enormous booty. The CID were even luckier when one of the victims of the Richardsons came forward to the police with a story of sadistic treatment, after a fight at Mr Smith's Club in Catford, in March 1966, where a member of a rival gang was killed. Widely and enthusiastically reported in the press, both trials had done much to maintain public confidence in the CID.

Then in the late summer of 1967, Sir Joseph Simpson died unexpectedly, and was succeeded by a one-time lawyer turned policeman, Sir John Waldron. It was no secret that Waldron was a stop-gap. His ambitious deputy, Peter Brodie, already had his eye firmly on his job and was hoping that another major CID success would help his chances. At a press conference soon after his appointment,

Assistant Commissioner Peter Brodie announced his intention of waging all-out war on organised crime in London. He hardly had to mention that this meant the Krays.

It was smart of Brodie to choose Nipper for the job. Quite apart from his proven keenness and ability, the fact that he was the new boy in the Murder Squad meant that he was not personally involved with the old guard who typified the spirit of Sir Joseph Simpson's CID. Nor did Nipper share the sort of defeatism in the face of the Kray Twins' reputation that had made even a detective of the eminence of 'Tommy' Butler pack his bags and leave the Cornell case unsolved. But only in an organisation as deeply flawed as the post-Boothby Scotland Yard would a newly promoted detective have been given the extraordinary brief that Brodie now gave Nipper Read.

For reasons of CID hierarchy, the officer immediately in charge of the Kray investigation was the head of the Murder Squad, Commander John du Rose. Nicknamed 'One-day Johnnie' after his knack of solving a murder in a day, he was another celebrated old detective like Tommy Butler. But unlike Butler, John du Rose had a justified reputation as a wily operator, and while he encouraged Nipper, it would perhaps have been too much to have expected him to take this newcomer entirely into his confidence – or tell him all he knew about the Krays.

Not that this seemed to matter at the time. Not only did Nipper apparently enjoy the full confidence of Assistant Police Commissioner Brodie, but he also enjoyed virtual independence for this all-important investigation. Brodie had told him that he could pick his own team, who could be free from the dubious security at Scotland Yard. It is some indication of how little trust Brodie can have had in the personnel within the CID that not only was Nipper's team given the anonymity of separate offices in Tintagel

House, a Civil Service office block on the south bank of the Thames, but Nipper was himself provided with a cover story to damp down any in-house rumours about what he was doing. It was announced that he was leading an investigation into a murder in Northern Ireland, which explained his absence from his desk. This was followed by a story which, though bogus, must have caused uneasiness in certain quarters: he was said to be hard at work investigating corruption against an unnamed member of the CID. Although du Rose knew the truth about Nipper's operation, he personally did little to assist him and after a while they saw less and less of one another.

The situation suited Nipper, who was very much a loner and happiest working with his team away from Scotland Yard. Leslie Payne, who got to know him well, used to call him 'the Little Gangster', which gives some idea of the single-minded way Nipper led his 'gang' of dedicated followers. The very nature of this self-contained investigation suited Nipper too. For in character he was different from old-style virtuoso detectives like Butler and 'One-day Johnnie'. Nipper was dogged and immensely methodical, working more like a field anthropologist than a traditional detective as he and his co-researchers started building up a data base of information on the Krays and all their followers. This was important in the way it helped to give the case against the Twins and their followers the form it eventually assumed.

Nipper's first breakthrough came in the summer of 1967, when he met the Twins' former associate, the con man Leslie Payne, and persuaded him to talk. Although Payne had now broken with the Twins, who had recently been issuing death threats in his honour, it was still a considerable achievement of Nipper's to gain his trust. Through conversations on every aspect of the Twins' activities,

Nipper was able to compile what he called his 'delightful index' of thirty-six potential witnesses, most of whom he'd need if he was ever to bring a convincing case against the Krays to court. Then, thanks in part to Brodie's backing and to favourable reactions from the Home Office to his inquiry, Nipper achieved another coup.

He told me later, 'I realised that the only way we'd ever nail the Twins was through villains' evidence.' He had several sessions with police and Home Office lawyers, who began by being shocked by what he told them. But Nipper had a way with lawyers and they finally agreed to give him the powers he needed to overlook the crimes of guilty witnesses in return for their co-operation. This could have happened only with the agreement of the Home Secretary, which meant that the Kray investigation had the full support of the government. In theory the investigation could now go ahead unhindered.

But the situation was not as simple as it seemed. While Nipper had been hard at work, setting up his operation with the backing of the Assistant Police Commissioner and the Home Office, no one had told him that for over a year, his boss, and the head of Scotland Yard's Murder Squad, Commander John du Rose, had been quietly conducting an undercover operation of his own to catch the Krays, and seems to have told no one else about it. Only in an organisation as riddled with distrust as Scotland Yard in the sixties could two totally separate operations against a pair of murderers as dangerous as the Twins have been carried out in such a way. I never did discover whether Brodie became aware of what du Rose was up to. Probably not. Nipper was certainly completely ignorant of what was happening.

Du Rose had always had a reputation as the slyest of old foxes, and as I discovered later, had established close professional contacts in America, with the FBI and the US

Bureau of Narcotics and Dangerous Drugs (BNDD) in their fight against the operations of the American Mafia. Early in 1966, in co-operation with senior members of the FBI and the BNDD, du Rose had been able to insert a pair of influential and potentially dangerous *agents provocateurs* into the very centre of the Twins' operations.

By early 1967, these agents had already involved the Twins in plans for three separate murder operations, which were actually continuing with John du Rose's blessing. And at the beginning of April 1967, again with the blessing of du Rose and the Americans, one of these agents arranged for Ron to fly to New York to meet representatives of the Mafia, hoping that this would incriminate them. A few days before this happened, I met this agent with the Twins in person.

By now it was becoming something of a habit for me to meet the Twins for a drink in their favourite pub, the Old Horns, before dinner, and I was with them one evening at the end of March, when a pale brown Rolls-Royce drew up outside and a small man with an expensive camel hair coat draped around his shoulders entered the pub. He was probably in his early forties, with a pasty face, a very pale moustache and thinning hair brushed forward to conceal a balding cranium. He was followed by a very pretty girl in a fox-fur coat clutching a Yorkshire terrier. It's hard to do justice to the effect the arrival of this expensive-looking pair had upon the clientele in Teddy Berry's bar.

Ron greeted them and introduced them to me. The man's name was Cooper. He was American, and the girl, who was introduced as Beverley, was his wife; the Yorkie's name was Sam. Ron clearly liked them, Reg as clearly didn't, and we chatted inconsequentially for some minutes. As the talk was all about New York, I assumed they were show-biz acquaintances of the Twins. When they left the Twins went with them, driving off together in the Rolls.

Before they left, I had had a brief conversation with Cooper.

'Are you in films?' I asked.

He shook his head and offered me his card. It was headed 'European Exchange Bank', with the words 'Alan Bruce Cooper, Chairman' underneath, and an address in Curzon Street.

Around this time I sensed that something out of the ordinary was going on. Reg, still drinking heavily, seemed more anxious than ever and Ron seemed permanently excited when I saw him now and was in the best of humour. One evening, he even talked to me quite freely about 'business', which he had never done before.

'There is this Pakistani diplomat who's offering to bring in drugs in the diplomatic bag. What d'you think?' he asked.

This was the only time I'd ever heard either of the Twins mention hard drugs, and I was non-committal. Then he mentioned something about six kilos of weapons-grade uranium, which were on offer in Switzerland.

'It's been stolen from the Russians, and I was wondering if there was anything we could do with it.'

I nearly said, 'You could always make yourself a bomb,' but didn't, and Ron never mentioned uranium again. All the same, it was clear that somebody was feeding Ron some very strange ideas.

After the meeting with Cooper I saw nothing more of him or Ron for a week or so, but in the second week of April Ron reappeared along with Dickie Morgan. Ron was mysterious over where he'd been, but in the end, as usual, Dickie told me. He and Ron had been off to New York together. When I asked him what they were doing there, he laughed and put a finger to his lips. 'To meet the Mafia,' he whispered, grinning slyly.

At the time I thought he was joking, as I couldn't see how a convicted criminal like Ron could have been allowed into the United States. It was only later that I learned that what Dickie said was true. Although Ron was supposedly under close observation by members of Nipper's team by now, he and Dickie Morgan had had no difficulty taking a scheduled flight from Heathrow to Paris, where they met a supposed member of the Mafia, who was arranging the trip for them. This was none other than the chairman of the European Exchange Bank, Alan Bruce Cooper, who was staying at the Ritz.

As I also discovered later, the European Exchange Bank was little more than a front, and Cooper was in fact a former big-time international drugs and gold runner who had been caught by the FBI and to avoid prosecution, agreed to operate as a double agent for the BNDD. The man who directed his activities was the Agency's Bureau Chief in Paris, a retired US admiral called John E. Hanly, who was attached to the US Embassy, and who happened to be an old and trusted friend of John du Rose.

When he was seeing the Twins in London, Cooper had been talking up the fortunes to be made from the international drugs trade, along with one of Ron's cherished fantasies – an international murder network operating closely with the Mafia and several European crime syndicates. Cooper also told him that if he wished to meet some of the leading members of the US Mafia in person, he could arrange it.

This was why Ron had been seeming so excited recently, and once he was in Paris, Cooper had been as good as his word. Telling Ron that he was working on behalf of the US Mafia, Cooper had fixed a trip to New York for him and

Morgan with extraordinary efficiency, paying for hotels and airline tickets 'by courtesy of our friends', and even taking Ron and Dickie to the US Embassy to get their visas.

By now, Reg, who was still in London, thoroughly distrusted Cooper, and would have nothing to do with him. But nothing in this fairly blatant sting appears to have worried Ron in the least. I think he genuinely believed by now that he was 'untouchable' and that his inner voices were infallible; as Dot Brown had assured him so often in the past, no one could harm him. The strange trio flew together to New York, where Cooper had already booked them into the Hotel Frontenac and set about introducing the man he was calling the most dangerous man in England to the top men in the Mafia.

It was in fact Admiral Hanly, working in conjunction with du Rose at Scotland Yard, who had arranged the New York trip to meet the Mafia in conjunction with the FBI, hoping that Ron would incriminate the Illianos and the Gallo brothers. But the Mafia was not that stupid and the plan simply didn't work. Cooper told me later, 'We were counting on Ronnie meeting Meyer Lansky, the Las Vegas people, Angelo Bruno and the Gallo brothers. But Ronnie was so hot that none of the important ones would risk seeing him.'

In the end, Cooper had to get an old actor friend to play the part of a top mafioso to have dinner with them and keep Ron happy. Ron was often drunk, and seemed more interested in finding boys than discussing business. Later he told me that he knew the trip was a set-up from the start, but only went along to enjoy it, convinced that the Americans could never catch him. By 6 April he and Dickie Morgan were safely back in London.

Despite the failure of the New York trip to incriminate

either the Krays or mafiosi such as the Gallos and the Illianos, back in England Cooper still had other plans to catch the Twins. For several months, with the active backing of Admiral Hanly and Commander John du Rose, Cooper had been organising on the Twins' behalf something that looked suspiciously like a London branch of Murder Incorporated.

As with the New York trip, Cooper had been extraordinarily efficient, supplying the Twins with serious weaponry, including hand guns, explosives and two traditional American gangster-style Browning machine guns. These held a strong appeal for Ron and he couldn't wait to use one. Presumably they were ultimately paid for by either the British or the US governments. Cooper had also been working on several other ingenious ways of killing that appealed to Ron. These included a spring-loaded hypodermic needle concealed in a suitcase, a high-powered steel crossbow and a car bomb.

Cooper had even recruited a mentally disturbed potential hit man who would work with Ron on these associated projects. His name was Elvey, and I saw him briefly. He was tall, thin and bespectacled, and spoke in a furtive, worried voice. I remember him having a long and heated conversation with Ron that I couldn't overhear. I also remember Dickie Morgan saying afterwards, 'Dangerous character, that Elvey. Just like Ron. Do anything.'

When Nipper's men finally arrested Elvey they discovered quite a cache of arms in his possession, together with a cyanide-loaded hypodermic in a suitcase. The hypodermic was apparently intended to kill a witness who was appearing at the Old Bailey against a friend of the Twins. Elvey didn't seem to know who was the target for the crossbow, but it could certainly kill. And the car bomb was primed and ready to be used on a Maltese gangster called

'Boxing had long been seen as a path to fame from the poverty of the Old East End, and by their early teens the Twins were already highly motivated fighters.' Reg (left) and Ron training at the Repton Boys' Club.

'Reg was good-looking in those days, and was already dressing the part of a movie gangster ... copying his favourite movie star, George Raft.' Reg, aged 24, on holiday, at the caravan site at Steeple Bay in Essex.

'"Esmeralda's Barn", a gambling club in Wilton Place, just down the road from Harrods in the very heart of affluent, "Swinging London" of the early sixties [...] proved to be of great importance to the lives of the Twins.'

Until the early sixties the Twins were still virtually identical, but as Ron's schizophrenia advanced, his features coarsened and the differences between them grew. Reg (left) and Ron in Bethnal Green in 1964.

The smartest young couple in Bethnal Green. Reg Kray, already the acme of early sixties 'gangster chic', with his teenage fiancée Frances Shea outside her parents' house in Ormsby Street just around the corner from 'Fort Vallance', the Kray family home in Vallance Road.

'The East End's wedding of the year.' A tense-looking Reg Kray (right) stands beside his 'trophy bride' Frances, the new Mrs Kray, while Ron raises his glass to their future happiness.

Neither drink nor the vivacious presence of a famous star can eliminate Reg's misery. Reg Kray, much the worse for drink, at a nightclub with Barbara Windsor.

Sparrows Can't Sing was the glittering premiere of 1963. Lionel Bart wrote the songs, Joan Littlewood directed, James Booth, Barbara Windsor, Roy Kinnear and George Sewell starred in the film, and Charlie and the Twins starred at the after-show party at the Kentucky Club.

The nightmare starts. Reg Kray (right) leaves St Pancras Coroners' Court after the inquest that has just recorded a verdict of suicide by his wife Frances in June 1967.

'I know Lord Boothby very well.' Ron Kray dines in style with Lord Boothby and an unidentified teenage boy at the old 'Society' Restaurant in the heart of Mayfair. From left to right, Charlie Clark, cat-burglar, Lord Boothby's butler, Goodfellow, Lord Boothby, unknown boy, Ron Kray and Billy Exley, member of 'the Firm', with his wife.

The crucial meeting. Ron Kray and Lord Boothby at Boothby's London flat in Eaton Place in May 1964. With them is Leslie Holt, the burglar son of a Shoreditch dustman whose affections were shared by both the older men.

Racehorse owner. Ron in smart tweed overcoat proudly holds the reins of 'Solway Cross', the horse he has just purchased for his mother. After Ron bought it 'Solway Cross' never won a race.

'The most fashionable photographer in London visits Bethnal Green.'
The photograph, taken by a member of 'the Firm' as a 'souvenir' of David
Bailey's visit to photograph the Kray Twins, in the saloon bar of the 'Old
Horns' in March 1968. From left to right, Teddy Berry, the landlord, John
Pearson, David Bailey and Checker Berry.

'In February 1968 the Twins bought themselves a country house.' This
picture of 'The Brooks', Bildestone, near Sudbury in Suffolk, is taken from
a snapshot
given to the
author by
Ron at the
time of his
visit that
spring of
1968, three
days before
his arrest.

Ron shortly before his arrest. This previously unpublished photograph was one which, for some reason, Ron particularly liked of himself.

The rival 'Firm'. The line-up of Nipper Read's team of detectives taken outside Tintagel House at the conclusion of the Old Bailey Trial in March 1969. 'Nipper' (in overcoat) has now made his peace with John du Rose, head of the Scotland Yard Murder Squad on his right. Other members of the team are (from left to right) Det. Chief Insp. Holt, Det. Supt. Mooney, Det. Insp. Cater, Det. Sgt. Eager, Det. Supt. Adams, Det. Sgt. Lloyd-Hughes, Commander du Rose, W.D.C. Liston, Det. Sgt. Travette, Det. Sgt. Hemmingway, Det. Supt. Read, Det. Sgt. Callagher, Det. Cons. West, W.D.S. Acton, Det. Con. McKay, Det. Sgt. Ness, W.D.C. Adams, Det. Sgt. Waite, Det. Sgt. Wright.

A last glimpse of freedom and a final wave. Ron at the window of the 'Black Maria' taking him to spend the rest of his days in captivity.

Vice. And Versa.

Mick Jagger.   And Mick Jagger.

performance.

See it soon at The Trans-Lux East. 3rd Avenue at 58th Street.

The legend starts. American publicity for Donald Cammell's film *Performance* (1970) with Mick Jagger in the dual part of pop-star and gangster. *Performance*, widely regarded as the key cult movie of the sixties, embodies much of the early legend of the Krays.

'Your children are all you have.' In this haunting picture taken shortly before Violet Kray's death in 1982, the recently released Charlie Kray stands with his arms around his parents. After so many years of unhappy marriage, old Charlie and Violet have found peace and a certain happiness together.

'Celebrities, gangsters and neighbours close ranks to pay a final tribute to the mother of the Twins.' Diana Dors with husband Alan Lake (right) and actor Andrew Ray arrive at Chingford Old Church on August 12 1982 for Violet Kray's funeral.

When Ron Kray made blonde ex-kissagram girl, Kate Howard, his second wife in Broadmoor, he was determined to celebrate in style. David Bailey took Reg's wedding pictures, so Ron paid the Queen's cousin, Patrick Litchfield, £2000 to take this wedding portrait of his wife.

THE KRAYS 18

Stars playing gods. Martin and Gary Kemp with Billie Whitelaw, portraying the Twins and their mother Violet in the film *The Krays* (1990), which mythologises the trio as Greek demi-gods, Castor and Pollux and their mother, Queen Leda, wife of King Tindareus.

'No David Bailey for the second Mrs Kray.' Roberta, formerly Jones, Kray leaves Maidstone Prison in her wedding dress after marrying Reg Kray in July 1997.

'Back at last among his own people.' The frail figure of sick, sixty-six-year-old Reg Kray, once more in immaculate dark blue suit, briefly returns from prison for the funeral of brother Charlie in March 1999. Note the handcuffs discreetly shackling him to the female prison officer (top left).

'Two down, one to go.' Reg bids a last farewell to Charlie's coffin. Directly behind him stands Wilf Pine, former manager of pop group Black Sabbath, keeping his promise to Ron, 'always to look after Reg'.

The last Kray funeral. 'Like a long black snake' the cortège of twenty-three black limousines follows the hearse bearing Reg's coffin to the cemetery at Chingford Mount for his funeral in October 2000.

'He cannot escape from Frances and kept visiting her grave.' Before witnessing Charlie's burial Reg pauses to kiss the grave of his dead wife, Frances.

Reunited at last. 'Kray Corner', Chingford Mount Cemetery.

Caruana, who'd been threatening a West End club-owner friend of Ron's.

The point about this whole bizarre operation, which Cooper was building up with the knowledge and participation of the head of Scotland Yard's Murder Squad, was that it was obviously immensely dangerous. Given the chance, Ron would certainly have gone into action with one of Cooper's Browning machine guns when he felt the inclination, and all of Elvey's lethal devices worked. Had the Twins used them and once again become involved in murder, the head of Scotland Yard's Murder Squad might well have found himself in court as an accessory.

In the event, Commander John du Rose was saved from this embarrassing situation by a simpler but equally dangerous operation by Cooper, this time to supply the Twins with dynamite. I never discovered who or what Ron wanted to blow up, but clearly these wildly dangerous schemes excited him with just the sort of cinematic gangster-style fantasies that had already caused the death of several people.

Little Tom Cowley had the misfortune to be picked by Ron to go to Glasgow to contact Cooper and collect the dynamite. But by now Nipper Read had had a tip-off about the journey from a Scottish gangster friend of Leslie Payne. As a result of this Nipper was shadowing him from the moment he arrived in Glasgow and arrested him red-handed as he received six pounds of dynamite from a man who turned out to be Alan Bruce Cooper. At that moment two separate operations, both emanating from Scotland Yard and both intended to entrap the Twins, dramatically collided.

When Cooper was arrested, Nipper told him he was charging him with attempted murder. To which Cooper gave the cool reply, 'If you contact John du Rose, he'll tell you that I'm his informant, and have been working for him for two years.'

Nipper would never tell me what he said to Commander John du Rose when the two men met the next day at Scotland Yard. I know that while du Rose was famous for his self-control Nipper was just as famous for his temper. Du Rose of course was at a total disadvantage, for by now Nipper had arrested Elvey too and discovered the cross-bow and the suitcase, and frightened, white-faced Elvey had, in gangster parlance, 'been singing like a choir-boy'. There was no question that Elvey, a psychopath, had been operating in deadly earnest, passing on the weapons given him by Cooper.

Whatever passed between du Rose and Nipper Read, the head of Scotland Yard's Murder Squad now effectively withdrew from the Kray case, leaving Nipper Read in charge of the investigation, together with the police side of the prosecution when it came to court. By the end of April it was action stations at Tintagel House, and the time had almost come to catch the Twins.

THIRTEEN

A Place in the Country

Beware what you set your heart upon. For it surely
shall be yours.

Ralph Waldo Emerson

In February 1968, the Twins had bought themselves a
country house, and in the second week in April, they took
possession of it. They bought it in their mother's name, on a
fairly hefty mortgage, from their old friend Geoff Allan, who
was still living at Gedding Hall. Violet seemed particularly
excited by the idea. So was Ron, and when we talked about
it, he invited me down for lunch on the first Sunday in May.

I remember feeling wary about going, since by then I
had few illusions about the Twins, but I was also fascinated
to see their house in the country, and as usual curiosity
triumphed over common sense. I arranged with a close
friend that if I hadn't called him by nine o'clock that night,
he was to contact the police, and drove off for Sunday
lunch in the country with the Krays.

Ron had given me the address the night before – The
Brooks, Bildestone, near Sudbury, Suffolk – and according
to my map Bildestone lay a few miles off the main
Lavenham-to-Sudbury road, fairly close to Gedding. The
Twins knew this part of Suffolk, having lived as wartime
evacuees at Hadleigh, which was just up the road from
Bildestone.

Sunday dawned bright and clear, and I set off early. The

journey could have been a re-run of the one I had made just seven months earlier, when the two Toms took me up to Gedding Hall and my involvement with the Twins began. But now I was on my own, driving a comfortable old second-hand Citroën I had bought, and this time I knew where I was going. I followed the same route as before, up across the flat green countryside round Newmarket, then right into Suffolk and left through Lavenham.

The last time I came here it was autumn; now spring had come. I was unprepared for the greenness and silence of this tucked-away part of Suffolk. After so many miles of motorway, it was a relief to be driving down winding, badly signposted Suffolk lanes, with great elms and shaded meadows and grazing cattle. The village of Bildestone was tiny, just a few unpretentious houses scattered around a village green, and so anonymous and private that I could see exactly why the Twins had come here.

Because Ron had talked so much about the house, I was imagining some sinister gangster hideaway, complete with guard dogs, security lights and electrified fences. Instead of which the Brooks turned out to be a run-down, yellow-and-white-painted, turn-of-the-century villa, with paddock, stables and a vicarage-style garden, planted with conifers and rhododendrons. An old man with a weather-beaten face opened a five-barred gate to let me in. No one else seemed to be about, apart from some chickens and a goose sitting on its eggs by the stables.

Then Ron appeared, waving a carved walking stick that he had brought back from Nigeria, and beaming at the world in general. This was a Ron I'd never seen before, Ron in an old sports shirt, with trouser-ends tucked in the top of his socks and white paint in his hair. He said he'd been putting the first coat of paint on the shelves of what he called 'the library', and couldn't wait to show me round.

The week before he had bought a donkey, which was grazing in the paddock. Out of nowhere two children from the village suddenly appeared and asked if they could have a ride.

''Course you can,' said Ron. 'Don't be frightened of him. His name's Figaro. He's a very nice donkey. He won't hurt you.'

Much of the house was still derelict, and builders had just started work on it. In Ron's 'library' the floorboards were up, and only a few of the shelves had been painted. But the kitchen was functioning. Violet was there and seemed very much at home. She was standing by the sink in a plastic apron, preparing lunch for the family. Reg had just arrived with an attractive red-haired girl he introduced as Carol. As Reg poured us out a glass of beer, everyone seemed relaxed and I suppose that this was the last time I saw any of them really happy.

Violet was in her element. She was cooking roast beef, roast potatoes and Yorkshire pudding. She had also boiled spring greens for us, and after she had drained them in a colander, she tried to make the Twins drink what she called 'greens water', as she had when they were children, saying it was full of vitamins.

We sat round the formica kitchen table, and everyone enjoyed Violet's good home cooking. Ron's sunny mood continued, but by the time we'd finished eating, Reg had become quiet and preoccupied. It was then that I mentioned that I'd recently seen their old headmaster, Mr Evans. Reg mumbled something about the way they always used to trick him in class because he couldn't tell the two of them apart. Then suddenly something happened that I've never forgotten.

'D'you remember how he used to make us learn things and recite them in class?' said Ron.

Reg nodded.

'What things?' I asked.

'Bits from the Bible.'

Then Ron suddenly rose to his feet and began reciting a passage from Isaiah. It seemed so out of place that it was quite extraordinary. In his flat voice I heard him speak the words of the prophet: 'But they that wait upon the Lord shall renew their strength: they shall mount with wings as eagles: they shall run and not be weary: they shall walk and not be faint.'

He then sat down, and no one said a word. Violet smiled at him proudly, and while we finished off the meal with a cup of tea, she talked nostalgically about the past. She said that now that the old Vallance Road had gone, she was hoping to spend more time in the country.

While she was talking, I wondered why the Twins had really bought this house. Had it been to keep their mother happy after the move from Vallance Road, or would they one day settle here themselves? Were they thinking of it as a bolt hole and a place to escape to? I had simply no idea.

Ron insisted on showing me the rest of the house and took me round the garden, but time was passing, and I suddenly felt anxious to be on my way. So I made my farewells to Carol and the Twins, kissed Violet on the cheek and drove away with a sense of relief. But my visit had left me more puzzled by the Twins than ever.

My first stop was at a motorway garage, where I filled up with petrol and called my friend in London, assuring him that all was well.

Remembering the Twins as they were that Sunday, I'm struck by how differently they were both behaving. Not only was Ron happier than I'd ever seen him, but he seemed almost childishly excited. I could see that living in the country, he had a chance of acting out yet another role – that of the Colonel in retirement.

While we were walking in the garden at the Brooks he had told me of his latest dream – 'to settle down and be a country gentleman like Geoff Allan'. I knew he had a handsome friend, an ex-bank robber called 'Duke' Osborne, who would soon be out of prison. 'Together me and Duke can live in the country, like two old bachelors,' he told me. But Ron had no intention of stagnating in the country. He could always take a holiday to Morocco and he was planning to buy himself a Rolls-Royce, like Geoff Allan and Alan Bruce Cooper. He said he would have himself driven up to London once or twice a week for 'business'.

Reg's life had become almost the exact opposite of his brother's, and I know he felt that for him there could be no way out. Even pretty Carol really made no difference. She told me later that they had already started having bitter arguments, just as he'd had with Frances. Carol told me he was often on the edge of violence, 'So I used to tell him, "Hit me if you want to. Show me what a brave man you are." But of course he never hit me.'

He had more important problems on his plate than his relationship with Carol. As he was not living in Ron's schizophrenic dreamland he knew exactly what was happening. He had seen through Cooper from the start, he knew what Nipper and his men were up to, and he knew by now that there was no escape.

Reg was no Colonel, no General Gordon, not even Al Capone or Meyer Lansky. He was a wretched, guilt-torn gangster, haunted by his dead wife's ghost and recurring nightmares of the killing of Jack McVitie. Not only did he know that he would soon be arrested, but part of him couldn't wait for this to happen.

Whenever I saw him now there was always the same

anxious face, the bloodshot eyes, the haunted expression. And when I had a chance to talk to him alone, there would always come the same worried small boy's question: 'Heard anything about the police? That Nipper Read, heard anything about what he's up to?' Once he even asked me, 'What d'you give for our chances?' I can't remember what I answered, but he must have known by then that I was aware that he and Ron were killers.

Not long before he was arrested, he suddenly asked me, 'D'you think I could go off and fight in Vietnam?'

'You're too old,' I answered. 'And anyhow, you're not American.'

'Where would *you* go if you were in my position and wanted to get away from everything?'

I don't know why I said it, but without thinking, I replied, 'Portuguese Timor. Part of Indonesia. Nice people. Interesting island. And unlike Spain, there's no extradition treaty.'

He smiled and thought about it for a moment, and then his face returned to the look of utter hopelesness I had seen so often.

'But I can't go anywhere,' he said. 'I can't leave Ron. Ron's my brother.'

After that Sunday at the Brooks, I was to see the Twins as free men on just one more occasion.

By now it was becoming clear that Frank Taylor's original enthusiasm for a book on the Krays was waning; the contract with McGraw-Hill was still not settled, and the Twins were becoming increasingly suspicious.

Deborah Rogers was still patiently at work, trying to sort things out with David Puttnam, who was still representing the Twins. He and Deborah had been in correspondence. Then something happened that revealed the perils of mixing violent crime with literature.

Two days after my visit to Suffolk, I became aware that something was going seriously wrong when brother Charlie rang me with the news that Ron urgently wished to see me with Deborah. So next day at around 5.30 p.m., I picked her up from her Goodge Street office, and we drove as arranged to meet the Twins, who were once more drinking at the Old Horns. As soon as I saw them standing by the bar, I knew that this was not going to be a sociable occasion. Charlie was also there, but as usual in awkward situations with the Twins, Charlie stood back and said nothing. Reg was stony-faced, and Ron was looking angrier than I'd ever seen him.

After the curtest of nods to Deborah, Ron asked in that dangerously quiet voice of his, 'Can you tell me what you mean by this?'

With that he slapped a piece of paper down on the bar. It was a carbon copy of a letter Deborah had sent a few days earlier to David Puttnam. In her efforts to make light of the Twins' growing suspicions, she had apparently ended up by writing, 'Perhaps this has all been dreamed up by Ron's paranoid fantasies, or else the Scotland Yard scrambler telephone must have been at work.'

As Ron read out these words, his voice was quieter than ever. Reg still said nothing, and the few drinkers around us in the bar fell silent.

'What d'you mean by my paranoid fantasies?' he asked. 'I suppose you know I was certified a paranoid schizophrenic and spent time in a lunatic asylum? And what d'you mean by Scotland Yard's scrambler? Are you in touch with the police or something?'

It was the one occasion when I saw Ron struggling to control his anger and just, but only just, succeeding. I was, I fear, completely useless, anxious to say nothing that might make things worse. But Deborah, faced with a situation few literary agents can ever expect to have to cope with, acted with extraordinary coolness and composure. I think she even called him 'Mr Kray'.

'Come now, Mr Kray,' she said, or words to that effect. 'We're all in this together. All the misunderstandings are coming from the Americans. We must be frank with one another.' To my surprise, Reg seemed conciliatory, and in the end Deborah managed to calm Ron down as well, apologised profusely for her tactless letter and quietly explained that she had had no wish to offend him.

Finally she persuaded him to agree to meet our English publishers the next morning so that we could calmly talk the situation over. Later Deborah and I tried finding out how he had got a copy of that letter. It was then that we discovered that, because of his suspicions, he had had Deborah's office raided, and all the letters in the 'Kray' file copied.

But as things turned out, our meeting with our publishers on the morning of 7 May 1968 was one appointment that the Twins would never make.

By the time Deborah and I were having our confrontation with Ron Kray, Nipper had made the decision to arrest the Twins and key members of the Firm. After arresting Alan Bruce Cooper, he was surprised and deeply shocked by what Cooper told him about the Krays; the new murder plots, the machine guns, the car bombs and the armoury of lethal weapons. Knowing the homicidal nature of Ron's obsessions, he also realised the dangers of playing games with a paranoid schizophrenic. Although the case he and his team had been building up against the Krays was far from complete, he knew that the time had come for a swift decision.

In the small hours of 7 May 1968, Nipper summoned

reinforcements from ten branches of the regional crime squads in and around London to Tintagel House. At 3 a.m. he briefed them, and gave each team their orders to arrest the Krays and the leading members of the Firm in a synchronised operation planned for 6 a.m.

That same morning, just before 9.30 a.m., I was driving through London for my appointment with Deborah and the Krays at my publishers' office when I heard a news flash on the car radio. 'In dawn raids across London this morning, members of Scotland Yard arrested the notorious Kray Twins along with other members of their organisation.'

Nipper himself personally arrested both the Twins when they'd been pulled from their beds in Braithwaite House, Bunhill Row. In one bedroom Ron had been sleeping with a fair-haired boy; in the other Reg had spent the night with Carol. Violet and her husband were still in Suffolk. Neither twin put up the least resistance. When Nipper told Ron he was under arrest, all he said was, 'All right, Mr Read. I'll come quietly, but I've got to have my pills.'

Once the Twins were arrested, Nipper's work began in earnest. Barely eight weeks later, on 12 July, there were committal proceedings before the Old Street magistrate, Frank Milton. It was then I got my first idea of the full police case against them. Standing in the dock were Ron, Reg and Charlie, together with eight key associates.

I remember sitting during the days that followed in that crowded courtroom, listening in amazement as the prosecution rolled out crime after often far-fetched crime alleged against the Twins. Some of these crimes I knew about already. There were the protection rackets, the large-scale frauds, the international trafficking in stolen bonds and the connections with the New York Mafia. I knew of the murders of Cornell and McVitie and the grim story of the release from Dartmoor of 'the Mad Axeman'

Frank Mitchell. I'd also heard most of the gangland stories, including the fights and woundings and gang warfare.

What I hadn't heard at this stage were Cooper's stories, which were coming out in court, about Elvey's steel cross-bow, his lethal hypodermic hidden in the suitcase and the car bomb intended to kill George Caruana. Still less had I heard anything before about the fantastic plots, which were also being described in court, about the Twins' alleged plans to release the Congolese President Tshombe from captivity in Algeria and to kidnap Pope Paul VI from the Vatican.

Something puzzled me about what was happening while these sensational revelations were being made. I knew that the law makes strict provisions against the media reporting details of preliminary court hearings, in order to avoid prejudicing the jury in a later trial. I also knew that this ban could be lifted only if requested by the defence, and on the very first day of these proceedings, I discovered that the Twins had done exactly that. As a result, reporting restrictions on the evidence were lifted. As the hearings continued, press and television had a field day.

By the time the hearings ended, it was inevitable that Frank Milton refused the bail applications, and ordered the Twins and their followers to go for trial at a later date at the Old Bailey. What hadn't been inevitable was the fact that by the time these hearings ended, the Twins and the members of their Firm had been established in the minds of the public as the most fearsome and audacious criminals in Britain.

I only understood why the reporting ban was lifted when I visited the Twins in Brixton Gaol soon after the remand hearings started. The Twins were sharing a cell, and as Ron sat on his prison bed in clean blue jeans and freshly laundered cotton singlet, I thought I'd never seen him looking better. Far from complaining of his fate, he seemed calm and philosophical, and was already treating the outcome of the trial at the Old Bailey as a foregone conclusion.

'The law's got it in for us,' he said. 'We both know that, so what's the point of arguing?'

When I asked him why he and Reg had lifted the ban on press reporting, he answered with a knowing smile. 'As nothing of what gets said in court will make a scrap of difference, we just wanted everyone to know the sort of rubbish we're accused of.'

Reg nodded but said nothing. He was looking more nervous and unwell than ever, and was clearly worried by rumours that one by one members of the Firm were turning against them.

'You know that rat Dickson's gone over,' he said bitterly. He lowered his voice. 'Have you heard anything about Donoghue?'

I shook my head. A few days earlier, 'Big Albert' Donoghue had been with them in the dock, accused of involvement in the Mitchell murder. Now there were rumours that he was siding with the prosecution.

'It isn't nice to be betrayed by people you thought that you could trust,' said Reg.

This time it was Ron who nodded, but apart from the subject of betrayal, there was one thing and one thing only that now obsessed the Twins – what the world outside was saying about them. Now that their days of secrecy were over, I believe they were really starting to enjoy their role as Britain's most notorious gangsters.

By now Nipper Read had come into his own. With the Twins and members of the Firm in prison, on remand, he could start building up the High Court case that would finally be brought against them. His most important work of all was to get witnesses who would testify in court. He was determined that whatever happened, this time there would be no mistakes.

This meant breaking down the East End's 'wall of silence', which had always previously protected the Twins and demolishing the traditional loyalty they had always relied on. Nipper got to work undermining the Firm and making as many of the Twins' associates and key supporters as possible 'turn' into witnesses for the prosecution in the trial, which was to be at the Old Bailey. In the end no fewer than twenty-eight deals were done on behalf of the prosecution.

As the investigation continued, Nipper's role became more like that of a grand inquisitor and a broker than an ordinary detective. As he admitted from the start, he was having to rely on 'villains' evidence', and dealing with such people was 'rather like going down into the sewers'. But it was necessary, and I had the feeling that he rather enjoyed it. He was certainly extremely good at it, as were the other members of his team, such as Harry Mooney and Frank Cater.

It was slow work. Mooney's particular coup was to gain the confidence of Mrs X, the barmaid in the Blind Beggar on the night of George Cornell's murder, and persuade her to co-operate. Some key members of the Firm, including Albert Donoghue and Scotch Jack Dickson had already been won over. Others were still to come. One by one, Nipper sought the Firm out, keeping up the pressure, especially on henchmen of the Krays who would otherwise stand trial for murder. Some of these, like Freddie Foreman, Ian Ritchie, Ronald Bender and the Lambrianou brothers, stalwartly refused to the last to 'go against their own, and betray them'. Others, faced with the choice, and unable to resist Nipper's arguments, agreed to go into the witness box against the Twins in court, as the price of their own immunity from prosecution. By the beginning of the new year of 1969, the 'Little Gangster' Nipper Read had finished his work. He had his own gang of witnesses by now, most of them former associates and close friends of the Krays. He was more than ready for the final showdown at the Old Bailey.

FOURTEEN

Trial

Hanging them would have been most suitable. They can't have been more clearly qualified for the gallows.

Sir Aubrey Melford Stevenson, speaking in 1982

Even before it started, on the morning of 7 January 1969, it was clear that this would be no ordinary trial, with the police already putting on a show of force that made the Twins and their followers seem more like urban terrorists than East End gangsters being tried for murder.

Just before 9.00 a.m. the traffic lights along High Holborn suddenly turned red. Then, with the traffic at a standstill in the freezing rain, an armed convoy of police vehicles went sailing past with headlights blazing, flanked by a motorcade of police motorcyclists in fluorescent jackets and marksmen in squad cars with blue lights flashing. At the centre of this convoy went two heavily armoured 'prison transportation vehicles', carrying ten prisoners the seven-mile journey to the Old Bailey from Brixton Gaol, where they'd been waiting on remand since 7 May. To make absolutely sure that nothing happened on the way, Nipper had worked out six different routes from Brixton to the City. Not until the moment of departure were the drivers told which route to follow.

Such precautions were new to London in the 1960s. In Palermo, where the last of a series of important Mafia trials was drawing to a close, they were standard practice. But in

London they were worrying, suggesting that in the heart of a once great empire the streets were no longer secure against the threat of criminals.

Something of this same uneasiness spilled over into the courtroom inside the Old Bailey as the trial commenced. One might have thought that nothing ever changed within this great cathedral of the law, with the gold and crimson sword of Justice awesomely suspended underneath the massive carved and gilded coat of arms of the City of London, the judge in scarlet robes and judge's wig presiding centre stage, like a medieval painting of God Almighty, and lawyers, reporters, court officials, deferentially ranked in the body of the court below him. But appearances had become deceptive.

In the past the Old Bailey's number 1 Court had been the most famous courtroom in the world, scene of many of the most celebrated murder trials in history. But when capital punishment for murder was abolished in 1964, less than five years earlier, the nature and atmosphere of murder trials had changed, and what was now occurring was something rarely seen in any English court of law. The resemblance to a Mafia trial was not to end with the cavalcade of armed policemen driving through the streets of London.

The presiding judge, Sir Aubrey Melford Stevenson, had a reputation as the toughest High Court judge in England. He was in fact a vicar's son, who began his career as a barrister in the rich pastures of libel and divorce; and among his fellow lawyers at the Garrick Club 'old Melford' was regarded as something of a wit. But his humour, like his attitude to law and order, was summed up in the name of the country house he bought in the ancient smuggling port of Winchelsea in Sussex – Truncheons.

On moving to the criminal bar, Stevenson was not as successful as when dealing with divorce. He defended Ruth Ellis for murdering her lover and she ended up being the last woman in England to be hanged for murder. He was later blamed for showing what was felt by some to be excessive sympathy with the prosecution, and for not contesting the judge's ruling against trying her for the lesser charge of manslaughter, which might conceivably have saved her.

As prosecuting counsel he could be erratic. In 1956 he was junior counsel to the then Attorney General, Sir Manningham Buller (known to fellow lawyers as 'Sir Bullying Manner'), in one of the last great murder trials in Britain – that of the Eastbourne doctor John Bodkin Adams, who was accused of poisoning a rich widow and her husband for their fortune and the family Rolls-Royce. Against the odds, and thanks largely to the courtroom brilliance of his barrister, the diminutive Geoffrey Lawrence QC, Adams escaped scot-free, and the prosecution was widely considered to have blundered. Stevenson was fortunate, two years later, to receive his High Court judgeship and the knighthood that automatically goes with it. Now, at the age of sixty-six, he had a chance to live down his failures with Ruth Ellis and Bodkin Adams, and to find his place in legal history at the centre of what already looked like being one of the most sensational murder trials of the century.

Together with that armed police convoy from Brixton, following on the heels of the whole extraordinary police operation under Nipper Read, the appointment of a judge as remorseless as Melford Stevenson to conduct the trial was taken as a further demonstration that the utmost rigour of the law was being brought to bear upon the Krays and their followers. For Melford Stevenson made no secret of the fact that he had no sympathy for violent criminals or murderers. Although he could no longer hang them, it was unlikely that he would show them any mercy.

It was also clear that the sheer extent, not to mention the improbability, of much of the police evidence against the Twins had been giving the prosecution problems. No court on earth could possibly have tried the Twins and the rest of the accused without the trial continuing for years. Also, much of the evidence, especially that concerning Alan Bruce Cooper's involvement with John du Rose, could have been highly embarrassing to the police.

So when the Twins and their followers arrived at the Old Bailey most of these accusations had been 'left on file', and they were being charged with three capital murders. Melford Stevenson was trying the Twins, and eight of their alleged accomplices, for committing or participating in the murders of George Cornell and/or Jack McVitie. Afterwards another High Court judge, Mr Justice Lawton, would take over in a separate trial of the same defendants for the murder of Frank Mitchell.

This meant that none of the most sensational crimes alleged against them at the Old Street hearings would be brought to court. The world would never know for sure how close the Krays had really come to releasing President Tshombe or kidnapping the Pope; nor would the Krays stand trial for the major protection rackets alleged against them, the commercial frauds and the complex web of criminality from which, according to the police, the Krays and their followers had made their living. More important still, the crucial point of whether they really were a British Mafia would never be argued out in court.

This was an important point for popular perceptions of the Krays in future, as the proceedings seemed to follow the pattern of a Mafia trial with ten men being tried together in the same court for two separate, very different killings. With the first of these killings only two of the figures in the dock – Ron Kray and his driver, Ian Barrie – were actually accused of murdering Cornell. As the prosecution admitted, the rest of those on trial had no connection whatsoever with this particular murder.

This unusual feature of the trial made it almost inevitable that, despite the drama staged by the police, the first day brought an instant anti-climax, with the defence immediately objecting to what appeared to be obvious rough justice. The judge had no alternative but to adjourn proceedings as he heard out the defence submissions. But when the court was reconvened two days later, it was to hear that, to no one's great surprise, Mr Justice Melford Stevenson had rejected them. The trial would continue as planned, but no sooner had it started again than the judge was facing trouble of a different nature.

Although I had observed when I visited the Twins in Brixton Gaol that Ron was less concerned about the outcome of the trial than with the impression he and Reg would make in court, I hadn't realised that Melford Stevenson was similarly concerned about the Kray Twins' image, and determined to do everything he could to cut them down to size.

I had a hint of Melford Stevenson's intentions when I opened the post on the morning the trial recommenced, and found a letter Ron had written to me the day before from Brixton. As I read the words laboriously spelled out in capital letters on coarse prison paper, I could almost hear his voice. 'Well now the trial has started they want us to wear numbers round our necks like catle. It seams that they dont want to leave us with any dignity.' [sic]

This was the first I'd heard of prisoners being numbered in the dock. Next morning when the trial was reconvened at 10 a.m., no one I spoke to seemed to know anything about it.

Despite its size, the court was packed to overflowing. Since each defendant had his counsel, and every counsel had his junior, I'd never seen so many lawyers crammed together. But despite this, and despite an air of keen expectancy, everything was very much in order, with lawyers, court officials and jurors in their places as the accused were led up from the cells. When the judge entered, everybody rose. When he took his seat, we all sat down.

Then, without a word of explanation, a group of prison officers suddenly appeared, carrying large, white, numbered cards, which they proceeded to hang around the necks of the prisoners with bright pink ribbon.

I watched them standing there in total silence with the numbers round their necks. There was a slight pause, then, without a glance in their direction, Melford Stevenson stated in his clear, no-nonsense voice, 'These numbers will be worn throughout the trial.'

Still in silence, and with considerable dignity, the prisoners removed the cards and placed them on the edge of the dock. Knowing Ron, I guessed exactly what would happen next.

'I repeat that the numbers will be worn by the prisoners in court,' said the judge, looking straight ahead. 'I order them to be replaced.'

The warders obeyed, but once the numbers were put back around those sturdy necks, the prisoners again removed them.

At this point, Ron's counsel, John Platts-Mills QC, already looking fairly ancient in his old black gown and very old grey wig, rose to object.

'My Lord, in what used to be called the British Empire, Hong Kong was the last place to make accused persons wear numbers of this sort, but on that occasion the learned judge ruled that it imposed such indignity upon them that the practice should be discontinued, which it has been ever since, even in Hong Kong.'

'Mr Platts-Mills, this is not a question of imposing indignities on anyone but of making the accused identifiable to witnesses. I repeat my order. Numbers will be worn – and kept on too, throughout the trial.'

Undeflected, John Platts-Mills rose to his feet once more, but was instantly cut short.

'Mr Platts-Mills, I have heard all you have to say and it makes no difference to my direction. The numbers will be worn.'

For the third time the warders went through the pantomime of placing the numbers with pink ribbons over the heads of the accused. This time there was something of a struggle, and Ron Kray made the move I knew he had intended from the start. Having removed his card, he slowly tore it up, as if tearing up the judge's authority. Reg followed suit, and threw the bits of cardboard into the body of the court.

'I thought this was a court of law, not a cattle market,' shouted Ron Kray.

Pandemonium ensued. Dignity departed – as did the judge. Looking alarmingly like the Red Queen in *Alice's Adventures in Wonderland*, Mr Justice Aubrey Melford Stevenson gathered up his papers, spectacles and scarlet robes, and, clutching them around his waist, stomped from the court. The prisoners filed off to the cells beneath, muttering among themselves. It was then that I realised that by attempting to be firm, the judge had made a terrible mistake.

Only by using force is it possible to make anyone, even a murder suspect in a court of law, wear something round his neck if he doesn't want to. And since the Krays and their followers had made it clear that they were refusing to obey him, the judge was left with only two alternatives – either use force or accept their wishes. It took an hour for him to reach the only possible conclusion.

At 11.30 a.m. the usher, in his long black gown, entered and bellowed 'Silence! Be upstanding in court.' And the little judge, looking smaller than ever now, resumed his seat, and announced, rather as if the thought had just occurred to him, that to help identify prisoners in court, numbers would henceforth be taped to the front of the dock. No one inquired how this would work – and in fact it didn't. John Platts-Mills expressed his gratitude for the judge's wisdom. Stony-faced, the judge accepted his thanks, and the trial went on with no quarter offered or expected.

The Cornell trial was the opening gambit in what would soon develop into a much wider game of legal chess. And as is the way with opening gambits, it began by seeming rather dull. Just as the most fearsome aspect of the law departed from the Old Bailey with the ending of capital punishment, so the great criminal barristers seemed to have vanished too.

The prosecuting counsel, Kenneth Jones QC, a Welsh-man with a tendency to overact, opened the proceedings by describing how Ronald Kray entered the saloon bar of the Blind Beggar shortly before eight o'clock one March evening in 1966 with another member of the gang called Ian Barrie. He described how the gangster, George Cornell, who was sitting at the bar, looked up, remarked, 'Well, look who's here,' and how, from a distance of five or six feet, 'Ronald Kray raised his gun, fired and shot him through the forehead. Two further shots were fired, probably by the second man. Cornell fell to the floor. The two men turned on their heel and walked out, leaving George Cornell dying on the floor.'

A pause followed as Kenneth Jones peered like an owl at the members of the jury over the top of his half-moon spectacles, as if to emphasise the drama of the moment.

'Gentlemen of the jury, think for a moment of the horrifying effrontery, the terrifying effrontery of this deed. That two men can walk into a public house on any evening and there in cold blood kill another human being.'

While he was speaking, I was watching Nipper Read, who was sitting perched, like a bright-eyed bird, behind the scrum of prosecution lawyers. I thought that he was looking anxious, as well he might be, with so much personally at stake. This was the culmination of two years' dedicated work by him and by his team. This was really Nipper Read's great moment. Now that the deals were done and the investigation was complete, he had become the impresario responsible for the police case and for the prosecution witnesses who were to follow one another through the witness box during the weeks ahead.

The success or failure of this trial was going to depend upon how well he'd done his job, and their credibility before the jury. But he knew that, however much he had prepared, in any trial there is always much that can, and often does, go wrong.

The first witness, always referred to as Mrs X, was the barmaid who was working in the saloon bar of the Blind Beggar, on the night Cornell was murdered. She was potentially the prosecution's strongest witness. Unlike the majority of those to come, she had no criminal record and was not an associate or friend of the Krays, and no one disputed her presence in the bar at the time of the shooting. Her only weakness was that at Cornell's inquest, eighteen months earlier, she had sworn under oath that she hadn't recognised his killer. Now she was saying she had lied at the inquest out of fear of retribution, but that she had definitely recognised the man who fired the shot as Ronnie Kray.

A small, rather mousy woman, Mrs X was not impressive when she started, but when Platts-Mills cross-examined her, he made the mistake of attacking her integrity. The way Platts-Mills handled witnesses set him increasingly at odds with Melford Stevenson as the trial proceeded. By the time the trial ended, judge and barrister were clearly loathing one another.

Platts-Mills began by inquiring, with heavy sarcasm, how Mrs X, as a self-admitted liar, could possibly expect any jury to believe her. Surely they could only conclude that 'lying on oath does not matter to you a scrap?'

At this Mrs X's whole demeanour changed. Having been called a liar, she was on her mettle. 'It matters to me a lot,' she said indignantly.

'What matters?'

'Having to tell lies. I was so terrified at what might happen to me or my children that I had to tell lies then. Now I'm telling you the truth.'

The way she said this suddenly conveyed intense conviction. For underneath her indignation, one could also understand the reasons for her fear. By the time her cross-examination ended she must have convinced the jury that here was a weak but honest woman, who had lied to a coroner for one simple reason – because she was terrified of the Krays. Indeed, what woman wouldn't be frightened after witnessing a man she had just served a pint of bitter being shot before her eyes by Ronnie Kray?

Thus, perversely, it was largely thanks to the way Platts-Mills made so much of it, that Mrs X's lie became a sort of proof of her honesty – and of the truth of her unshakable insistence that Ronald Kray was George Cornell's murderer.

Mrs X was the lynchpin of the prosecution case against Ron Kray for the murder of George Cornell, and also against Ian Barrie as an accessory. Her demeanour in court, coupled with her previous independence from the Krays, made her evidence powerful enough to render their conviction virtually certain. But the prosecution case for the murder of McVitie was more complex and was going to be more difficult to prove in court. Since it involved not only Reg Kray but also Ron, their brother Charles, and other accused men who were allegedly the nucleus of the Firm, it was far more important to the prosecution than the Cornell case, and rapidly became the crux of the trial.

After the appearance of Mrs X, the trial became more than ever like a major show trial brought against the Italian Mafia. In such trials, much of the evidence usually comes from so-called *pentiti*, 'repentant ones' – indicted former members of the Mafia who have been persuaded to show 'repentance' by giving evidence in court against their former friends, in return for leniency by the authorities.

As I sat in court, and a succession of 'repentant ones' passed through the witness box, I found the proceedings totally engrossing. I'd never realised before the voyeuristic fascination of observing human beings in the act of betraying one another in public. It was all the more fascinating as I knew most of those involved and remembered them as loyal buddies, drinking partners and staunch allies of the Twins in the days before they were arrested.

Although I knew that Scotch Jack Dickson had 'turned' and was appearing for the prosecution, it was dramatic to see his transformation as he stood in the witness box; this former Gorbals gangster who had served many years in the Marines had always struck me as one of the most unshakable of men.

On the night Cornell was murdered, he had driven Ron and Ian Barrie to and from the Blind Beggar. He had originally lied to the police about this, in order to provide his comrades with an alibi. By offering him his virtual freedom, Nipper had persuaded him to come to court as a key prosecution witness against his former friends. At the same time, Dickson was also ready to confess to his involvement in freeing the Mad Axeman, Frank Mitchell, from Dartmoor, and on the strength of these confessions he was awarded a nominal prison sentence. Having now spent eight months in prison on remand, he had all but served his sentence and would soon enjoy his freedom.

Under cross-examination from Platts-Mills, Dickson gave as good as he got, and there was nothing remotely cowed or apologetic in his manner as he gave Mrs X supporting evidence by relating how Ron Kray had casually informed him as they drove back from the Blind Beggar that he had just shot George Cornell.

The next group of witnesses were very different. These were three brothers, all of them street-traders, who had been friends of the Kray family and particularly of Ron. They had all spent holidays with the Kray family and even been abroad together. Soon after Cornell's murder they had gone off drinking with the Twins. They gave detailed evidence of how Ron had told them all about the shooting, and how one of the brothers had been 'forced' to hide him in his flat for several days. Later I discovered that one of these brothers had in fact been 'turned' by the police, and had been supplying the police with information for nearly a year before the Twins were arrested.

Listening to their evidence, I began wondering how such formerly close friends as these could have been turned against the Twins. As they followed one another through the witness box, I found it painfully pathetic as, one by one, they insisted that they had all been forced into friendship with the Krays simply by the threat of violence.

Under cross-examination by Platts-Mills, the truth emerged. One by one, each of the brothers admitted to having blackmailed rich homosexual clients in the past, and there was no denial when Platts-Mills suggested that there had been a deal with the police over charges pending against their mother. She was described in court as having been 'a housekeeper to a noble, titled person' and had apparently confessed to letting a burglar into the house when the owner was robbed of £25,000. The police can't have found it too difficult to persuade the three brothers to turn against their former friends.

By the time the court had heard all the evidence over the killing of Cornell, no shadow of doubt remained that Ron was guilty of his murder and that Ian Barrie had been an accessory. Now the case against the Twins and their accomplices for murdering McVitie was about to start. The atmosphere in court changed dramatically as all the defence lawyers suddenly appeared like birds at feeding time, and the first of the prosecution witnesses took the stand.

Although she was McVitie's wife, for some reason the first witness was addressed in court by her first name only – Sylvie. She seemed desperately vulnerable, a waif-like figure standing in the witness box in a blue silk dress with very thin blond hair. There was actually little that she could contribute in the way of evidence, apart from describing how her husband Jack had left her on the evening of the murder, saying he was going out for a drink with the Krays. She swore that she had never seen him since. Then she started sobbing, telling the court how much she missed him. As she finished her evidence, she suddenly swung round and faced the figures in the dock.

'You murdering bastards,' she shrieked at them.

Everyone in court was suddenly reduced to total silence. Even Melford Stevenson seemed lost for words, and I remember wondering how spontaneous Sylvie's outburst really was. Perhaps I was being cynical, but the distraught girl's evidence came at such a crucial moment in the trial that it made the perfect curtain-raiser for the gruesome tale that followed. As little else could possibly have done, it seemed to make the point that, faced with such human misery, the law was justified in using any means to bring the cause of it to justice – even if this meant relying on the evidence of someone as deeply compromised as the next witness for the prosecution, who followed white-faced, weeping Sylvie into the witness box.

I've never forgotten my surprise at the sight of the figure in the pale blue suit who took the stand, gripping the Bible firmly in his hand and swearing 'before God to tell the truth, the whole truth, and nothing but the truth'. This was the prosecution's key witness to McVitie's murder. After Ron himself, this was also probably the one member of the Firm who was most deeply implicated in what had happened, and his appearance in the witness box was the ultimate act of betrayal. The figure in the pale blue suit was the Twins' own cousin, who had told me once that he had joined the Firm because of his longing for adventure – the tall, still boyishly good-looking Ronald Hart.

In his evidence Hart admitted having been present at the killing of McVitie, and it was undeniable that had he not been standing in the witness box, he would have been in the dock beside the Twins facing a charge of murder.

Renegades have always made the bitterest accusers, for

only by being unforgiving can they justify their own betrayal. And the fact that, by his own admission, Hart had been an accessory to McVitie's murder made his testimony particularly chilling. Although he denied any part in the actual killing, he told how the unsuspecting McVitie had been led into the flat by the brothers Lambrianou.

I remember the stunned silence in the court as Hart related what had happened to McVitie: how he had arrived at the flat expecting a party, how Reg had unsuccessfully tried to shoot him, and how a member of the Firm then offered Reg a kitchen knife. Then came the description of the actual killing: the way Ron grabbed McVitie from behind, how he screamed encouragement at his brother, and how Reg began to stab his victim, first in the face below the eye, then in the stomach, finishing him off by stabbing him through the neck and leaving him pinioned to the floor like a flailing animal.

It was one of the most horrible first-hand accounts of cruelty I've ever heard. And by describing the murder in such horrendous detail, Ronald Hart and the succeeding witnesses did more than just establish the guilt of Jack McVitie's killers: they were also acting out in court a gripping tableau of sadistic wickedness. It was now that the image of the Twins as exceptionally evil murderers was born. By the time the prosecution case was over, the only explanation for the Twins' behaviour seemed to be lurking in the very depths of human depravity.

While this story was unfolding the increasingly bad-tempered judge was dismissing every interruption by the Kray defence – 'Really Mr Platts-Mills, must we go through all this again?' – and the one person in the court whose satisfaction clearly grew with every day that passed was Nipper Read, as he watched the conclusion of his long investigation. I must admit to finding him impressive, particularly in contrast with so many of the barristers with their courtroom flummery and self-importance and the way some of them could even get their facts wrong. Nipper got nothing wrong. Who else but Nipper would have brought his big grey filing cabinet into court to help with the deft production of the evidence, as he steered the (then) longest police investigation in Scotland Yard's history to its destination? But as he did so I also suspected that, although the Twins were undoubtedly guilty, the full story behind their crimes was not appearing.

As witness after witness added to Ron Hart's account of Jack McVitie's murder, the Twins themselves remained the two most enigmatic figures in the court. In their dark blue suits, with spotlessly clean white shirts and tightly knotted ties, they showed little sign of emotion and rarely bothered to so much as glance at the witnesses. Never uttering a word, they seemed to grow more remote with every day that passed, brooding figures standing in the dock as they listened impassively to the recitation of their crimes and an aura of extraordinary evil built up around them.

On 30 January, day seventeen of the trial, the prosecution case finished, and early in the afternoon, John Platts-Mills began the case for the defence. At first I wondered what he could be up to, for this was Platts-Mills at his most pedantic, quoting from Shakespeare's *Henry IV Part One*, and then comparing the prosecution case to the progress of a juggernaut. Being Platts-Mills, he proceeded to tell the court exactly what a juggernaut was – 'a great chariot employed in pagan religious festivals, and as it continues people in a state of hysteria or ecstasy are thrown beneath its wheels'. Not for the first time I noticed that the judge was yawning. As Platts-Mills turned to what he called a 'police vendetta' against his client, and described how

'Ronald Kray has been so foully abused that he may be forced, possibly against his interests, to enter the witness box himself,' I suddenly realised what he was up to. He was marking time while Ron decided whether to give evidence in person.

Impatient as ever, the judge attempted to compel Platts-Mills to show his hand, which produced the classic Platts-Mills reply: 'My Lord, I know, but I'm not in a position to say what I know.'

At which point Ron Kray suddenly cut short all further argument by speaking to the judge direct.

'I'll go in the box, sir.'

It was one of those abrupt decisions, full of drama and surprise, that so often happened in his life. If giving evidence in court can be made a violent act, Ron did so now, as the bulky body in the dark blue suit lumbered from the dock and thrust itself towards the witness box. Ron had made up his mind. After seventeen days of listening in silence to other people abusing him, *he* was now going to have his say and the court would listen.

Until this moment all the other figures in the dock had been looking more and more dejected, accused by their former friends, and having to listen to whatever case they had presented for them by condescending gentlemen in lawyers' wigs, as if they were incapable of speaking for themselves.

But now the Colonel was taking over.

To begin with he seemed highly nervous, gulping for breath as he answered Platts-Mills's routine questions about his previous convictions. But then his true character started to come over stronger than ever. I had never realised before how threatening that strange voice of his would sound in public. But although it sounded threatening it also sounded like the voice of a child, a very wicked, wilful child who had been caught out over some act of wickedness and who was cunningly complaining at the constant unfairness of everyone against him.

'Yes, sir,' he said, agreeing with his counsel, 'Mr Read was in charge of the McCowan case, and ever since we was acquitted, he's had it in for us.'

He answered suggestions that he and his brother Reg had run a gang involved in violence and protection rackets with all the feigned innocence of a guilty child. 'All we have are drinking friends we go out with in the evening.'

And how did he and his brother get their money, Platts-Mills asked him.

'From the club game, sir, and I give my father money to gamble with on fights on my behalf.'

As I listened to him going on about the way he and his family had been endlessly picked on by the law, I was sure that in his paranoid way Ron totally believed what he was saying. Since he was able to put the violence and the murders out of his mind, they could be totally ignored because they no longer really worried him. He made it clear that what really mattered in the mind of Ronald Kray was an overwhelming sense of bitterness and anger at the way he and his family had been treated. The real victims in this case, he implied, were not McVitie and Cornell, but he and his brothers, because of how the law and all those former friends had turned against them. I'm sure that to him the two murders were irrelevant, when set against the injustice of the law, the low-down dirty tricks of the police and the shameless ingratitude of former so-called friends. Thus, by a curious logic, the more powerful the prosecution case, the more it proved, if not exactly the Twins' innocence, at all events the supreme nature of their role as victims.

What also clearly came over as Ron continued with his

'evidence' was the importance of his 'legend'. A sense of betrayal is a key ingredient in many legends, and soon he was saying how wrong it was for police and the court to persecute two innocent East Enders as evil doers, when they were actually public benefactors, who had given tens of thousands of pounds to the old folk of Bethnal Green, and who had been honoured with the friendship of the great and famous during their careers.

'I took Joe Louis to Newcastle, and Rocky Marciano and Sonny Liston to the Repton Club. If I wasn't standing here today I'd probably be drinking with Judy Garland now. I've also drunk with Lord Boothby and Lord Effingham and Sophie Tucker,' he boasted.

But the effect of 'evidence' like this was the exact opposite of what Ron presumably intended. Coming so swiftly after all the images the witnesses had just presented of two sadistic killers wading through a sea of blood and violence, his words appeared extraordinarily sinister. Evil can be defined as human wickedness beyond belief and explanation, and it was as if Ron was determined to complete the story of the murders by exhibiting himself as the sort of grotesque villain that a plot like this demanded. By the end of his time in the witness box he had established himself as a figure emerging from the murky depths of age-old East End crime, violent and coarse and cunning, the very embodiment of evil.

Ron's appearance in the witness box was almost certainly the turning point in the case. Until then, I was convinced that the Twins' only possible choice would be to change their plea to one of guilty. Had they done so, their counsel would have been free to argue out the extraordinary motives and the mitigating factors that lay behind the murders.

And had this happened, I am convinced that the outcome of the trial would have been different. Ron would have had to have been recertified insane as a dangerous paranoid schizophrenic, and sent to Broadmoor – which was where he ended up anyway, nine years later. And whatever the court's final view of Reg, and the influence his schizophrenic identical twin brother may have exercised over him, it is almost inconceivable that even Mr Justice Melford Stevenson would have 'recommended' him to thirty years in prison.

But by appearing in the witness box Ron had made it certain that this wouldn't happen. Since he believed so firmly that he was in the right, how could he possibly admit he wasn't?

I noticed a contrast now between the Twins. Ron was obviously enjoying acting out the greatest public role of his career. He was still the Colonel, valiant to the last, showing no concern for his countless enemies around him. But the fight had gone out of Reg, and he refused to follow his brother into the witness box. He didn't make much sense, although at times he became overcome with frustrated rage. The only words he uttered to the court came later when Kenneth Jones, in his summing-up, happened to refer to the brother of his dead wife Frances. 'You fat slob,' Reg shouted at him, then buried his face in his hands.

As the trial drew to its close and the lawyers completed their summing-up, the difference between the accents of the Twins and the East End witnesses, and those of the judge and the lawyers who were trying them became more noticeable than ever. In the accents of the lawyers, particularly of Kenneth Jones, one heard the voice of upper-class England confronted with a world it didn't know and would never really understand.

'Gentlemen of the jury,' he began. 'There are many motives for murder. High passion, emotion, greed, lust and jealousy have been known through the ages as reasons for one human being to kill another. But you may decide, gentlemen of the jury, that none of these motives was present in these two cases. The reason, in my submission, is that these two men, these twin brothers, Ronald and Reginald Kray, sought to demonstrate the lengths to which they would go. It is a terrible thought that murder was committed, not for profit, nor for gain, but as a matter of prestige.'

And so it was, but looking at Ron at that moment, I could see that something else was on his mind. He was looking not at Kenneth Jones but into the body of the court, where a few favoured visitors were sitting, and I realised that this had to be Ron's proudest moment since the trial started.

For sitting there hearing the case against him and attracted by his fame was his greatest hero, General Gordon – or rather, the man who had played him in the memorable film about Gordon's life. None other than Charlton Heston in person was sitting in court.

At the conclusion of the trial, on 8 March 1969, Melford Stevenson got his revenge for the way the Twins had made a fool of him at the start of the trial over his wretched numbers, as it was obvious he would.

'Society needs a rest from your activities. I intend to ensure that you don't trouble society for a very long time. Life, which I would recommend, should not be less than thirty years. Take them down.'

Since the Twins had refused to admit their guilt (as they both did some years later) this meant that none of their followers, standing by them, could do so either and plead the mitigating factors raised by Ron Kray's madness. All had to share the Colonel's fate, and received swingeing sentences in line with those awarded to the Twins – twenty years for Ian Barrie, and for Ronald Bender as an accessory in McVitie's murder, fifteen years apiece for the brothers Lambrianou, ten for Charlie Kray and Freddie Foreman, and seven for Cornelius Whitehead, a minor member of the Firm who had 'cleaned up' the flat following McVitie's murder.

Nipper, of course, was happy at the outcome of the trial, as he had every right to be. His strategy had worked and the long reign of the Krays was over. As a show trial for the police, and particularly for the CID, the case against the Krays had succeeded beyond Scotland Yard's wildest expectations, the proudest feather in their cap since the Great Train Robber trial and the Richardson case. It had been a skilfully staged and managed show of power by the police, a public demonstration that showed that the criminal organisation of the Krays had been destroyed for ever, and that the law was back in charge.

It had also been a show of force against the mores and traditions of the old East End. The spectacle of criminal betraying criminal in the witness box was a very public demonstration of how flimsy had become the traditional loyalty of the old East End.

So it seemed as if the trial had gone exactly as Nipper Read and the police had intended. The idea of Bethnal Green as a no-go area was over. With the Krays' so-called 'wall of fear' demolished, Nipper's work would be completed by the bulldozers which were already crashing over Vallance Road and the changing of the whole area where the Twins grew up.

Melford Stevenson was also satisfied. He would clearly have preferred to have hanged the Twins, but thirty years apiece appeared an acceptable alternative. From the bench he officially thanked Nipper Read, who had been the real star of the proceedings. But in fact Nipper Read had done too well and put far too many backs up for his superiors ever to forgive him, and he would never know success like this again. Instead of ending up at the very top of Scotland Yard as he deserved he was finally appointed Assistant Chief Constable at Nottingham.

Ironically, the real winners were the Twins. What no one seemed to notice was that they also got what they wanted. Certainly Ron did. Just as the trial had established Nipper Read in the role of Britain's supercop, so it caused the Krays to become enshrined as the nation's supercriminals, the most notorious, evil men in Britain. What mattered to them was that the Twins had stood together, and not only had their legend as the most dangerous criminals of the sixties remained intact, but the dramas of their murders had been acted out in the most impressive theatre in the country – the Old Bailey. In the twisted way that such things work, the trial also formed the basis of their later celebrity. Those killings, sordid and senseless as they really were, had been elevated out of all proportion, thus giving the Twins what they had always longed for – fame and notoriety. They had also been betrayed, and betrayal is a strong ingredient in producing martyrs. The legend of the Twins had almost taken wing.

At the time of the trial I could never understand why the defence was so inadequate. Although I asked both Twins this question later, neither seemed inclined to tell me why and it was nearly thirty years before I learned the answer.

In 1999 my friend Tom Tanner was working on a television programme about Reg Kray, who was still in prison. He told me that he had just interviewed John Platts-Mills, who was not only very much alive, but at ninety-two was still working as a barrister from his old chambers in the Middle Temple. As I was still fascinated by the trial I went to see him.

At first sight he appeared to be the ultimate eccentric English gentleman, although he had actually been born in New Zealand and had spent much of his life fighting for unfashionable causes, the Krays included.

When I asked him what he thought of Ron, his reply was rather strange.

'Ronald Kray was a jolly good fellow.'

He seemed equally enthusiastic about Reg, and was incensed at 'the disgusting way the parole board and the Home Secretary conspire together to keep him in prison even though he's served the thirty years Melford awarded him.'

Then I asked him the questions that had always foxed me. 'Why was it never brought out in court that Ron had once been certified insane and was a classic example of a dangerous paranoid schizophrenic? And shouldn't someone have said that when he killed McVitie, Reg was on the edge of a nervous breakdown after his wife's suicide and that he was drunk, drugged and dominated by his homicidal twin brother? And why did no one mention the fact that they were identical twins, bearing in mind the influence one identical twin can have upon another?'

The directness of John Platts-Mills's reply surprised me. 'Oh, but we wanted to,' he said. 'From the very start, Wrightson [Paul Wrightson QC, who defended Reg] and I had both decided it was the obvious line to follow. It would have been hard work, of course, arguing a case like that in front of Melford, who wasn't the most liberal of judges. But you're absolutely right. The facts were undeniable. As Ron had already been certified insane as a paranoid schizophrenic he would have been sent to Broadmoor, where he ended up anyhow. And Reg, who knows? He would have certainly received a much reduced sentence on the grounds of diminished responsibility. *Folie à deux* between identical twins, one of whom was a paranoid schizophrenic. Absolutely fascinating. Both of us would have liked the chance to argue it out in court.'

'So why didn't you?'

'My dear fellow, why do you think? The Twins, of course. The Twins. They simply wouldn't hear of it.'

'Why not? Why should they have objected?'

'Their legend, of course. It would have destroyed their precious legend and all their credibility as famous criminals. Besides, for Reg it would have been a terrible betrayal of his brother. To be fair to Ron, during the trial he urged him to, on several occasions to my certain knowledge. "Save yourself, Reg," he said. But Reg wouldn't hear of it. I've always admired him for that, but he paid a very heavy price.'

He paused. 'More than thirty years in prison, and he's still there to this day with little hope of freedom. It's a dreadful story.'

FIFTEEN

Top Security

At present, the most efficient way for a man to survive in Britain, is to be almost half-witted, completely irresponsible, and spend a lot of time in prison, where his health is far better looked after than outside.

Charles Darwin

When the trial ended, the Twins were parted and consigned to start their sentences in maximum security in two of the most formidable penal institutions in the country – Ron at Durham Gaol and Reg at Parkhurst on the Isle of Wight. From now on they were effectively 'banged up for life'. The lid had been firmly put in place and screwed down as tightly as the Prison Service could manage on the Krays and all they stood for.

Had they been 'normal' murderers, that would have been virtually the last the public would have heard about them. Almost invariably, when a trial ends and the prison gates clang shut on even the most sensational killers, their interest to the public and the media subsides. Convicted murderers are rapidly forgotten, apart from notorious child murderers who antagonise the public and whose unspeakable crimes we never seem able to escape from.

In theory then, the Twins should have been slowly forgotten, but for some reason they were not. Just as their trial had played a crucial part in establishing their public image as the ultimate in dangerous criminals, so their time in prison, far from diminishing their interest, would see it grow and flourish in ways that have happened with no other modern killers in captivity. In this, as in much else, the Kray Twins were virtually unique. Therein lies much of their enduring fascination.

I had a glimpse of what was happening very early on, when, only a few days after the Mitchell trial ended, my phone rang at eight o'clock in the morning. It was Violet, sounding remarkably composed for someone with three sons who had just been sentenced to seventy-five years' penal servitude between them.

'I'm all right,' she said. 'Can't complain. After all, it's worse for them. Terrible what's happened to 'em, isn't it? The things people said about them, after all the Twins have done for them.' But as usual on the telephone, she was brief and came quickly to the point. 'Ronnie wants to see you. He says to say it's important as he's something to tell you. So I've booked you in for a visit next Wednesday morning. Mr Kray's going too, so you can go up on the train together. Ron'll be expecting you. That all right, John?'

If it hadn't been all right, I had a feeling it would not have made the slightest difference. Ron Kray wished to talk to his biographer.

'What time's the train?' I asked.

'It leaves King's Cross at seven-thirty in the morning.

'I'll be there,' I said.

Sure enough old Charlie was waiting on the platform in his electric-blue suit and gleaming winklepickers, and I helped him on to the train with the enormous yellow leather holdall he was carrying. Luckily the train wasn't crowded, and we had a compartment to ourselves.

'It's his,' he said, pointing to the holdall. 'Ronnie's. Brought it back from Tangier, didn't he?'

Despite its size the bag was crammed to bursting. I was inquisitive about the contents.

'Take a look,' he said, unzipping it and showing me what

Vi had packed for her favourite son.

I found it curiously touching. It was as if Ron, far from embarking on thirty years' imprisonment for murder, had just gone off to boarding school, and Violet, most loving of mothers, was sending him everything he needed for the term ahead. Six bottles of Brylcreme, a dozen tubes of Signal toothpaste, silk underpants, special weight-lifting boots and – a mother's touch – his favourite bedspread.

'Typical of 'er to make me carry all his clobber, but what can I do? The Twins is all she thinks about.'

Despite his lifelong role as absent father, old Charles had sat in the public gallery throughout the trial, and I remember seeing him on the last day, very drunk, being slipped a pound by Violet to keep him quiet, while we were waiting for the verdict.

I asked him if he felt relieved that the trial was over.

He nodded glumly and said yes, he felt freer now than at any time since the Twins came out of the army. 'Never knew what was going to happen during all those years, did we, me an' their mother?'

He lit a cigarette and stared sadly through the window at the passing countryside.

'I tell you something. That Ronnie was definitely mad, an' he made life hell for me. An' for her too, for 'is mother. That was the trouble. I'd tell her, but she'd always say, "If you're too strict wiv 'em they'll leave home. My father was too strict wiv me, so I cleared off and married you. I don't want the same thing happening with Ronnie and him leaving home because of you." So either I'd hold my tongue or I'd escape to the country when things got too bad at home. All three of them have given me a slap in their time. I've even 'ad Reggie frothing at the mouth against me. But she never minded what they did, as long as they were *her* boys and on *her* side.'

We sat in silence, and I suddenly felt immensely sorry

for him. At least Violet loved the Twins and they loved her, but Charlie hadn't even that strange consolation. And yet at sixty-three he was still tied to them and acting as their errand boy.

'I'd like to go off now an' take her to live in Spain – or even Bristol – Bristol's nice, you know. But how can we? She won't hear of it. They're still her life. She's still tied to 'em, and has to visit them every fortnight, or whenever they can have a visit.'

At Durham Gaol, we had to pass through two sets of doors, the second one electrically operated like an air lock in a submarine, from which one emerged into another world. Durham's maximum security block is a prison within a prison, isolated from the world outside. An elderly warder with a bushy grey moustache led us to a room where Ron was sitting at a table waiting for us.

Ron was looking thinner than when I had last seen him in the dock at the Old Bailey. He'd had his hair cropped very close, and there was something slightly trance-like about him. His movements weren't co-ordinated, and I imagine he must have been heavily sedated. He certainly seemed calmer than I'd ever seen him. As we sat and talked, the only thing that seemed to interest him was still his all-important legend and the story of his life. He was clearly obsessed about the book – and the prospects for the film.

By now Deborah Rogers had sorted out the deal for publication. Frank Taylor had been struck by a bad attack of publishers' cold feet, and just before the trial, McGraw-Hill had withdrawn from the deal. But another US publisher was in the offing, while in England Jonathan Cape, who had made a considerable success of my biography of Ian Fleming, remained enthusiastic about the project.

Although the Twins were now in prison, I felt it wise as

well as right to stick by our agreement to a fifty-fifty split on the profits from both the book and the film. The book would be my copyright, I would have total freedom over what I wrote, and since the Twins had legally no right to gain financially from their misdemeanours, I would pay their parents under a separate agreement.

Old Charlie had had to hand over the holdall to the warders on entering the prison, but when he told Ron what he'd brought, Ron merely grunted and more or less ignored him for the rest of the visit. I soon realised that the point of the visit was to get started on the book as soon as possible, and ensure that I understood his version of events. I took the opportunity to ask him as many questions as I could, not knowing when I could arrange another visit.

I remember being anxious to discover why he had risked going to New York with Dickie Morgan only a few weeks before he was arrested, and whether he suspected that the trip had been set up by Alan Bruce Cooper on behalf of Scotland Yard.

''Course I knew. Soon as we walked into the American Embassy in Paris to get our visas I knew at once. The whole thing was too easy, but I thought, well, what the fuck? We've come this far so, we might as well use 'em. It would have been kind of babyish not to, an' I met a lot of interesting people from the Mafia in New York – Frank Illiano at a club called the Mousetrap, and the Gallo brothers. I liked them. It was good to meet them. Since I realised the FBI was trying to plant stolen bonds on us, I wasn't 'aving it, an' we both came back early.'

'Tangier? I've been there three times, and Reg an' me would've liked to have settled there. But the law was on to us by then and wouldn't let us settle anywhere so we was thrown out. What was so special about Tangier? The boys, of course. I like Arab boys. I could do with one right now.'

He laughed slyly, and I felt he said this to upset his father who, unlike Violet, was always embarrassed by Ron's homosexuality. Throughout our conversation Ron rarely stopped going for him. 'Where's my record player? Why isn't it here? Just shut up, can't you? Stop telling *me* what to do. I'm not a fucking baby.'

Having got this off his chest, he continued with his story and his version of events. How sorry he had been for his friend Frank Mitchell and how he and Reg had finally decided that they had to get him out of Dartmoor.

'And then? What happened then?'

'That's something I don't want to talk about,' he said, and he switched the conversation to relations with the Richardson gang. He and Reg had had nothing against the Richardsons, 'except for a little misunderstanding'.

'So why did you kill Cornell?' I asked.

'I didn't like Cornell, but that wasn't the reason why I killed him. I'd said I'd kill him, so I did. It would have made no difference if there'd been a death penalty. It was easy and it made me feel good. I remember the blood spurting from his forehead like a red flower. It turned me on. I'm still glad I done it.'

'Stupid bastard,' said his father suddenly. 'Your Aunt Rose always told you you'd be topped for murder.'

'Shut up, you silly old cunt!' said Ron.

Charlie muttered something under his breath and fell silent.

'So why did things go wrong?' I asked. 'If you hadn't killed Cornell and the rest of them, you could have been running London.'

'Nothing went wrong,' he said and smiled knowingly. 'We just did what we had to do, me an' Reg, like we always did. I've told you already, me an' Reg is really the same person. Always have been, always will be. We might seem different on the surface, but underneath we're the same. Our only real mistakes were the people we chose, an' that was my fault. I was a bad judge of character. Everyone let us down when it came to it. Besides, the law was always after us. That Read just wouldn't let us be. You see, John, we was ambitious, me an' Reg. Make a note of that when you write the book. Put it all down to our ambition.'

Two or three weeks later I made a journey to the Isle of Wight, this time to visit Reg in Parkhurst. For some reason, Violet couldn't accompany me as promised, and I went instead with an old friend of the Kray family called Jim Harris. I never discovered what his racket was, or even if he had one. He currently owned several mini-cabs, and I knew him simply as a kindly, good-looking older man of considerable dignity who, for whatever reason, had stayed faithful to the Twins. He was one of the very few who had, the last of the old retainers. One of his self-appointed tasks was to look after their parents.

We had a drink among the holiday-makers as the Newquay ferry steamed across the Solent, and talked about the Twins' plight. Violet was apparently desperate to keep the mortgage paid up on the house in the country, although it cost nearly £5,000 a year. 'She wants her Twins to have something to look forward to when they come out,' said Harris.

'After thirty years?' I said.

He shrugged, and said that money had become a problem.

'But what about the clubs, and the pensions, and all their rich friends like Billie Hill? What about the money they're supposed to have salted away?'

He shrugged again. 'You have to understand: the Twins are has-beens, history, and none of their old friends want to know. I know I shouldn't say this, but it would've been better for everyone if they'd both been topped. Then the old couple could have mourned them and remembered them, and that would have been that. Better for the Twins too, being honest. What sort of life can they look forward to? Thirty years inside? I'd rather be dead myself. As it is, old Vi and Charlie have to go on visiting them and paying for all the expenses and worrying themselves to death about them, knowing they're responsible for them till the day they die.'

I understood more of Jim Harris's point of view when we finally reached Parkhurst and passed through the successive gates, like the seven gates of Hell, and found ourselves in the empty visiting room in maximum security, face to face with Reg. There was a little garden outside with ripening tomatoes and a small cement birdbath, where the twenty- and thirty-year-old men like him were allowed to exercise.

As at Durham, the warders seemed extremely kind in a distant sort of way. I found it touching how they looked away when Jim passed Reg his tobacco tin, and he quietly transferred two ounces of Old Holborn from Jim's tin into his.

'More tea, Reg? Biscuits?' said one of the warders. Reg shook his head but said nothing.

When I mentioned the book, he showed little interest, unlike Ron, and for the next ten minutes talked about Ron endlessly, quizzing me about my recent visit to Durham. Then he talked about himself, and in particular about the three or four hours a day he was spending in the gym, working out on the parallel bars, the medicine ball, toughening himself in frantic efforts not to weaken and to preserve himself for freedom, however distant.

'I'm under eleven stone now, and have never felt fitter.'
He may have done, but his appearance disturbed me. He

looked desperate, with drawn cheeks and mottled skin, and his eyes perpetually darting round the room. Unlike Ron, at this stage he was not sedated, and he seemed almost unable to control the suppressed violence of his nature, which was always there beneath the surface.

While Ron was dreaming on about his precious legend and Reg was trying to preserve his body by his punishing exercise routine, something odd was happening. The Twins were on the point of achieving one of their fondest and wildest ambitions. Their emergent legend was about to be embodied in an extraordinary movie, which some film historians now claim to have distilled much of the essence of the sixties. By 1967 Donald Cammell, the tall, good-looking portrait painter, who had been studying under the royal portrait painter Pietro Annigoni, had decided that his future really lay in making movies. He had a younger brother, David, who was already in the business, and had just written a successful script for a film about a young criminal, entitled *Duffy* and starring his friend, the promising young actor James Fox. Now he was determined he would write and direct a film himself.

Having lived for some time in Paris, Cammell was strongly influenced by the work of the homosexual thief turned playwright Jean Genet, and in particular by his book, *The Thief's Journal*. And in Chelsea he had got to know the whole unlikely set of aristocrats and artists who were loosely grouped around the most charismatic rock'n'roll star of the day, Mick Jagger. Only within this highly charged, incestuously interlocking and strangely influential little world of late sixties Chelsea could the sort of film that he was envisaging have been produced, let alone have taken the unusual form it did.

He began working out a plot involving several of the

more glamorous and bankable people among his friends. It involved a reclusive, upper-class pop singer to be played by Jagger, while his friend James Fox would play the part of a dangerous young criminal on the run who takes refuge in Jagger's house and becomes involved in a real-life situation with the pop star and his two girlfriends. This being Chelsea, the story included hallucinogenic drugs, bisexuality, rock'n'roll, three in a bed, an upper-class English background and the ever-present threat of very violent crime.

Cammell was persuasive and obsessive, and as he talked among his friends, the film started taking shape. For along with drugs and way-out sex, the whole idea of crime and evil held a particular fascination for his gilded friends. Several of them had been present at the notorious 'Redlands Bust' when the police had blundered into Mick Jagger's country home, searched him and many of his guests for possession of drugs, and arrested him and several guests. Jagger was imprisoned.

Along with Jagger, Marianne Faithfull was to be in the film. She finally backed out, her place being taken by one of Cammell's many mistresses, the beautiful Anita Pallenberg, who would bring an extra touch of realism to the movie by switching her affections from Keith Jones to Mick Jagger while the shooting was in progress.

By now another of Cammell's many friends, Christopher Gibbs, had agreed to do the decor, and this in turn brought in his friend, the arch-talker, one-time East End villain, friend and victim of the Krays – David Litvinoff.

The film, *Performance*, was Litvinoff's lasting contribution to the culture of the sixties, since it was he who effectively provided whatever in the way of script the film possessed. Once shooting started, he also became what Marianne Faithfull called 'our instructor in evil' to Donald Cammell and his cast.

Today it seems amazing that the project ever got off the ground at all. The key to this was probably Mick Jagger. Someone knew a promising young American film agent called Sandy Lieberson, who agreed to act as the film's producer. On the strength of Jagger's appearance in what was being scripted as a highly original British gangster movie, Lieberson was able to arrange a contract with Warner Brothers. At this point the director and camerman Nicolas Roeg joined Cammell as his co-director. For the interior shots, Lieberson rented a house in Lowndes Square in Kensington from Brigadier Lennie Plugge, a former Conservative MP.

But what made the film unique was the merging of this world of druggy, upper-class erotic daydream with David Litvinoff's violent re-creation of the ethos and behaviour of the East End of the Krays.

As Cammell's catalyst and co-conspirator, Litvinoff was simply doing what he had done so many times before in Chelsea pubs and dinner-parties – talking compulsively about one of the great obsessions of his life, the Twins. Cammell later called Litvinoff 'a great scriptwriter', and he put a lot of his own experiences into the film. James Fox's character is on the run from a dangerous East End gang boss, just as Litvinoff had been from the Krays; the chauffeur is shaved as Litvinoff had been himself; and the Rolls is defaced as the Krays had smashed up cars on rival gangs' car sites in their youth. He also modelled the East End gangster boss, played in the film by Harry Flowers, on Ron, and even acted as Fox's voice coach, taking him to various East End pubs to help perfect his East End accent.

A more useful contact, which has missed the notice of film historians, was provided yet again by Francis Wyndham. For not only did Francis know the Twins, but he also knew James Fox, and in the late summer of 1968, when shooting on the film was just about to commence, he took Fox to Brixton Gaol to meet Ron.

It was clever of Donald Cammell to pick up on Litvinoff's own situation as a villain on the run, and it was cleverer still to have the villain played by the obviously upper-class James Fox, whose character took refuge in the pop-star world of Mick Jagger and his women. When the film was finished, it offered a mesmerising vision of the intermingled world of homosexuality and drugs and class and the lure of violent criminals which was somewhere at the heart of the whole strange movement of the sixties.

Remembering Ron's words to me at our first meeting at Gedding Hall about wanting to become the subject of a film like *Bonnie and Clyde*, I was intrigued to read one critic claiming later that *Performance* helped to create a new image of the violent criminal in British gangster movies for the post-*Bonnie and Clyde* generation.

In his study of *Performance* published in 1993 the British Film Institute's historian Colin MacCabe claims that the film's originality and power come from 'its precise and accurate recording of two separate worlds', that of East End crime and swinging sixties Chelsea. MacCabe goes further, claiming that the film 'bears the mark of a true classic'.

Personally I don't agree with him that *Performance* is a particularly good or even particularly convincing movie. To me the plot seems self-indulgent, the actor Harry Flowers, in a role based on Ron, has little of the chilling sense of ever-present schizophrenic violence that I remember about Ron. As for the cockney accents, they are frankly laughable.

But MacCabe is right in his insistence on the enduring nature of *Performance*. When it was finished, Warner Brothers were so shocked that they tried to disown it and insisted on a much hacked-at version appearing at its premier in 1971. Subsequently the restored version of the film has been immensely influential as an underground movie, and has had a lasting influence on the way British film makers have come to depict violent criminals, on the screen and in endless television serials.

MacCabe believes that it is thanks to *Performance* that the image of the Krays has indelibly imposed itself upon the national consciousness as the dominant image of the violent criminal. My own feeling is that the way in which this happened is more complex than MacCabe would probably allow for, and that besides *Performance* there were several other sources feeding this whole weird phenomenon. The development of the image was a gradual, rather complicated process. Part of it was undoubtedly stimulated by the Bailey portrait and the media reaction to the Boothby scandal. Part also was caused by the work of Nipper Read and public memories of the sensational evidence endlessly presented at their trial. And yet another contribution to the process was, I fear, the much delayed and debated biography that I had just started writing.

The Profession of Violence

If anyone opposes me I will make his wife a widow, his children fatherless, and his home a dunghill.
Admiral 'Jackie' Fisher

If there's a moral to the story of my long involvement with the Krays it has to be that biographers with families to support should never get involved with criminals. Or if they do they should always pick dead ones.

In strictly practical terms, it was only the fact that the Twins were now in prison that made it possible for me to write my book at all. Indeed, had they not been arrested when they were, my life would have become impossible. By the time of their arrest I knew too much about them to have simply smiled a sheepish grin and muttered, 'Sorry, boys, but I can't quite see this working out. It's been a great experience getting to know you, and I'll always remember you, but I just don't think that I can write the book you want, let alone do you justice.' I had learned by then that tougher men than I had died for considerably less than that. All in all I was in a most unenviable position.

Two members of the Firm had separately warned me that before their arrest Ron had been getting suspicious of my behaviour and wondering what I was up to. In fact, with my marriage over, I had fallen in love with someone else, and the romance was entailing endless late-night telephone calls, secret rendezvous and frantic drives around the countryside. The Twins had become aware of my comings and goings but, lacking in romantic imagination, had failed to realise what I was up to. Ron, being Ron, was seriously wondering if I was working for MI5 or Scotland Yard. Had I been, it would have placed too great a strain on someone of my simple nature, and I would certainly have been found out – with dire consequences.

I say this to emphasise the fact that my conscience *vis à vis* the Krays was crystal clear. But by the time of their arrest, I was in what might be termed 'a biographer's logjam'. I could see no way at all of writing the book they wanted me to write without bringing in the fact that they were murderers. And if I gave up on the whole idea and tried to disappear abroad, I guessed the Twins, with their Mafia connections, would eventually have found me. Besides, not only would a further spell abroad have meant me leaving my beloved, which was unthinkable, but on top of everything, I was running short of money, now that Frank Taylor had left me in the lurch.

Thus the arrest of the Twins by Nipper Read and his team on that bright May morning came as a considerable relief to me, as I guess it did to many others; and their trials – first at Old Street, then at the Old Bailey – came as a godsend to a biographer trying to understand their story. Their imprisonment opened up a whole new gallery of witnesses and untapped sources, who were finally prepared to talk.

Now more than ever, I was obsessed with finding out the truth about this pair of highly complicated cockney murderers. I was also learning fast that lies and fantasies are as much part of the stock-in-trade of the criminal fraternity as they are among journalists and lawyers, and while I had no intention of writing a PR book for the Twins, I felt a certain obligation to treat them both as fairly as I could.

So, with my new-found freedom to write as I pleased I went cheerfully ahead, and was soon building up an extraordinary dossier, not only on the Twins, but also on Nipper Read and his colleagues, on the nature of identical twins and on schizophrenia, with as much about the history of East End crime and criminals as I could cope with.

I had obviously stumbled on a unique opportunity to observe and write about two of the most unusual criminals of our time, and the more I learned and thought about the book, the more involved in it I became. Deborah Rogers negotiated a deal for the book with a reasonable advance from the publishers Jonathan Cape and, more important, a deal with the *Observer* newspaper, which was offering an enticing £17,000 for the serial rights. The sum of £17,000 spelt riches in the 1960s and suddenly the future brightened.

There was, however, one perilous area in my search for truth that I should have had the sense to avoid. Had I been wiser I would never have listened to Frank Taylor's suggestion that I wrote about the Kray Twins in the first place. And had I been sensible now I'd have curbed my curiosity about Lord Boothby and the Krays and stuck to safer areas, such as who they had murdered, when and why. But alas, I didn't.

Here I must backtrack and explain that ever since that evening in the Turkish nightclub near Liverpool Street station with Ron and the aging belly-dancer, I had become fascinated by his relationship with Lord Boothby. Frankly, I found it bizarre to think of that figure at the very heart of the Establishment – former protégé of Churchill, and long-time lover of Harold Macmillan's wife, Dorothy (who also happened to be the daughter of the Duke of Devonshire) – taking somebody like Ronald Kray for dinner at the House of Lords and afterwards for drinks at White's, his exclusive London club. And apart from the strange socio-sexual overtones of this event, there were those all-important inconsistencies between Ron's assurance that he had 'known Lord Boothby very well', and Boothby's own denial of the fact, in his letter to *The Times*, which had earned him £40,000 in libel damages from the *Sunday Mirror*.

While I was working on the *Sunday Times*, I'd occasionally interviewed Lord Boothby, and knew him well enough to tell him about the book and arrange to go and see him on the evening of 2 December 1968, in his second-floor flat in Eaton Square. As always, he was immensely affable, even when I started quizzing him about his Kray connections. He stuck firmly to his story of those three brief business meetings.

'But why,' I asked, 'should Ronnie Kray, who was someone you've said you'd never met before, have rung you out of the blue and asked you to be the chairman of a company in Nigeria?'

His lordship bellowed with laughter. 'But of course he knew me! *Everyone* knew me in those days. That was all there was to it.'

When I mentioned that Ron had told me that he'd taken him to White's he seemed less amused.

'Bless my soul,' he said. 'You know I think you may be right. It had slipped my mind, but I seem to remember that I did take someone to White's on a Saturday and it might well have been, yes I think it was, Ron Kray.'

He quickly changed the subject, and offered me a drink; the affability was firmly back in place. I seem to remember that we talked about his recent holiday, and ten minutes later the interview was over. I wrote later in the journal I kept at the time, 'Still nothing specific. Just everything totally unlikely and a definite feeling that I had throughout the interview that I was being taken for one long but extremely serious ride by this most adroit old politician.'

A few days later something happened that confirmed my suspicions about Lord Boothby.

I'd had a message from Deborah that Violet wished to see me, as she had something to tell me. Violet often sent me messages from the Twins after visiting them in prison. These messages rarely added up to much more than lists of professional boxers the Twins had shaken hands with in their teens, but one never knew if something more important might suddenly crop up, so I thought I'd better go and see her later that evening.

When I got to Braithwaite House and rang the bell at number 43, there was the usual scene inside the living room – the television set turned on full blast, and old Charlie with his feet up, snoring on the sofa. Violet, wearing a smart blue dress, started telling me the latest news about the Twins and how both of them were doing their yoga exercises and enjoying the hot meals she was sending in to them (at Brixton, where they were then on remand) every day. I always got on well with her and we stood chatting in the kitchen waiting while the kettle boiled to make us our usual cup of tea.

'Who've you been seeing?' she inquired.

I had in fact spent the afternoon talking to Nipper Read, but I could hardly tell her that.

'Oh, various people.'

'Ronnie told me he wants you to see our old neighbour Queenie, who's moved to Harrow.'

'I will when I've a moment. I've been very busy. I saw Lord Boothby a few days ago.'

'That's funny you should mention him,' she said. 'I found a couple of letters from him when I was turning out the kitchen drawers the other day. Like to see them? Think I've got them somewhere.'

She rummaged at the back of the dresser and produced

two envelopes with House of Lords crests on the envelopes. The first was addressed to her at 178 Vallance Road. The short note inside was typed, and simply thanked her for her donation of £5 which she had sent to the National Heart Foundation, of which Lord Boothby was president. He'd signed the letter 'Boothby'.

Given the circumstances, this struck me as a little odd, but on its own it proved nothing. She was obviously rather proud of it.

'You really did meet Lord Boothby, then?'

'Oh yes. With Ronnie, several times. He liked Ronnie and was always very nice to me, very polite. A real gentleman.'

Then she handed me the second letter, which was addressed to Ron. It read as follows:

Dear Ron,

This is just a line to thank you and your brothers most sincerely for your generous donations to the British Heart Foundation. I do appreciate this action on your part and in due course you will receive a receipt from the secretary of the Fund.

Kindest regards and all good wishes for '64

Yours ever sincerely,

Bob Boothby

By now the kettle had come to the boil, and Violet was busily warming the pot – otherwise she would have noticed my excitement. What surprised me was not so much the letter, although that was strange enough – 'Ron' and 'Bob' didn't quite tie in with Lord Boothby's dismissive references to the three strictly business meetings that had supposedly taken place between them – as the date typed so clearly at the top of the letter: '7 January 64'.

So the peer and the gangster were on Christian name

terms four months before the meeting in Lord Boothby's office in Eaton Square which he insisted was the first time they had ever met. As I wrote in my journal that evening:

> It was this insistence by Lord Boothby that had averted a national scandal, saved his political and public reputation, humbled the wealthiest newspaper in Britain into an apology and earned him massive damages of £40,000. It was this insistence that had brought the future Lord Chief Justice Gerald Gardiner, Lord Goodman and Harold Wilson in on his side. And it was this insistence that made Lord Boothby appear the innocent victim of gutter journalism at its worst.
>
> And it was all a lie.

I was in a serious dilemma, and there was really no one I could turn to for advice. Clearly the implications of the fact that Lord Boothby had lied over his relations with the Krays played an important part not only in my story but in the political history of sixties England.

I felt nothing personal against Lord Boothby; nor had I any great belief in the probity of politicians. But I found something offensive in the whole idea of this bland cover-up of such a blatant scandal which had involved so much of the Establishment, and had produced such dire results – including the temporary invulnerability of the Krays and the incidental death of several East End villains. I was still young enough to find cynicism in high places squalid, particularly as those involved were not just Lord Goodman or his supporters, like Harold Wilson and Tom Driberg, but also included Sir Alec Douglas-Home and the Metropolitan Police Commissioner Sir Joseph Simpson.

The point was that they all *knew*. They knew that Boothby's £40,000 compensation was fraudulent, and this was so crucial to my story that it was something I could simply not ignore. But even more clearly I realised I had to be enormously careful not to land myself in a libel case, as the *Sunday Mirror* had.

So I did the best I could. I'd worked in newspapers long enough to know how to write a piece avoiding libel. Nevertheless, trouble duly came ...

I sent my finished manuscript to my publishers, who liked it and went ahead with production, even to the point of designing a jacket, which I liked. It was a picture of the Twins as babies, both wearing fluffy white hats. It still hangs framed on the wall of my study.

My first warning of trouble was completely unexpected and took the form of an early morning call from Lord Goodman himself. He came swiftly to the point.

'I think you should know you've gone too far in these irresponsible and highly libellous allegations you are making against Lord Boothby.'

I tried to argue, but he would not listen. After saying what he had to say he hung up. Later I tried to call him back at his office. I also wrote to him on numerous occasions over the coming years, but never got an answer.

My publisher sent the manuscript to the *Observer* for their approval. After a short delay I was told that they had decided to cancel our contract. To my horror after a few days Jonathan Cape made the same decision, with no explanation – only a demand for my advance.

Suddenly I was left high and dry. I had just completed the most difficult book I had ever had to write and I was broke. The only reason I could come up with to explain Lord Goodman's intervention was that as well as being Boothby's lawyer, responsible for the settlement with the *Sunday Mirror*, he also happened to be chairman of the Observer Trust. I suddenly found myself without a publisher, and with a book which no one seemed to want.

A month later Deborah Rogers came once more to my rescue by introducing me to the dynamic Tony Godwin, who was working as editorial director for the publisher George Weidenfeld.

It was Tony Godwin who saved my book – and probably my sanity. He liked my manuscript and agreed to publish it. He even came up with the title – *The Profession of Violence*. He made one condition. After the trouble with Lord Goodman, Weidenfeld's lawyers insisted that we dumbed down the Boothby chapter. I had to agree, as I had no choice. At least I'd tried to tell the truth, but the Establishment is powerful.

The Profession of Violence was finally published in 1972, after all the original trouble from the lawyers over the manuscript, I was surprised at how calmly it was now received. A reviewer in *The Times* thought it 'brave and useful', while one in the *Express* went so far as to call it 'brave and disturbing'. It was the first time in my life that anyone had called me brave, and I rather liked it. Several other reviewers patted me on the head with the remark that my book was 'well-written', and that, it seemed, was that.

The only strong reaction that I got was from the Krays themselves. They loathed it, and I was reliably informed that they were furious. As all but the blandest of biographers will confirm, this tends to be a common reaction from living subjects when they see their lives in print. Ron was quoted in the *Daily Telegraph* saying that 'Pearson's book is all a load of rubbish', and someone else reported Violet as saying that I'd betrayed her boys, and told an awful lot of lies about them. She never spoke to me again. Reg hated it too, especially for the references I made to his dead wife, Frances.

But in the months following publication, something happened which surprised me, as it must have done the Twins. By taking them seriously and trying to find the truth about their crimes and characters, far from damaging their all-important reputation, I seemed to have increased the 'respect' with which their fellow inmates and the prison staff regarded them. What other Category A prisoners could produce such formidable a CV as *The Profession of Violence* and copies began to circulate in prison libraries. The Twins may not have liked what I had written about them, but they were sharp enough to realise the new celebrity status the book was giving them.

To my surprise I received a note from Ron inviting me to visit him. All was suddenly forgiven. Later he apparently told his friend Wilf Pine that my book had 'taught him a lot', and had helped him come to terms with his schizophrenia. When I saw him, he seemed unusually agreeable – so agreeable in fact that he made me a rather worrying proposition.

'When I get out of prison, John, I'll get us a couple of nice boys and we'll go on a cruise around the world together.'

'Ron, that's very kind of you,' I said, 'but I don't like boys.'

'You will by then,' he said. 'You will.'

I quickly switched the conversation to a topic that obsessed him almost as much as sex – the film prospects for the book. He seemed particularly concerned about who could play his part.

Almost as a joke, I suggested Rod Steiger, who seemed to be the right shape and had a frightening presence on the screen. He took the suggestion seriously.

'Nice idea,' he said. 'I'll think about it.'

To show that all was now forgiven, a week later I received

the ultimate accolade from Ron: one of his paintings. Later it was lost when moving house, but I wasn't all that sorry, as I'd always found it most disturbing. Painted in vivid, child-like colours it showed a yellow house surrounded with flowers on a bright green hill. Behind the house the sun was painted black.

SEVENTEEN

In the Name of Kray

Establish a character for strangeness. There is nothing like it. Then one can do what one likes.

John Stuart Mill

Two things ruled the waking hours of the Twins in prison: their battle to stay sane and their passion for celebrity. Here one must understand the strange position they were in during the early years of their 'recommended sentence', with Ron still up at Durham and Reg in Parkhurst.

As Category A prisoners in top security, all normal life was over for them both for the foreseeable future. Night and day, they were under total supervision and could not shower, eat, excrete or sleep without some member of the prison staff observing them. Behind the razor wire and the elaborate electronic locking systems that controlled the prison gates, they inhabited a tiny cloister of mainly homicidal monks – their fellow long-term inmates, most of them also in for murder.

Like many monks of old, both Twins began suffering accidie, acute depression, Reg especially. Early on, Violet began lobbying the Home Office through her local MP arguing that it was cruel to keep identical twins like Ron and Reg apart. Early in 1972, without publicity, the Twins were quietly reunited in Parkhurst Prison.

As might have been predicted from their early history as discordant identical twins, this didn't work. Once together, the old pattern soon started to reassert itself. As in the past, the Twins united were more dangerous than they'd ever been apart. Later that year it was reported that Reg had attacked and nearly killed a fellow prisoner with a broken bottle. He was dragged off in time, and the prisoner received more stitches to his face and shoulders than one would have thought that human flesh could bear. Word of the attack reached the press, together with the news that the Twins had been reunited. An MP complained to the Home Secretary, and once again the Twins were parted, this time for ever.

During the three years after the publication of my book in 1972, interest in the Twins began to grow along with steadily increasing sales of my book. And I realised that *The Profession of Violence* was being read not just by sober citizens wishing to understand the threat of organised crime in Britain, but also by members of a younger generation.

Part of the reason for the book's popularity was undoubtedly Bailey's famous portrait of the Twins, which was on the front cover of the paperback, and I found it strange that this picture from the sixties, which Bailey had taken in 1964 and sold in a box together with pictures of Mick Jagger and Jean Shrimpton, could still cast its spell over the new punk generation of the seventies.

I believe that what was happening was a repetition, on a wider scale, of what had happened around the Twins in Chelsea in the early sixties. What seemed to fascinate so many of the young, just as it had fascinated those wild creatures of the sixties, was what they saw as the dark side of the Twins. Once more it was the weird attraction of the monster in our midst. Provided there's no real danger – and there wasn't any, now that the Twins were in prison – there is a certain thrill in being frightened. And just as the fact that they were killers had given the Twins their credibility as gangsters, so the mindlessness behind their crimes endowed them with the flavour of authentic evil.

Apart from my book, there was another crucial element in this surge of interest: the growth of punk and the latest developments in rock'n'roll. Back in the sixties, the Krays had been unique among big-time London gangsters in the way they had followed the US Mafia with their close affinity with show-biz personalities. And when Donald Cammell made *Performance* there was something eerily prophetic in the way he had picked the most famous rock star in the country, who had recently recorded 'Street Fighting Man', to star in a film that was permeated with the reputation of the Krays.

Curiously, few middle-aged male Anglo-Saxons were less in tune with the new punk generation than the Twins themselves. True, they had killed people, which might seem hip. Just as sixties cult writer William Burroughs killed his wife while high on LSD, so drugs and some sort of nihilistic frenzy would appear to have led Sid Vicious of the Sex Pistols to kill his girlfriend, Nancy Spungen. But, apart from their associations with homicide and their homosexuality, the Twins were actually extremely square. They were nostalgic, deeply anti-feminist, right-wing Little Englanders. As we have seen, they loved their mother and were deeply sentimental about their family. Their heroes were not Elvis Presley or even the Beatles, but Winston Churchill, Lawrence of Arabia and General Gordon; Ron's favourite music was Puccini ('Nessun Dorma' and 'Your Tiny Hand is Frozen').

Nevertheless, many of the up-and-coming generation, which was being weaned on groups like the Sex Pistols and the Ramones, with their message of rejection of accepted social values, could see in the Twins the ultimate in violence and anti-social conduct. They saw the Twins as the ultimate in anti-heroes. For in a sense the Kray Twins really had it all: along with murder, one had driven his wife to suicide, both were sexually unconventional, and both had unquestionably fucked the Establishment and loathed 'the Pigs' (as the young called the police). Among the young who disliked authority and especially the pigs, and were out to shock the older generation, my book had suddenly become a cult book. Whatever it was about the Krays, their legend was not only surviving, but flourishing, and my book was actively promoting it. Certainly the Twins were being talked about and becoming more famous than ever. Already, like the character in one of Henry James's novels, they had reached the stage of being 'famous for being famous'. But before their fame could reach its true potential, something else was needed.

Because of their tendency to try touching me for money during my visits, there was a period when I almost gave up visiting the Twins. Then in 1978 I heard from Ron, who wrote to tell me he'd had a breakdown and asked me to come and see him. When I went, I was shocked by his appearance. He'd apparently been suffering from deep depressions, tried to kill himself and lost five stone in weight. He looked far thinner than I'd ever seen him, but he assured me he'd been cured of 'the problems with my nerves' by electric shock therapy.

He went on to explain that he was facing a difficult decision. Should he soldier on in maximum security hoping for eventual release, or get himself certified insane and go to Broadmoor? If he chose the latter course, he would probably never be released. On the other hand, as a hospital for the criminally insane, Broadmoor would mean a freer, more comfortable way of life than that in a high-security prison. Theoretically he'd be a patient, not a prisoner. His next remark, in that familiar flat, depressive's voice of his, made me realise that he'd already made his decision. 'In Broadmoor, I could have sex with anyone I fancied.'

Faced with a choice between sex or the possibility of freedom, Ron was choosing sex. A few months later I read that because he had become so dangerous he had been certified and sent to Broadmoor.

Reg, who was still enduring all the rigours of being a Category A prisoner, was said to be upset at Ron's decision. He need not have been, for his brother's move to Broadmoor held more important implications for their joint future as celebrities than any improvements that it brought to Ron's sex life.

I saw Ron soon after he went to Broadmoor late in 1979. Father Hetherington had recently been to see him, and reported that he was turning back to Christianity. Perhaps he was. He certainly looked a lot better than when I saw him last, but I felt that this probably was due less to religion than to the fact that the Broadmoor doctors had finally got his medication right. Instead of prison uniform he was now allowed to wear his own clothes. Violet had, as usual, turned up trumps, ordering him a dark blue double-breasted suit from his favourite tailor, Woods of Kingsland Road. I noticed that the solid gold Rolex was back on his wrist.

But the most important thing about his new situation was his virtual freedom over visits. In maximum security, visits from outside were strictly limited and controlled. Before visiting either of the Twins in prison, I remember always being made to sign a fearsome document, promising on pain of instant prosecution never to use any words or information I obtained from my visit for the purposes of journalism. At Broadmoor there were no such restrictions.

By 1980 Ron was reported in the *Sun* to be 'delighted with life in Broadmoor', which clearly rather suited him. He was being looked after and kept firmly off the booze. His depressions were being dealt with, and on top of this he was being treated more than ever as a celebrity.

The Twins' brother Charlie appeared to be helping the Twins in their quest for celebrity. He had been released in 1974 and had started a pop group which, like most things Charlie did, had failed. For a while he was reduced to working on a friend's silverware stand at the Ideal Home Exhibition. After his release he had thought of changing his name. But now he had second thoughts. As brother of the Kray Twins he was kept far busier signing autographs than selling silver. Thanks to the name of Kray, he was soon earning money from other sources. He had started a 'minders' agency, specialising in lightly veiled protection. He was also seeing people in the pop world and the movie business, and around this time talk began in earnest once again about turning *The Profession of Violence* into a film.

Bill Curbishley, who had known Reg in prison while being wrongfully sentenced for armed robbery, had now cleared his name and was out of gaol and managing the immensely successful pop group The Who. As a fellow East Ender, he was grateful for the Twins' support in prison, and had been talking to Charlie Kray about the film. So was Roger Daltrey, the lead singer of The Who. Another contender for the privilege of playing Ronnie was Robert Duval, the American star of *True Confessions*. Even Richard Burton seemed to be in the running. Not long before he died in 1984, he visited Ron in Broadmoor, and Ron seriously suggested he should play him.

In media terms, the Krays were now 'hot', and for potential movie makers, there was something unusual and authentic about discussing a film about a murderer with the man himself in a psychiatric ward in a hospital for the criminally insane. The long procession of the great and famous beating a path to Broadmoor started.

Whenever I saw Ron now, he was sitting in the hospital visiting room, which in those days was like the lounge of some very old decaying grand hotel. Most of the other 'patients' looked like human ghosts, but not Ron. With his well-cut dark blue suit and rather worrying rimless spectacles, he could well have been a depraved movie mogul himself, as he nodded to an attendant inmate to bring us both a drink. Although this turned out to be non-alcoholic lager, it looked authentic, as we talked yet again about 'the film of the book'.

Reg was, as usual, having a far tougher time of it than Ron. He was now in Long Lartin maximum security prison near Birmingham, and in February 1982, he slashed his wrists.

A few days later Violet made a lonely journey to Whitehall and asked to see the Home Secretary. He was not available, but she saw one of the permanent secretaries and pleaded for 'more humane treatment for my boy'. As she put it later, 'Reggie is now a broken man. It looks as if I'll be visiting him in prison to the end of my days. The system has broken him, and I don't want him to lose his reason.'

Reg didn't lose his reason. Later he admitted that 'a Moroccan fellow had introduced me to cannabis' and that it was this, and 'the effects of a curry dinner', that had made him cut his wrists.

But over one thing, Violet was proved right. End her days she did while still visiting her Twins in prison. Anxious not to add to their worries, she never told them she was suffering from cancer, and died early in August 1982. Her funeral was the most valuable legacy she could have left them.

Both Twins naturally applied for permission to attend, which now presented the Home Secretary with a genuine dilemma. One of his officials was quoted as saying that 'a refusal would look pretty cold-hearted' but by letting the Twins attend, 'It might turn into a circus and be undignified.' Brother Charlie Kray apparently agreed with him. 'I just don't want it to be a spectacle,' he said. But that was not how the Twins were thinking.

After thirteen years' exclusion from society, this was their first chance of a public appearance together. Nothing could possibly make them waste such a heaven-sent opportunity and as always, it was their decision, rather than Charlie's, that prevailed. From inside prison the two of them organised the entire proceedings.

The funeral was held in Chingford Old Church on 12 August and once the Twins arrived, they were the spectacle. As one newspaper put it, 'It was the Twins' arrival that switched the attention of everyone from their devotions to an extraordinary lady – as by all accounts she was – to her 48-year-old twin sons.'

Acting on the Home Secretary's advice, the prison authorities had tried to make the best of things – making the Twins look small and insignificant by having them handcuffed to two of the tallest members of the Prison Service. It made no difference. Their stature may have been diminished, but what mattered was that the two most celebrated murderers in Britain were making a unique personal appearance before the most appreciative audience in London – the congregation gathered in the Old Church, Chingford.

According to the *Daily Telegraph*, 'The result came close to being a state occasion in the East End, when gangsters and neighbours closed ranks in a final tribute to Mrs Kray.' One reporter, Paul Callan, described the scene as the

Twins entered the church, and 'Men with hands as large as babies' heads grabbed at the passing brothers, hugging them with a wild East End tribal passion.'

Reg responded like the star he always longed to be. 'Bless you all, bless you all,' he said as he raised his one free hand in benediction.

The service began with Violet's favourite psalm, 'The Lord is my Shepherd.' Then, in the words of the *Daily Telegraph* reporter, 'It soon turned into an emotional lap of honour for the Twins.'

When the service ended and Father Hetherington had delivered his blessing on the congregation, Diana Dors, encased in deepest mourning, led the mourners, as she knelt and crossed herself before the coffin. She was closely followed by the Twins, who kissed their mother's coffin and then knelt in prayer, 'each man,' according to the front-page story in next morning's *Daily Express*, 'a picture of supplication, with their right hands holding a prayer book, and their left hands cuffed to a prison warder.'

The funeral cost the taxpayer £30,000 for policing the event. For the Twins themselves, however harrowing the occasion, it must have been a wonderful reminder of their growing status as true criminal celebrities. It was also a potent demonstration of the undeniable connection of the world of crime with the people of the old East End, which formed the bedrock of the Kray Twins' popularity.

Seven months later, the Twins' father, Charlie, died. It seems that he had pined for Violet ever since her death, but according to a spokesman for the Prison Service, 'The Twins did not seek permission to attend his burial.'

For both the Twins this demonstration of unfading popularity among the people that they called 'their own' seems to have led to an important development in their growing personal publicity campaign. This campaign had only started up in earnest after Ron arrived at Broadmoor. Brother Charlie had been doing his best to speak out on their behalf since his own release in 1974, and had even hired personal PR to lobby for the Twins. This did little for their chances. But all this changed once Ron was in Broadmoor, where he was completely free to entertain journalists himself. It was a privilege he made the most of as he and Reg began to reinvent themselves.

The point of the campaign was essentially to change their image, in the hope of gaining parole. Ron knew that he had little hope of getting out and was reconciled to ending his days in Broadmoor. But he was hoping that sufficient good publicity might one day bring his brother freedom.

In its way, the line that he adopted was adroit, although much of it went back to the stories they were putting round before they were arrested. It started with a sustained attempt to demonise their long-dead victims. Since neither McVitie nor Cornell had anyone to speak on their behalf, this wasn't difficult. Early in 1983, a long interview from Broadmoor published in the *Daily Star* began with Ron, the born-again Christian, holding forth on the subject of the murdered George Cornell whose son and widow were both living. 'He was vermin,' he began. 'He was simply nothing. I reckon I did society a favour ridding it of him and the East End in particular.' He spoke similarly of Jack McVitie, calling him 'a drunken slag' and a danger to decent women.

The Twins had been talking on and off like this for years, but at the end of the interview Ron reiterated the message that had formed the underlying theme to Violet's funeral. In contrast with scum like McVitie and Cornell, the Twins were truly lovable, user-friendly gangsters who had loved their mother and the people they grew up with. As the reporter ended his article, 'East Enders speak very affectionately of the Kray Twins. They are regarded, if not as Robin Hoods, certainly as people who maintained peace and safety in the streets.'

In the words of Ron, 'We never hurt ordinary members of the public. We only took money off other villains and gave a bundle of that away to decent people who were on hard times. Old people didn't get mugged either. It didn't happen when we looked after the East End. Ordinary people just thought we were businessmen who gave a lot of money to charity.'

This would remain their message for the next few years. Little really changed in their situation, apart from the fact that Reg was finally downgraded from being a Category A prisoner and moved to the more relaxed regime of Lewes Prison on 18 April 1989. This encouraged him to hope that things were slowly turning to his advantage in respect of his parole. But he was in a somewhat tricky position.

When capital punishment was abolished in 1965, Parliament decided that the only punishment for murder was a mandatory life sentence, but since it was unrealistic to keep every convicted murderer in prison for his natural life, at a certain point the Home Secretary would review each mandatory lifer's situation. According to the circumstances of the crime, the judge's recommendation on the time the prisoner should serve, and his behaviour while in prison, a decision would be made as to when the prisoner should be released. In practice this decision was usually made on the recommendations of one of the government's parole boards, whose task it was to see each prisoner, study his records and assess his suitability for release.

None of this applied to Ron now that he was in Broadmoor. With two murders to his credit, and having been officially certified insane, it was almost inconceivable that he'd ever be released. Reg, however, would soon have served twenty years of his 'recommended' sentence. Apart from his suicide attempt and the cutting of the fellow prisoner in Parkhurst in 1972 his behaviour had been good, and his chances of the parole board recommending him for early release seemed not unreasonable.

The chief argument against this was that, like his brother, he was probably at least partly schizophrenic; this, coupled with his history of violence, could mean that although he was now past fifty, he remained a potential danger to the public.

One thing parole boards demand from convicted murderers is some evidence of repentance. This may seem reasonable, but the fact is that nothing is easier for a convicted murderer than to put on a show of penitence when he knows his freedom could depend upon it. Repentance was something Reg would never consider; to state publicly that he was sorry for murdering McVitie would contradict what Ron was saying about having done society a service by murdering Cornell.

But the real case against paroling him was tied up with his status as a criminal celebrity. This was a problem, for as I'd seen myself, the quest for fame had been the driving force behind the Twins' whole criminal career, and while in prison, Reg had sustained himself on his role as a celebrity. I often felt he couldn't have survived those endless prison years without it. But his fame made the possibility of parole remote.

However much Ron might claim that he and Reg had been the East End's Robin Hoods, it simply wasn't true, and few were really taken in by it. Public perception of the Twins was of a pair of highly dangerous if glamorous criminals, which of course they were, and films and media publicity about them had done little to diminish it. What neither of the Twins would ever understand was that the final decision on their fate would always lie with the Home Secretary, who was first and foremost a politician. Whatever party was in power, one of the jobs of the Home Secretary was to reassure the electorate that his government was being 'tough on crime'. Being realistic, no Home Secretary could ever think he would achieve this by releasing one of the most famous killers in the country.

In spite of this, nothing could suppress the Twins' passion for publicity – nor the ever-growing skill with which they managed to pursue it. Their flair for personal PR was undiminished. They could always seem to find a way to keep themselves in the news, and it was largely thanks to this that, even twenty years after they were 'ruling London', the public seemed as fascinated by them both as ever.

Celebrity status has a way of building up like capital in the bank, and the Twins now had a lot to draw on. In his famous book *The Image*, published in 1961, the social historian Daniel Boorstin defined the celebrity as 'a person who is known for his well-knownness'. The Twins' 'well-knownness' was something they continued to exploit in every way they could.

This was obviously easier for Ron, who enjoyed holding forth to the journalists who were delighted to visit him in Broadmoor, and became a constant source of celebrity-style gossip in the popular press. His liveliest coup came in 1985. For whatever reason, both the Twins attracted fan mail from lonely and frustrated women, which meant that Ron especially always had a following of adoring female correspondents. He invariably asked them for photographs, and if he liked the look of them, invited them home to Broadmoor.

Although he was still claiming to be bisexual, and genuinely liked female company, his real reason for encouraging these ardent friendships was probably to find somebody to take the place of Violet. He formed a particular friendship with a homely 29-year-old divorced mother of two called Elaine Mildener, and suddenly got the bright idea of marrying her.

He managed it extremely well. Only recently the government had permitted inmates to marry while in prison, and he was more than aware of the news value of the Broadmoor marriage of the country's most famous homicidal madman. The fact that he was also homosexual gave added lustre to the story.

He knew exactly how to deal with offers from the press, and is rumoured to have obtained a fee of £20,000 from the *Sun* for exclusive coverage of the marriage, plus a further reproduction fee for the marriage photographs.

For a year or two he shamelessly exploited the press interest in his marriage. One of the best stories he sold was the announcement that he wanted to become the father of twins, and had asked the authorities for 'facilities' to consummate his marriage. One can imagine his relief when they refused, and bearing in mind the possibility that consummation might have succeeded, this was probably a wise decision. Before long the first Mrs Ronald Kray began finding all the publicity and fuss too much for her. She stopped her visits, and three years after he married her, Ron sold a story to the press giving all the details of his divorce.

Throughout this time Reg also had his female fans. Around the time of Violet's funeral there had been press reports that he had been seeing 29-year-old Beverley Derbyshire and that wedding bells might follow. A few weeks later an embarrassed Mrs Derbyshire was reported to be 'laughing off reports that she is to marry the jailed killer. "I went to visit him out of curiosity and sympathy," she said. "I found him very quiet, gentle-mannered and witty. My husband is proud of my prison visiting."'

Apart from promoting his romantic stories, Reg earned a lot of interest and sympathy from his flair for picking extremely newsworthy deserving causes for high-profile acts of charity. Early in 1985 he and Ron were widely reported to be footing the bill for hospital treatment for fourteen-year-old David Lee of Liverpool, who was dying of a rare brain disease. 'Do not ever give up,' Reg wrote to David. 'I'll be saying a prayer for you.' When a reporter went to interview David's mother, the result was a front-page story. Mrs Lee, mother of four, was quoted saying, 'Reggie's offer really choked me when I heard it. He can't be all bad.' There would be several other newsworthy charitable exploits from both the Twins to keep them in the public eye over the years ahead.

During the early eighties there was fairly regular press speculation that Reg was also about to marry. At one point the lucky lady looked like being the blonde East End model Flanagan (real name Maureen Cox). As well as writing her romantic letters, Reg had been collaborating with her by post on a keep-fit book which may have originated with a slightly flippant suggestion I had made to Reg that he should write 'a book of exercises for people in confined places'.

Although Reg's prison romance with Flanagan came to nothing the press soon became interested in another of his marriage prospects, thirty-year-old Gill Gibson. His brother's marriage to Elaine must have made Reg want to follow suit, and news of his proposal to Miss Gibson reached the press.

'"Reggie is so kind. He is the most interesting and

sensitive man I have ever met. The whole Kray family is lovely. What they did in the past is history, as far as I'm concerned." He calls her "Brown-Eyes", she calls him "Rabbit" and she says she gets on wonderfully with Ron's new wife, Elaine.' Reg seemed to be just about to pop the question, when he discovered that Miss Gibson was in fact Mrs Gibson, with a husband called Andy.

It seems unlikely that his heart was broken, for the truth was probably that, publicity apart, Reg was using his would-be mistresses as what were known in gay parlance as 'beards' to cover up the current love of his life. This was Peter Gillett, a 25-year-old fair-haired criminal he met in Parkhurst and had fallen deeply in love with.

Gillett's ambition was to be a pop star, 'like Roger Daltrey', whom he rather resembled, and like a doting father 52-year-old Reg started trying to promote him. Such was the freedom at that time in Parkhurst that Reg used to take him his breakfast in bed each morning, and when news of what was going on began to reach the ever-eager media, he admitted he was in love. 'Peter is the best friend I have ever had. He makes me feel young again,' he said. It was left to Gillett to deny that the relationship was gay. 'It's an intimate relationship,' he told a journalist, 'but we're not bent. It's like a homosexual affair without sex, and I'm closer to Reg than I've ever been to anyone – even my wife.'

Apart from drugs, I heard that the two platonic lovers enjoyed a regular gin and tonic together in the evening, and when Gillett left prison on four days' parole, Reg ordered a white Rolls-Royce to meet him at the gates of the prison.

Like several others, I used to wonder where the money came from, but the truth was simple. In conjunction with their brother Charlie, both the Twins were using their extraordinary freedom to continue various quite lucrative rackets from inside. Early in 1986, they were said to be earning up to £3000 a week from 'authentic' Kray Twins T-shirts, selling at £7.99 each. (A company marketing 'pirated' Kray Twins T-shirts was forced to withdraw them rapidly following threats to any shops or stalls with the temerity to stock them.) Earnings from the Twins' business were paid into Krayleigh Enterprises, run by Charlie, which also collected 'pensions' from various 'minding' businesses.

But although the Twins were still able to some extent to 'do the business' from inside and were 'doing very nicely thank you', so that they had all the money they required for their simple needs in prison, they still had their hearts set upon the movie. So too had a lot of other influential people, who suddenly saw the chance of making their reputations and their fortunes from the name of Kray.

Had Reg's parole and subsequent release really been the Twins' top priority at this time, nothing would have induced them to have agreed to a full-scale feature film about them. But with the film version of *The Profession of Violence* still not made, potential producers were once more growing interested in the book. So too were potential stars, anxious as ever for a chance to play the Twins. Despite difficulties over the script, the Twins remained enthusiastic. And in 1989 production of the film finally began.

EIGHTEEN

The Krays

Mythical figures lead many lives, die many deaths, and in this they differ from the characters we find in novels.

Roberto Calasso, *The Marriage of Cadmus and Harmony*

On 22 April 1990, the *Sunday Telegraph*, in a lengthy article on the recently completed film, *The Krays*, reported that:

> for a long time Roger Daltrey from The Who owned the film rights to John Pearson's book *The Profession of Violence* and in 1989 he sold the rights to Pearson's book to Jim Beach, the manager of another pop group, Queen. Beach brought in two young video producers, Ray Burdis and Dominic Anciano, and they cast Martin and Gary Kemp of yet another pop group, Spandau Ballet, in the lead roles as the Twins.

When I read the piece it genuinely puzzled me for it was news to me that Roger Daltrey had ever owned the film rights to *The Profession of Violence*, let alone that he had sold them on as the basis of what became an immensely profitable movie.

I remember feeling curiously let down, particularly by the Twins – which was in the circumstances a slightly gratuitous emotion – and remember discussing the situation with my then literary agent, Ed Victor, who, as an American, had close experience with the movie business.

Probably wisely, he firmly advised me not to sue, saying that with the Krays involved it could be dangerous, and that for writers, law suits over film rights usually become a nightmare. Not entirely convinced, I asked the advice of the doyen of theatrical lawyers, Oscar Beuselinck, who gave the following advice. 'It's always a dangerous business trying to sue a movie company. It can also be prohibitively expensive. You'll probably win in the end, but there's always a chance you won't. If you're willing to risk ruining yourself, then go ahead.' It was there and then that I decided not to sue.

The truth was that whatever had happened over the sale of the film rights, this was not the only thing about the making of the film *The Krays* that was questionable. Even the Twins themselves ended up being deceived by one of the very few people they had always trusted, their own brother, Charlie.

With a budget of £3 million, Jim Beach's company, Parkfield Films, weren't being extravagant, and production costs were kept to a minimum. Although Roger Daltrey forfeited his ambition to act in a film about the Krays, Martin and Gary Kemp were eager to take on the part. Parkfield paid them £30,000 each to play the Twins, and the same fee went to a young novelist called Philip Ridley to write the script. The producers gave firm assurances that the Twins had not been paid a penny, which was true. Since convicted criminals are theoretically not permitted to profit from their crime, £250,000 was paid instead to their brother, Charlie, who split the money evenly between the three of them, the Twins' share being paid to a lawyer, who kept the money for them. In addition, lucky Charlie received £500 a day as technical adviser, together with a chauffeur-driven limousine to take him to and from the studio throughout the shooting.

But like the Twins themselves, Charlie could never resist the chance of a deal and he secretly earned himself an extra £10,000, in return for all his and the Twins' share of future profits from the film, then pocketed the proceeds. As with most of Charlie's business deals, this wasn't very bright, as he and his brothers came to realise when *The Krays* went on to gross something over £10 million, including video earnings, and none of them earned a penny from the profits.

My first reaction to *The Krays* was that almost everything about it was ludicrous and that the characters bore no relation to the actual characters of the Twins or those around them. Even the simplest facts were misinterpreted in the film. Cornell was in fact murdered before, not after, Frances died; Reg's honeymoon was spent in Athens, not picnicking on the white cliffs of Dover; Violet, as Ron indignantly pointed out, never swore. All this apart, I also remember thinking that this had to be the weirdest gangster movie I had ever seen.

The weirdness was evident from the beginning. Following the opening credits, one watches as a large swan flies from right to left across the screen. Cut to Billie Whitelaw's Violet, looking slightly dazed and dreaming that she is a swan who has just laid an egg. She hears children's voices in the egg. It hatches. The dream ends, and she noisily gives birth to two beautiful twin boys, Ron and Reg.

Like, I'm sure, the great majority of the several millions who would see this film, I found all this distinctly puzzling. None of the film critics I read ever mentioned or explained it. Nor, as far as I know, did Philip Ridley, who has spent his subsequent career writing tales for children. He did, however, offer one mysterious hint of what these references to swans and eggs were all about.

His film, he said, was the moment when 'Jean Cocteau meets the East End'. In the mood I was in at the time, it struck me as, shall we say, pretentious of Mr Ridley to compare himself to the greatest magician of the cinema, but as I brooded on his words, the penny dropped. My favourite Cocteau film, *Orphée* is a reinterpretation of the Greek myth about the poet Orpheus whose wife Eurydice is killed, descends to Hades and is finally brought back to earth for six months every year. In the film, Orpheus has become a fashionable young Parisian writer played by Jean Marais, whose wife is killed in a Paris street by a passing motorcyclist. Philip Ridley, I realised, was doing something similar with the story of the Krays. Once I grasped the connection between swans and twins, the film began to make some sense.

In classical mythology the beautiful Leda (wife of King Tindareus and mother of Clytemnestra and later Helen of Troy) is abducted from her husband by a swan, who makes love to her while in flight. This is no ordinary swan, of course, but the father of the Gods, great Zeus himself, in disguise. One of Zeus's favourite ploys was to transform himself into an animal for sexual purposes, most famously when he made himself a bull and carried off the nymph Europa, on whom he fathered the goddess Venus. With beautiful Leda, Zeus decided he would be a swan, and following the aerial copulation, Leda gave birth to two demi-gods, the heavenly twins Castor and Pollux – just as in Philip Ridley's film *The Krays*, Violet, having dreamed about a swan and that she lays a massive egg, gives birth to Ron and Reg.

I remember thinking, Mr Ridley, even as a joke, you can't be serious. But then, why not? After all, most stories from Greek mythology tend to be outrageous and the extraordinary thing about this film is that in its own strange way it almost works. It certainly worked well enough to earn Ridley a BAFTA award for his script, and the film a less credible prize from the *London Evening Standard* as the best British movie of 1990. More to the point, in relation to the Twins, I'm now convinced that *The Krays* played an all-important part in the process of turning the Kray Twins into modern myths.

For this was what the film was really all about. By using material from *The Profession of Violence* to flesh out this original Greek myth about Castor and Pollux, Ron and Reg were being mythologised before our eyes; and it was this that gave the film its touch of strange religiosity, which had also puzzled me. The underlying message of the film was that Violet, like the Virgin Mary, had been inseminated by a god, and produced two god-like creatures in the form of twins. This meant that Ron and Reg weren't ordinary murderers at all, but beings set apart. As a final twist, in Greek mythology one of the heavenly twin demigods, Pollux, became the tutelary deity of pugilists and Roman gladiators.

With the film's treatment of the murders of McVitie and Cornell, the implications of the myth became more interesting still. Here there was no pretence at presenting a true account of what had happened. The killings, as I have said, were out of sequence, the two victims, particularly Cornell as played by Stephen Berkoff, were grotesque caricatures, and the insults they were shown heaping on the Twins just never happened.

But once one understands that this is 'Greek mythology' it more or less makes sense. Even the studied acting and unKraylike faces of the Kemp boys don't really matter. For this is essentially Greek drama, not the story of the Krays at all. These twins are actually the heavenly twins, Castor and Pollux, and the reason McVitie and Cornell must die is simple and inevitable: both have been guilty of the one unforgivable offence in Greek mythology – *hubris*, contempt for the gods, which always brings *nemesis*, justified destruction. Or as Ron said in real life, 'Cornell was scum, and I did society a favour getting rid of him.'

What I still find fascinating about the film – and where Philip Ridley was actually extremely clever – is in the way it fits in so neatly with what the Krays had been trying to do themselves ever since I first met them, by making themselves, as the cliché has it, 'legends in their lifetime'. In doing so he perpetuated what Francis Wyndham noticed about them back in the sixties in the piece he wrote to accompany Bailey's famous photograph, that they were 'already East End legends, Bethnal Green's own answer to Jesse James'.

Ron had been comparing himself and Reg with Robin Hood. Robin was in fact too benevolent a myth for the Krays to have been mistaken for him, and those two inexorable demi-gods, Castor and Pollux, seeking vengeance, came closer to the truth.

As the history of religions shows, you don't need to understand a myth to believe in it. Similarly, no one had to understand the film's connection with the gods of Greece in order to accept what it was saying on the subject of the Kray Twins' mythic status. *The Krays* is in fact an up-market religious movie loosely spun around the story of two famous gangsters, and apart from earning its producers a cool £10 million for a few months' work, it helped seal Reg's fate, like Ron's, for ever. For with all the publicity and success around the film, whatever chances Reg had ever had of being paroled and finally released were over.

The Twins themselves were deeply disappointed by what they considered to be inadequate remuneration from the film, and refused to speak to their brother Charlie for several years. Nevertheless £85,000 had its uses, especially in Broadmoor.

By now Ron had almost totally adapted to the safe and surprisingly tolerant regime within the country's most famous hospital for the criminally insane. Now, thanks to his money and the further status that the film would give him, the last and certainly the funniest period in his life began. Even as the myths about the Krays were building up around him, a new Ron Kray was taking shape. In place of the Colonel someone different was emerging: Ron Kray 'the Duke of Broadmoor'.

Already he had his own room and a regular supply of lovers, and did very much as he wished. Even in Broadmoor no one wanted to stand up against him. But it was only in 1989 when money from the film became available that he really started to enjoy himself. Cockneys are traditionally great spenders, and Ron never had much difficulty in following their example, even inside Broadmoor. 'Who wants to be the richest man in the graveyard?' as he used to ask. Not Ron Kray, for certain.

There was, of course, no question of wasting good money on former members of the Firm, who had stuck by them through the trial and suffered so unnecessarily with him and Reg through all those years in prison. Not even the ultra-loyal Ian Barrie or the invaluable Freddie Foreman received a cheque from the Kray Twins' lawyers. Now that he was Duke of Broadmoor, Ron had better uses for his money. Since he was officially a patient rather than a prisoner, he was allowed considerable discretion over what he did and how he spent his money. Some of it went on things like having his teeth recapped for £900, ordering more suits from his tailor, and hiring cars to bring his important visitors to Broadmoor. Since the influence of gangster chic had reached Broadmoor, he started buying Gucci watches to reward his current lovers. He even found himself a personal masseur from among the other patients, whose hands, he told one visitor, were 'the most wonderful hands in all the world'. What he didn't tell him was that his masseur was in Broadmoor for strangling his family.

Now that Ron was rich in prison terms, his thoughts began to stray once more to marriage. Although his union with publicity-shy Elaine had ended badly, it made him realise that for a paranoid schizophrenic homosexual murderer, marriage in a hospital for the criminally insane could be both fun and highly profitable, as it could generate endless publicity, which was always welcome. Love really might be nicer the second time round.

His only problem was how to find a girl who was worthy of him, and here, once more, *The Profession of Violence* proved useful to the Krays. Around this time an attractive blond kissogram girl called Kate Howard bought a copy of the book on a station bookstall, read it, and was so fascinated that she wrote Ron a fan letter. He replied, inviting her to come and see him. She went to Broadmoor, and during that first visit he asked her to marry him.

Kate Kray, as she soon became, is the sort of girl they used to call a 'good sport' who is game for almost anything. On the one occasion that we met, rather to my surprise, I found her enormously likable. As Ron must have realised at once, she was type-cast for the part of gangster's moll, and as well as being considerably prettier, there was a further difference between her and plump Elaine: like Ron, Kate had a flair for publicity, and she knew its value.

It's only now that I realise what Reg meant when he used to talk about his brother's sense of humour – a quality which, incidentally, Reg lacked himself. The marriage of

Ron was in its way a perfect sitcom and he milked the in-built humour of the situation. For here was the most famous inmate of Broadmoor, a homosexual and a murderer, order-ing a white Rolls-Royce for his bride and paying a member of the nursing staff to act as her chauffeur. When he couldn't get Lord Snowdon to take the wedding pictures for him, he asked the Queen's cousin, Lord Lichfield instead, and paid him £2000 for a wedding portrait of his bride.

From the days when he purchased his pythons from Harrods pet department, Ron had become a valued customer of the Knightsbridge store, and Harrods were delighted to arrange and deliver the wedding breakfast – which took place, in the absence of the groom, at a hotel close to Broadmoor. Ron bought his bride a house nearby as a wedding present.

It was clear that for the Duke of Broadmoor almost anything could be arranged – including 'facilities' for the discreet consummation of the marriage should the happy pair have wished it. But, although Ron had already had himself checked in advance for AIDS, as he put it 'just to set Kate's mind at rest', it turned out that this was one privilege that wasn't needed. One of his new bride's many advantages was the fact that, since she'd had a hysterectomy, there was no talk of little Kray Twins.

On one occasion when she apparently inquired if he was contemplating sex, he answered, 'I'm not particularly fussed.'

'If you're not fussed, then, fuck you, I'm not either,' she replied, at which the happy pair both roared with laughter.

Marriage with Ron was not entirely a bed of roses. At times he used her as an errand girl. Apart from asking her to order him new suits from Savile Row and buy him fresh shirts from his old supplier, Turnbull and Asser, he often asked her to bring him in several of the latest Gucci watches. One of her jobs was to arrange a special lunch at

Broadmoor once a month, when Reg would be brought over to see his brother. Again she relied on Harrods, and usually ordered their seafood platter – lobster, shrimps and jumbo prawns, which she knew Reg loved and couldn't get in prison.

Ron still suffered from acute depressions, and when gripped by paranoia he could become suspicious of anyone around him. Occasionally he might still attempt to kill someone, but this was something that the nurses could apparently cope with. However, he was also able to get people outside hurt – and those who knew him seem to have believed that, had he wanted, he could still get anyone he wanted outside Broadmoor killed. He was never short of money to pay a contract killer, and as one of his close associates put it, 'With the name he had by now, there were always people outside who would have considered it an honour to have done a spot of GBH for Ron for free.'

When there were press reports that Reg's friend, Peter Gillett, had committed the 'ultimate disrespect' to the Twins by having sex with Ron's wife Kate in the back of a Ford Escort, he was beside himself with rage. Kate and Gillett, however, both vehemently denied it, but Ron's fury simmered on. Although he accepted Kate's assurance that nothing had happened, he still thought Peter Gillett should die. To calm things down, Wilf Pine arranged for Gillett to visit Ron during one of Reg's monthly visits. It passed off peacefully. Reg told his brother that he was sure it was all a misunderstanding. But although Ron had apparently been dissuaded from ordering Gillett's execution, he told Wilf he'd still appreciate it if someone shot him in the foot, 'just to teach the flash sod a lesson'. Ever the peace-maker, Wilf finally convinced Ron that this wasn't necessary.

Wilf was an old friend, and a former manager of several

pop groups, including Black Sabbath. He had helped the Twins arrange the negotiations over the film deal, and now became a regular visitor to Broadmoor, managing a number of Kray enterprises and helping create a sort of Kray cottage industry from inside Broadmoor.

There were numerous possibilities which could be legitimately exploited. Official pictures of the Twins' faces and the Kray logo could be franchised. The Kray Twins T-shirt had become a steady earner. There was a new computer game called 'The Firm' which, according to the literature, was 'based on the Kray Twins' Reign of Terror in the Sixties'. Krayleigh Security provided 'minders' for clubs throughout the country, for the Kray name carried considerable weight in the 'minding' business. After the film, which was good publicity for them, earnings for the Twins were conservatively estimated to be running at around £100,000 a year. Money was paid on the Twins' behalf into offshore companies and nominee accounts.

Ironically, it was only now he was in Broadmoor that Ron could see himself becoming the 'Godfather' figure he had often dreamed of being, and in Broadmoor he was even starting to look the part. As he drank his alcohol-free lager, listening to records of 'Your Tiny Hand is Frozen' and dreaming of the boys in far-away Tangier, life, for Ron, still had its consolations.

He was certainly doing better than his brother Reg, who as always had a rougher ride than Ron. But Reg too was benefiting from his share of their money.

Geoff Allan, the squire of Gedding Hall, who more than twenty years before, had sold the Twins the Brooks, their retirement house in Suffolk, had finally disposed of his stately home to Bill Wyman. But squire Geoff was still living comfortably near by, and as he was in the property business, he offered Reg another country house. But Reg wasn't interested in retirement houses any more. Now that Peter Gillett was out of prison, Reg wished to buy a house for him instead. Rumour has it that Gillett personally collected £50,000 in notes from a London solicitor who acted for the Krays, to finance the down payment. Money was also helping to improve the quality of Reg's life in Maidstone Prison.

Since 1989, when he was moved from Category A to the slightly more relaxed regime of a Category B prisoner, Reg's life, including his sex life, had improved considerably. If Ron was the Duke of Broadmoor, Reg was rapidly becoming the King of Maidstone Gaol.

He was in many ways a model prisoner. He could now speak to Ron daily on the telephone, and as passes for visitors were easier at Maidstone than at Category A prisons, he could see virtually anyone he wanted, including members of the old criminal fraternity.

Reg gave a lot of his money away – generally to other criminals and to correspondents who he thought could do with it. He also used it to sweeten the prison staff into providing him and his favourite fellow inmates with anything they needed.

Sexually he was continuing the uncomfortable double life he had always maintained for the sake of appearances. As far as the press was concerned, he still publicised his relationships with women, and every year when spring was in the air there would be talk of marriage. But without Peter Gillett, the place in Reg's heart was vacant and it was now that what was probably to be the deepest love of Reg's life began.

Bradley Allardyce was tall, willowy, twenty-eight years old and very handsome, with an uncanny resemblance to the love of Oscar Wilde's life, Lord Alfred Douglas. During his short but eventful life, he had served with and been rejected by the French Foreign Legion, and robbed twelve post offices; when he was finally caught, he had been given a twelve-year stretch for armed robbery.

When he arrived in Maidstone Gaol, Bradley appeared so vulnerable and boyishly good-looking that he must have seemed irresistible to Reg. By all accounts it was an extraordinary time at Maidstone. With a governor who wanted a relaxed regime rather than the harsh discipline of the past, Reg was soon ruling those around him like a feudal monarch. Bradley's role was that of the royal favourite who could do no wrong. Whatever the physical nature of their relationship, it was unquestionably a love affair, which lasted to the day Reg died.

During their time together in prison Reg spoiled his friend and enjoyed flaunting their relationship, for Reg was proud of him. Bradley inevitably became unpopular with other inmates, but no one dared to show dislike towards him. Such was Reg's reputation that he appeared all-powerful. In fact his power in prison came from two things – fear and money – both of which he could command in abundance. Fear gave him power over the other prisoners, and money got him almost everything he wanted from the warders.

According to Bradley, inmates could have any alcohol they wanted as long as they could pay for it, and 'the screws were bringing us in gin at £50 a time for half a bottle'. Few prisoners could afford these prices, but since Reg could, he and Bradley started looking forward to their evening gin and tonic. If there was any food that Bradley wanted, Reg would see he had it. Drugs too were easily available, and at one point Bradley, unknown to Reg, became hooked on heroin. Bradley says that when Reg found out, 'He went mad, and hit me on the jaw. He made me promise I would give it up, and sent out a message to all the dealers in the nick that if anyone supplied me from now on, he'd kill him.'

Bradley came off drugs, but after a while the prison authorities decided that, in the circumstances, it would be wiser to separate this dangerously devoted couple. Bradley was sent to another prison and Reg remained at Maidstone, missing Bradley bitterly.

NINETEEN

Deaths and Entrances

Better a somebody than a nobody.

Ron Kray

By the mid-1990s, Ron was running out of energy. He looked dreadful, and was smoking sixty – some said over a hundred – cigarettes a day. When his marriage ended early in 1994, it left him strangely saddened and depressed. It was ironic that just as publicity had helped create his marriage, so now it helped to end it. This happened when his wife, like almost everyone around the Krays, became an author.

Her book, entitled *Murder, Madness and Marriage*, did not particularly worry him, even though it gave an alarming picture of his activities from inside Broadmoor. What upset him was when he saw the book serialised in a Sunday newspaper and read Kate's claim that 'Ron says I can make love with other men until he can get out.'

Ron didn't have a jealous nature and with no shortage of lovers in Broadmoor he was scarcely in a position to complain. But since he claimed to have asked her to keep the details of their marital arrangements secret, he said he felt 'betrayed'. Reg was reported to be furious with Ron, his attitude being that, whatever the situation, the wife of a criminal should stay 'loyal' to her husband while he was 'away', and that his brother had shown weakness in granting her such sexual freedom. Ron felt that by publishing what he'd said, Kate was 'making me look silly'. Worse still, her behaviour showed a lack of that all-important quality, 'respect', and undermined his image. 'I won't slag her off, but I will never see her again,' he told a friend, and angrily declared his marriage over.

When Kate calmly accepted this, he became angrier still, and fell into deep depression. For the truth was that, however bizarre his marriage, he had grown genuinely fond of life-enhancing Kate; if nothing else, she'd always made him laugh, and acted as an antidote to the other murderers and human wreckage all around him.

It was about this time that he noticed Lee Kiernander, a fellow Broadmoor inmate and former drug addict, smiling to himself at breakfast. Just to show him that there was nothing in life to smile about, Ron suddenly attacked him and nearly killed him. Afterwards, for once in his life, he seems to have felt genuine remorse. The next day he was quoted as saying, 'I want to go on record as saying that this is the last act of violence that Ron Kray will ever commit.'

By now he was suing for divorce, and since the marriage had not been consummated, and Kate was not counter-claiming for money, the divorce soon went through without a hitch. Apathy started to affect him. At one point Kate had persuaded him to take up gardening, which at the time improved his health, but now he gave it up and took no further exercise. After a minor heart attack in 1994 he seems to have accepted the fact that he'd end his days in Broadmoor.

It was appropriate that, just as another of his heroes, the Mafia leader Lucky Luciano, was finally sent to prison for not paying his taxes, so Ron's last recorded joke was to an inspector from the Inland Revenue, who arrived at Broadmoor to collect £370,000 from Ronald Kray in unpaid taxes. 'I can't pay taxes,' muttered Ron. 'I'm a madman.' (I never discovered on what basis the Inland Revenue made the assessment, but I do know that he never paid them.)

After this, he went into decline and on 16 March 1995, following a major heart attack, he was rushed by ambulance from Broadmoor to nearby Wexham Park Hospital, where he died the following day while still in a coma.

By now he was immensely famous and his body began to be treated accordingly. When Alfred Einstein died in 1955, Dr Thomas S. Harvey of Princeton Hospital, who performed the autopsy, removed the great scientist's brain and carefully preserved it for future students who might wish to study it in years to come for clues on the origins of scientific genius. Similarly, when Dr Mufeed Ali performed the official autopsy on Ron at Wexham Park Hospital, he felt it might be possible that Ron's brain might hold the answer to the problem of what makes a violent criminal.

Having carefully removed it, Dr Ali studied the brain of the famous murderer, but, as he told me later, he could detect no sign of any abnormalities. No lesions or inherited distortions, and significantly, no damage to the brain's frontal cortex – which, according to the influential nineteenth-century criminologist, Cesare Lombroso, and his many followers, held the secret to violent criminal behaviour. (This would suggest that the origin of Ron's schizophrenia indeed lay in metabolic changes in the nervous system caused by his prolonged diphtheria in early childhood.)

Having found out all he could, Dr Ali sent Ron's grey matter on to Oxford's Radcliffe Infirmary for further analysis by Dr Brendan Macdonald at the Neuropathology Laboratory. But Dr Macdonald apparently discovered little more than Dr Ali.

And there Ron's brain would probably have remained,

preserved for ever in formaldehyde in a large glass jar, but for the action of Kate Kray, whose last service to her former spouse was to save him from this sad indignity. When she went to plant a farewell kiss on Ron's cold brow, as he lay in state in the funeral parlour of W. English and Son, Bethnal Green's favourite undertaker, she noticed something that other grieving relatives had missed – a thin incision running just below the hairline, where Dr Ali had trepanned the skull in order to remove its contents.

Realising what had happened, she was understandably indignant and, backed by a Sunday newspaper, she launched the call, 'Give Ron Kray back his brain.' Faced by the power of the press, the authorities backed down. However much they might have wished to retain it for future scientists in the interests of forensic pathology, Ron's brain was decanted from its preserving fluid, placed in a plastic box and returned to Charlie, who made sure it was buried with Ron's body.

Some years later, when I questioned Reg about his reaction to his brother's death, he was non-committal, as he often was on the subject of his relationship with Ron. 'I knew something bad had happened, when I got this strange feeling in my back and had a sudden premonition that my brother, Ron was dead,' was all he'd say.

But according to Bradley Allardyce, the way he learned about his brother's death was more traumatic. 'When Reg found out, he went crazy, and was in such a state that the screws were unable to control him. They had to lock up his entire landing to stop the threat of violence spreading.'

It was some months since Reg and his Bradley had been parted and Bradley moved to another prison. Now, to calm Reg down, the authorities brought him back to Maidstone. Bradley told me, 'As soon as I saw him I held him and cuddled him and tried to show him that I loved him. It's at times like this in prison that even the hardest man needs real affection.'

If Reg really was as shattered by his brother's death as Bradley says he was, it makes what happened at Ron's funeral, a few days later, even more remarkable. Helped only by Paul Keys, the representative of W. English and Son, who went to the prison to consult him, Reg knew exactly what he wanted and made all the funeral arrangements down to the last minute detail. Just as Reg's marriage to Frances had had to be 'the East End's wedding of the year', so this had to be the East End's funeral to end all funerals. For Ron, no expense was spared. But there was more to it than that. What Reg was planning was nothing less than an extraordinary example of what has been called 'the invention of tradition'.

Unlike America and Sicily, where the Mafia has evolved a definite tradition that tends to be followed at important gangster funerals, Britain, not even the old East End, has ever had a similar tradition of how the burial of famous criminals should be conducted. But with Ron's funeral this was to change. Leading members of London's so-called 'criminal fraternity' were invited to participate in a demonstration of dignified solidarity at the Kray family church, St Matthew's, Bethnal Green, just round the corner from Vallance Road, where criminal protocol was being quietly created. The Church of England, adaptable as ever, happily went along with this, lending the ritual of the high Anglican funeral services to the new traditions, most of which had been carefully devised by Reg.

Ron, in a £950 coffin, was carried into the church by six trusted pallbearers: brother Charlie, fight-promoter Alex Stene and four representatives of the four criminal quarters of London, Joe Pyle, Johnny Nash, Freddie Foreman and

Ginger Dennis. It was a solemn moment as these famous old criminals bowed their heads in silent prayer before Ron's coffin. With a choir, two priests in full canonicals, and the smell of incense wafting through the church, the vicar of St Matthew's gave Ron's eternal soul his final blessing. The funeral service ended with what would become yet another criminal tradition – the playing of Ron's signature tune, which had now become his anthem – Frank Sinatra singing, 'I did it my way'.

Tradition went on being reinvented all the way to the cemetery. There was the long cortège of over twenty black limousines carrying family, close friends and celebrities. One Mafia tradition was adopted – enormous banks of wreaths and floral tributes showing how much the senders had loved and respected the dear departed. Amongst the sea of flowers two wreaths passed unnoticed – one from John Gotti on behalf of the New York Mafia family, the Gambinos, and the other from Danny Pagano, reputedly a capo from a rival Cosa Nostra family, the Genoveses. There were none from Messrs Burdis, Beach and Anciano, but apart from the tributes sent by such celebrities as Barbara Windsor, and the ever-faithful Roger Daltrey, the flowers that everybody noticed came from Reg. Spelled out in a huge arrangement of blood-red roses on a background of pure white chrysanthemums was the message, 'To My Other Half'.

The horse-drawn hearse that Reg had insisted on for his brother's funeral had become such a thing of the past that even W. English and Son could not supply one, and they had to get it from another undertaker. What Reg had not realised was that the horses would have to pull the lumbering hearse all the way from St Matthew's church to Chingford Mount Cemetery and, foaming at the mouth, the horses were exhausted by the time they got there. Here again, tradition entered into it, this whole bizarre affair drawing its charisma from the greatest funeral seen in London since the death of Wellington – the funeral of Ron's old hero, Winston Churchill.

By now almost everything around the Twins was being reinvented – the myths about the good old days in Bethnal Green, their generosity to the old East Enders, their decency and kindness, and how sadly they'd be missed by nervous widows, clean-limbed youngsters and law-abiding Londoners. Even so it was a stroke of considerable daring for Reg to try to make his brother's funeral the East End's answer to the funeral of 'the greatest living Englishman', thirty years earlier.

In a bizarre way it almost worked. The crowds turned out in their thousands and reverently lined the route. Young mothers born long after Ronnie was arrested lifted their own young children to catch a glimpse of the historic moment as the cortège passed. Old cockneys in the crowd talked intimately about their friends 'The Twins', when most of them had never met them.

The theme of history in the making was one that many of the mourners would pick up on later. Reg himself set the tone. 'When I saw Ron lying there he looked so peaceful it was like looking at a great statesman,' Reg told one journalist. These sentiments were echoed by Dave Courtney, who had organised 'security' in the form of several hundred burly 'minders' in long black overcoats – what he called 'well-dressed muscle' – who lined the route in considerable dignity, alongside the police. 'Dodgy Dave' spelled out what the funeral was all about. 'Losing someone like Ron is like losing the monarch,' he told a journalist. 'For me he has been lying in state, and his funeral is like Sir Winston Churchill's.'

But as when monarchs die, the praise is less important for the dead than for the living. Certainly as far as the East

End was concerned, this most impressive celebration was not only a tribute to the dear departed but also a ritualised endorsement of his clear successor. This was the moment when Reg took on his brother's mantle.

So that no one missed the connection between Ron's funeral and Winston Churchill's, it even ended with a reminder from the Battle of Britain. Reg would never tell me how he did it, but he somehow managed to arrange that, at the very moment of interment, as Ron's gleaming coffin was lowered into the grave, one of the few surviving Spitfires in the country flew over Chingford Mount Cemetery and dipped its wings in final tribute.

Ron was buried as he would have wanted. What other son of Bethnal Green would have brought such crowds out on to the streets to see his coffin passing? Truly one would never look upon the like of Ron again. As if to emphasise for ever what the funeral was all about, beneath Ron's name on the black granite tombstone is just one word, in large gold letters – 'LEGEND'.

In terms of the tortured private history of the Twins, Ron's death marked the end of the everlasting battle for supremacy that had waged between them. In the past, the undisputed winner was nearly always Ron. Ron had dominated Reg, and had always beaten him in their endless competition for celebrity and success. It was Ron who had helped destroy his marriage and because of whom he killed McVitie. It was for the sake of Ron's all-important image that Reg had even sacrificed his hopes of eventual freedom at their trial.

But now Broadmoor and those sixty cigarettes a day had given Reg his freedom and a sort of victory. He made the most of it, and assumed his rightful place as Ron's successor with considerable panache and absolute determination to maintain the legend of the Krays.

With Ron dead, for the first time in his life, Reg found that he was totally alone. And so it was perhaps predictable that he would find a wife to give him consolation. What wasn't predictable was that she would be a 36-year-old, middle-class, former English graduate from Southport, Manchester. Roberta Jones was the daughter of a college lecturer. A serious, very private individual, she ran her own small company making promotional videos. She had met Reg when he hired her company to make the video of Ron's funeral. As soon as he saw her he must have known that she was unlike any girl he'd known before.

Why did Roberta marry him? The simple answer is that she fell in love with him. Would she have done so if his name had not been Kray? I wonder – not because she loved publicity, like Ron's extrovert ex-wife Kate, but because, as a Kray, Reg offered her something that she needed, a cause, a dream, a way of life that would from now on totally obsess her. She was determined to dedicate herself to him – and Reg was more than willing to accept her dedication.

When she met him he was a 62-year-old criminal who had spent nearly half his life in gaol, but he was different from any man that she had ever met. He was very famous, it seemed that he was being badly treated, and he rapidly became the *raison d'être* she was seeking.

The wedding took place in Maidstone Gaol on 14 July 1997. By then Bradley Allardyce had been released from prison and had married Donna Baker, a girl whom Reg had chosen for him out of several of the young ladies who regularly visited him in prison; like a caring father, Reg wanted someone who would love and look after Bradley once he was out of prison. And now that Reg himself was getting married, who better than Bradley for role of best man at the wedding?

To show that this was no ordinary prisoner who was getting married, Reg somehow managed to arrange a laser show on the eve of the wedding outside the prison spelling out his bride's name in the night sky for all to see – 'ROBERTA'. The prison authorities were determined that Reg would not repeat his brother's wheeze of making large sums of money from selling the wedding photographs to the press, so someone had the bright idea of letting the photographs be taken by a warder and making them Crown Copyright. No David Bailey for the second Mrs Reg Kray. There were few wedding guests, but, judging from the photographs, the bride looked radiant in white. The short ceremony was performed by Ron's former 'spiritual director' from Broadmoor, the evangelical minister Dr Ken Stallard who, three years later, would deliver the eulogy at Reg's funeral.

After the wedding, whether or not Reg was in love with Roberta, he certainly came to depend upon her, as he had on no one else since the death of Violet. Although Roberta was allowed to visit him only once a month, they spoke to each other several times a day on the telephone, and it was through these endless phone calls that she really came to share his life. Over the telephone he also gave her his instructions, along with messages for those he wished to contact. Soon she became his secretary, his personal assistant and his confidante.

One thing Roberta did have in common with Kate Kray was that both were extraordinarily determined women. Roberta said that she intended 'to serve his sentence with him'; and to show that this was no idle boast, she sold her company, used the capital to help finance the campaign for his release and lived in a small, barely furnished rented room near the prison, where at nights she slept on the floor.

When Reg was moved to Wayland Prison, twelve miles south of Norwich, she followed faithfully. 'Although I see him only once a month, I feel uneasy when I don't live close to him,' she told me. Wayland had once been part of a US Airforce base, and she rented one of the tiny houses used by the wartime personnel. She joked to me about her 'hermit-like tendencies', as a mile or two away from Reg, she remained in nun-like isolation, her whole life now devoted to the murderer she loved.

It was through Roberta that in 1998 I started seeing Reg again. Reg's 'recommended' thirty-year sentence was drawing to a close and I'd written a piece for *Esquire* magazine, describing how I came to meet the Krays and ending by writing that, once he had served his sentence, clearly he should be released.

Roberta telephoned me soon after the article was published, and having introduced herself, said, 'Reg would like to see you.' Whatever anger I had felt about the way I was treated over the film seemed pointless now, and I suppose I was curious to see him. Possibly I felt I ought to help him. Together with my wife Lynette, who had met the Twins with me in Bethnal Green all those years ago before they were arrested, I made the journey up to Wayland.

We had both grown older, and for just a moment, in the crowded visiting room of Wayland Prison, I thought it was his father, old Charlie Kray, who stood before me. Reg seemed to have shrunk, he mumbled more than ever and he was slightly deaf. But what really struck me were those thirty years that hung between us, and I was terribly aware of all that he had lost through the cult of violence.

For me those thirty years had been the best years of my life, years during which I had remarried, travelled, lived in Italy and watched my children and my grandchildren growing up.

And Reg? During those same years his one undeniable achievement had been to turn himself, along with Ron, into a criminal celebrity. One thing and one alone distinguished him from all the other inmates in that crowded room in Wayland Prison: the unmistakable fact that he was famous. And just as fame had marked him out, so I knew that fame had also kept him going during all those years in prison.

On his wrist he wore a gold chain identity bracelet, which Bradley Allardyce had given him. On the name tag was the word that Reg had chosen for his brother's tombstone – 'LEGEND'. In his days of freedom Reg would never have thought of wearing so much jewellery, but around his neck he wore the heavy gold cross and chain that I had last seen on Ron. He also wore another chain with a gold medallion, which he made a point of showing me. It was engraved with a hologram, on one side a picture of Ron, on the other a portrait of his parents, Violet and Charlie.

Since Ron had died, he seemed to have become more than ever a conscious celebrity. One saw this in the way he talked, and how the other inmates treated him. He'd also changed in his demeanour. In the past I'd seen him break someone's jaw who 'took the liberty' of touching him. Now for the first time since I'd known him, he greeted me with a warm, Mafia-style embrace.

During our conversation in the prison visiting room he suddenly broke off. Good-mannered as ever, he said, 'Excuse me, John. I'll only be a moment, but I've promised to say hello to this fellow's family.'

A young coloured man was sitting at a nearby table with his wife and the young child she had just brought in to see its father. Reg went over, warmly shook them by the hand and chatted amiably for a few minutes. It was then I

289

realised that not only had he made their day but that he was unquestionably the star prisoner of Wayland Prison.

He talked about the twenty or thirty fan letters he was getting every week. Roberta answered most of them on his behalf. He told me that he was writing lyrics for the pop group Fun Lovin' Criminals. Just this week somebody had asked him if he could name a nightclub after him. We talked about his chances of parole and Roberta, who was with us, mentioned their hopes of living in a cottage on the south coast by the sea.

The only thing that seemed to trouble him was the thought of dying like his brother Ron in prison. He told me that his health was bad.

'I get this terrible stomach trouble. I was frightened at first that it was cancer, but the doctors tell me all I've got is irritable bowel syndrome.'

'What does the doctor give you?' I asked.

'Milk of Magnesia,' he answered.

He kept returning to the subject of his chances of parole – he should have got parole by now, and undoubtedly would have done, had it not been for his fame and status as a criminal celebrity.

Roberta had, as always, done her best and found the money to finance an independent psychological assessment by two of the most distinguished forensic psychologists in the country. After extensive tests they had concluded that he was probably no danger to the public or himself, and in their judgement was 'fit for decategorisation'. If this happened, it would mean that he would spend a maximum of a year in an open prison, followed by parole and freedom by the time he was seventy. His idealistic, left-wing lawyer Trevor Linn worked indefatigably without payment for his release, believing that not only was his case a grave injustice but that it had become an important human rights issue.

It was because I agreed with Trevor that I first decided I would write a sequel to *The Profession of Violence*, in which I would put forward the whole case for Reg's freedom. Reg was anxious to co-operate, and the first and most important person he wanted me to meet was Bradley Allardyce. Typically he set this up himself, and a few days later Lynette and I were giving Bradley and his wife Donna lunch at a restaurant near their home in Romford, Essex.

It was a most extraordinary occasion. Bradley and Donna were both charming, and spoke of Reg as of some much-loved relative. As I had known him so long, it was almost as if we were old friends already. As we sat down to eat, Bradley's mobile phone rang and I realised that there were not four of us present at the meal but five. The call was from Wayland Prison. Reg was checking up that we had met, and were enjoying one another's company. When Bradley finished speaking, he had to pass his mobile round the table, and one by one we spoke to our absent guest.

'Enjoyin' yourselves?' Reg asked anxiously. 'Having a good meal? What do you make of Brad? Lovely, isn't he? And Donna's all right, isn't she? Only wish I was with you all.' With Reg's order to 'enjoy your meal', we started eating.

After all I'd heard about him, I was surprised to find Bradley so cool and so sophisticated. There was no problem over conversation since there was one topic that fascinated all of us – Reg. Bradley spoke quite freely of their time in prison and of their devotion to each other. But among all the things he told me, the most disturbing was a quite casual remark.

'You know,' he said, 'Reg is a real killer and he still really loves the idea of it. It still switches him on. When we were in prison he once took me through the whole McVitie killing. It was scary. He couldn't wait to tell me every detail, and by the time he was telling me how he shoved the knife into McVitie's neck and twisted it, his eyes were staring and he was sweating and foaming at the mouth.'

While we were having coffee, my wife talked to Donna about her wedding, and she proudly showed her engagement ring with a large solitaire diamond. 'Reg gave me this when we got engaged,' she said. 'It used to belong to Frances, and he told us he wanted me to wear it, as it was one of his most treasured possessions.'

At this point, Bradley's mobile phone rang again. It was Reg, of course, and he sounded in the best of spirits. 'Just checking you've enjoyed your meal,' he said. We passed the mobile once more round the table, and one by one we spoke to Reg, assuring him that we were having a great time together, and that we really had enjoyed our lunch.

Relations between the Twins and their brother Charlie never fully recovered after the way he treated them over the film. Ron had been slower to forgive than Reg. Until well into his sixties, Charlie had carried on the sort of would-be playboy life he'd always wanted. He had enjoyed the high life on Billie Hill's old territory, the Costa del Crime in southern Spain. But Charlie also had his share of real unhappiness, particularly when he discovered that his only son, Gary, shared his brothers' homosexuality and in 1996 Gary died of cancer.

The last straw came when Charlie was arrested for involvement in a plot to market several million pounds' worth of cocaine. Charlie would always claim that because his name was Kray he was framed by policemen hungry for promotion. What no one could deny was that Charlie had been very foolish, but then, Charlie had been foolish all his life, and nothing could be more foolish than to find yourself back in Parkhurst, as the oldest man in Britain in maximum security.

He really was too old for this sort of thing, and by now he also had a heart condition too; the good life was catching up with him. I remember Reg ringing me late one night to tell me that Charlie was dying; which he did a few days later, in the prison hospital. He died in the arms of his best friend Wilf Pine, former pop group manager, honorary villain, and trusted friend and business associate of Ron throughout his years in Broadmoor.

'Charlie's wishes were very plain.' Wilf Pine told me. 'Whatever happened, he didn't want a celebrity funeral. He wanted his coffin to be taken to the home of his girl-friend Diane, then buried quietly beside his son and his parents at Chingford Mount. Above all, no fuss and no media circus. That's what Charlie wanted.'

But as usual, Charlie's wishes didn't count. As Wilf also told me, 'Nothing was going to be allowed to stop the Reg Kray road show.' Too much depended on this funeral for Reg to waste it. He knew exactly what had to happen. Paul Keys, the faithful undertaker from Mr English's, visited the prison for a second time to discuss the logistics of the funeral and take Reg's instructions. No horses this time, but at least twenty limousines for as many celebrity guests as they could muster. And, naturally, he had to be buried in an 'Opal' coffin of solid carved mahogany with cast brass handles, just as Ron had been.

Being an expert in such matters, and seeing Reg's own appearance, Mr Keys took the liberty of ordering not one but two 'Opal' coffins while he was about it.

The funeral was set for the morning of 19 March 2000. Reg had telephoned me two days earlier with our instruc-tions. Honoured mourners, among whom my wife and I discovered we were now included, were to foregather at Mr English's funeral parlour at 10 a.m. before proceeding to St Matthew's Church for the service, then afterwards to

Chingford Mount Cemetery for the burial. Roberta had booked us places in one of the leading limousines.

On the morning of the funeral, as usual, one of the trains on our local line to London Bridge was cancelled, and we arrived at Mr English's more than half an hour later than intended. Bethnal Green Road was closed to traffic. Two police helicopters were buzzing overhead, and the pavements were jam-packed with people. They were carefully held back by massed police in yellow jackets, matched by equal numbers of the Krays' official minders. Large bald men, mostly in long black overcoats and dark glasses, these were professional security men and bouncers from the Reading area, who had given their services free of charge and had been bussed in early in the morning for the great occasion. Each wore a small red and white plastic badge with the letters 'CKF', which one of them told us stood for 'Charles Kray's Funeral'.

Inside Mr English's, the crowd was even denser than without. I recognised a few familiar faces – Tony Lambrianou, of all people, the smiling murderer Freddie Foreman, the genial torturer Mad Frankie Fraser, and Charlie's closest friend and Ron's constant Broadmoor visitor Wilf Pine, with his nautical grey beard and ivory-handled walking stick. Charlie himself already seemed forgotten. He was safely in his 'Opal' coffin in a secluded room at the back of the establishment. The person everyone was waiting for had been staying overnight along the river at HM Belmarsh Prison.

Like everyone that morning, Reg was late making his appearance, but the waiting increased the crowd's expectancy. 'The bastards are keeping him in Bethnal Green Police Station, instead of letting him be here with us,' muttered Frankie Fraser. Then one heard a distant cheering from the crowd outside, and just before eleven I saw the top of a metallic blue Renault 'people carrier' with blacked-out windows drawing up against the pavement. The crowds surged forward. Bouncers and police joined hands to hold them back. Then Reg stepped out amid cheers and cries of 'Good ol' Reg', and ''Ow yer doin', boy?' Reg Kray was back at last among his people.

There was no disguising the excitement and affection of the crowd, as this grey-haired, frail figure in the inevitable dark blue suit walked slowly up the steps and past the cheering ranks of his enthusiastic welcomers. To point up the strangeness of the moment, he was handcuffed to a buxom female prison officer, suitably attired in black.

He appeared tired but curiously elated as he shuffled past us to give brother Charles his last farewell. There were brief handshakes and ''Ow yer doin''s for those privileged to touch him, and even some Godfather-style embraces for surviving old companions. The keynote of this whole extraordinary gathering of criminals and old associates like us was the conscious dignity with which everything was conducted. This was important, since it made the heavy presence of the police outside, which apparently cost all of us £2 million, appear like some alien force intruding on the grief of this close-knit community.

From Mr English's the cortège made its slow way up Bethnal Green Road, before turning left down Vallance Road and past the block of modern flats now standing where Fort Vallance used to be. As we passed them, even I began to feel an indefinable nostalgia for that long-lost world of the old East End, from which Reg was now appearing as the last of the great survivors, part of a tougher, rougher, but more real world than anything we see around us.

The atmosphere changed in the church, and as at Ron's funeral the mingling of the ritual of the Anglican burial service with the presence of the criminal fraternity gave a strange solemnity to the proceedings. Many of the well-known villains from the past were on parade. Since Charlie was always popular, they came to speed him on his way, but primarily they were there to honour Reg, who sat at the front of the congregation, with Roberta on one side and his female warder on the other.

We were sitting in the third row, directly behind Reg. In the seat in front of us I spotted the end of a chain dangling from its owner's back pocket, and realised that it belonged to a prison officer entrusted with the key to Reg's handcuffs.

But within the church, this was the only sign that I could see of Reg's status as a prisoner. As for Charlie, now safely in his highly polished coffin, all the references from the clergy and from those who knew him were to his little acts of kindness and his role as a lovely human being. Here before God, the cocaine conviction and the time that he spent inside for helping to dispose of Jack McVitie's body seemed of minimal importance. The address was given by an eloquent Roman Catholic monk, Father Ken Rimini, who grew up in Bethnal Green, and in his teens once boxed with Charlie, and I found myself thinking of the police outside as he declared, 'It is not up to any of us here today to pass judgement on Charlie, now that he stands before a far greater jurisdiction than any judge on earth.'

There were the same pallbearers as those who bore Ron's coffin to this same church for his funeral and Freddie Foreman's son, the actor Jamie Foreman, read out the tributes sent by Charlie's absent friends. Then as a final gesture to Middle England, somebody read 'Stop all the clocks', by W.H Auden, which had recently been given a celebrity status of its own by featuring in the film *Four Weddings and a Funeral*.

Once we were on our way to the cemetery, Reg took over. Although he was travelling in the Renault with the darkened windows, the long cortège was flanked with police outriders, and he could not have failed to hear the people crowded in the streets who called his name. During this brief outing from his thirty-one years of captivity, he had become a cause. Men raised their caps, women and children waved and there were banners in the street calling for his release.

But his greatest moment was still to come when we reached the cemetery. Descending from the darkened van, and surrounded by his friends, he bore a wreath of a broken heart made up of red and white roses. But these were not for Charlie. Pausing by the grave of his long-dead first wife Frances, with tears in his eyes he laid them on the grass beneath her tombstone. Then he paid his last respects to his brother, as the coffin was lowered into the ground. But even this was his great moment, rather than Charlie's.

'Three cheers for Reg!' someone shouted from the crowd, and, led by Freddie Foreman, Frankie Fraser and Charlie Richardson, the cry rang out across the cemetery.

With this the show was over. The blue Renault with the darkened windows was already waiting. On this peak of high emotion, with shouts of acclaim still ringing in his ears, Reg and his handcuffed companion stepped aboard. He raised his free hand to the crowd and waved. The door slammed shut, and he was gone. At that moment I realised why Charlie couldn't possibly have had his final wish fulfilled, and been allowed to 'go quietly'.

TWENTY

'A Vexation to the Spirit'

I came to the conclusion many years ago that almost all crime is due to a repressed desire for aesthetic expression.

Evelyn Waugh, *Decline and Fall*

Charlie's funeral was Reg's grand finale as a living celebrity, and just as he had arranged it to enhance his legend, so it exceeded all his expectations. Whenever I saw him afterwards in Wayland, he seemed buoyed up by what had happened. His sole obsession now was his release, just as it was for Roberta, who encouraged the idea in every way she could. She so desperately wanted a happy ending for their story. She still believed that as soon as he was free, life could begin at last for both of them.

But Paul Keys, the undertaker, was not far wrong when he ordered that second coffin. Although Reg didn't know it yet, he was in fact a dying man by now. Throughout his endless years in prison, death had always been his real enemy. Release would have left him free to enjoy his notoriety and make the most of his celebrity; but fame had rigged the odds in death's favour, and with every year that passed, his chance of ever savouring his freedom lessened.

We had talked about this in the past, and I had always realised how much he revelled in his role as a celebrity and that it was what had kept him going all those years in prison. But time was closing in on him. He was particularly worried by the way statistics showed that on average identical twins die within six years of each other. For once, statistics did not lie, and as he always guessed it would, it was his body that finally betrayed him – with powerful assistance from the prison medical service.

Had he been released in the spring of 1998 as he should have been, having by then served out in full his thirty-years sentence, he would have been free to seek whatever medical advice he needed, and the cancer he was already suffering from would almost certainly have been discovered in its early stages. Instead, during those last two years, while the prison doctors were dismissing his complaints of agonising pain and chronic constipation, and prescribing Milk of Magnesia, followed by yet more Milk of Magnesia, the cancer had been advancing like a cunning enemy, moving on from his bladder to his bowel, and then working insidiously through his body.

The crisis came in the second week in August 2000, when he suddenly vomited black bile and blood while in his cell. An ambulance rushed him the twelve miles from Wayland Prison to hospital in Norwich. At last the doctors had to take his medical condition seriously. Investigations confirmed a major intestinal blockage needing instant surgery.

Roberta was summoned to the hospital, and those few hours at his bedside were the longest and the closest period they'd spent together since their marriage; but even now she was not allowed to spend the night with him. That privilege went to two prison officers, who guarded him night and day, sitting in opposite corners of his private room on the seventh floor of the Norfolk and Norwich Hospital.

Next morning, when he was wheeled through the hospital to the operating theatre, he was in handcuffs and one of the guards went with him. Only when the anaesthetic was administered were the manacles removed. During the four-hour operation, the doctors discovered a tumour the size of a grapefruit in his bowel, and at one point they thought that he was dying from a heart attack. In fact, because of loss of blood, his heart had faltered. When he came round from the operation, hope continued for some sort of recovery.

On the journey back from the operating theatre he was no longer handcuffed, the doctors having made it clear that they would not permit it. But the warders were still there, waiting in his room when he returned. So was Roberta, with her anxious smile and unwavering devotion.

Regularly each morning a prison governor came to his room to check on his state of health, in strict accordance with prison regulations, just in case he recovered sufficiently to be placed in a prison hospital and then returned to Wayland. The chances of this happening were never great, but when the laboratory results came through a few days later, it was clear that this would never happen. The laboratory reported that the excised cancer was secondary, and that the primary cause of trouble still lay undiscovered. This meant a second major operation. The doctors thought that it would probably kill him, but Reg was determined to survive.

'I've always been a fighter,' he said. He was also very tough and the surgeons knew their job.

'What are my chances of recovery?' he asked when he came round from the anaesthetic.

'Slight,' replied the surgeon.

The cancer was aggressive and the blockage total. He couldn't eat. He couldn't even drink. His life was measured out through plastic tubes. His only nourishment was through an intravenous drip, and a drain was inserted from his kidneys. Morphine controlled the pain. Slowly but inexorably Reg Kray was dying.

* * *

Pressure grew on the Home Secretary to grant Reg compassionate release. Trevor Linn, his lawyer, drafted yet another letter to the Home Office which was sent on the Friday afternoon before the August Bank Holiday. After waiting, year in year out, for the Home Secretary to recommend him for release, it now came so swiftly that it was like a door he'd pushed against for years which suddenly swung open. Even before the Bank Holiday began that Friday evening, it was announced that, as an act of mercy, under Section 31 of the Criminal Justice Act, Her Majesty's Secretary of State for Home Affairs had seen fit to grant Reg Kray his liberty.

The Minister's humanity was overwhelming. Now that Reg Kray could barely stagger to the shower, with the tubes still attached to him trailing on the floor, he was free. Now that he could barely move, he was at liberty to enjoy life, eat the food he couldn't swallow, go where he wanted although there was nowhere he could go.

But his release would no longer be a political embarrassment to Her Majesty's Home Secretary. That night the first item on the BBC television news was the announcement that 'Gangster Reg Kray, the last remaining member of the notorious Kray brothers,' was free.

Next morning the papers were full of it. Most were favourable, some even praising the Home Secretary. But there was one letter in *The Times* saying, 'How outrageous that a dangerous murderer like Kray should be released. Life should mean life.' Of course.

It was now that the last and in its way the most macabre performance in the violent and convoluted life of the most famous criminal in Britain started – part black farce, part cockney tragedy, part sick saga in the overheated culture of celebrity.

This should have been Roberta's moment. She had waited long enough, and to start with she seemed to be entering into her most important role at last. For these last few precious weeks her husband had to live, the two of them would be together, and however briefly, they might be romantically united. But whatever else he may have been, Reg Kray was no romantic. His mother apart, he'd always had his problems over women, even those who loved him, like Roberta. And now, in addition, there was Bradley.

Bradley had finally arrived from London and was staying at a nearby pub. When I saw him, he said he'd promised Reg that he would never leave him. 'He said he'd leave me first,' said Bradley, somewhat sanctimoniously. And from now Bradley as well as Roberta maintained the bedside vigil, sitting either side of him.

Each seemed desperate to demonstrate affection. While Roberta mopped his brow, Bradley would tenderly stroke his thigh. It was a curious way for anyone to die, but Reg seemed happy.

Bradley, meanwhile, was discreetly selling stories to the press. Roberta resented this. But although Reg also said he hated the publicity and the pictures, he was always ready to forgive him. Roberta resented this so much that on one occasion even she lost her temper, hitting the beloved Bradley on the chin. But in the end Roberta had to become reconciled to the situation. She knew that she and Bradley loved Reg in their different ways, and since Reg depended on them both during these final days there was nothing she could really do about it.

There was still one further problem. Despite his fame and all the money he had earned for himself and others in the past, it seemed that Reg genuinely had no money. I found this hard to credit, and to this day I'm still not absolutely certain that there isn't something tucked away in some offshore fund or numbered account in some foreign bank or other. But if there is, someone has kept it very quiet. Reg was an old East Ender, and old East Enders used to pride themselves on not doing anything as middle-class as saving money. But during those last few weeks, shortage of money made dying difficult for this old gay gangster, dreaming of a grandiose East End funeral with all the trappings.

'Unless you do something fast, you'll have no limousines, no fancy wreaths, no fucking black plumed horses. You'll be cremated, my son, and end up on Roberta's mantelpiece,' said Wilf Pine. Although he didn't really like Reg, Wilf said that he respected him and that he'd promised Ron he'd always be there to look after his brother.

Although he now weighed less than five stone, Reg's will power was considerable. Free at last, he was determined not to die in hospital. Whatever happened, he was going to go out in style. The manager of the Town House Hotel on the outskirts of Norwich offered him his 'honeymoon suite' with riverside views and a four-poster bed for £37.50 a night. Reg accepted. And what other dying criminal would have insisted even now on hiring a black Rolls-Royce to drive to the back entrance of the hospital to act as a decoy to distract the waiting journalists?

Luckily a generous supporter was on hand – Bill Curbishley, the wealthy manager of the pop group The Who, who was still grateful for the way that Reg had looked after him in prison all those years ago before he cleared his name. One good turn deserves another. Curbishley was always grateful and from now on he picked up the bill at the hotel.

Similarly, true to his promise, Wilf Pine was still there, and despite being half crippled with arthritis, he saw Reg out of hospital and drove him to the hotel. Once in the suite, he helped him into the bathroom, where Reg caught a glimpse of himself in the mirror for the first time since leaving prison. A tear rolled down each cheek.

'Christ, Wilf, I look as if I'm dying.'

''Course you are, you silly bugger,' Wilf replied.

Reg had less than two weeks left, but even in these last few days of his life, unforeseen trouble suddenly erupted, which threatened to destroy the image he had tried to create at both his brothers' funerals. Now that he was dying, people were fighting for his soul and what it represented.

The trouble began over the question of the pallbearers at his forthcoming funeral. At both his brothers' funerals, the choice of who carried the coffin came to symbolise the whole connection between the Twins and the criminal fraternity. Since the pallbearers came from rival gangs and different parts of London, by carrying the coffin they became united in a way they had never been before. So to them this had become a ritual of extreme importance. Since Reg had instigated this himself at Ron's funeral, and the same pallbearers were there at Charlie's, he clearly knew the score, and would presumably have wanted them there again. Indeed, according to Wilf Pine, who was at the hotel throughout this time, Reg spoke to the previous pallbearers on the telephone, asking them to carry his coffin, but this time they were told that they had to include Bradley Allardyce among them.

Reg also made a public declaration of defiance to the world in general. Few knew that this was happening, but he summoned Bill Curbishley and told him that, to thank him for all he'd done for him and Roberta, he would offer him the rights to a final death-bed television interview. It was also part of his self-obsession. Even when so close to death, Reg could not resist this chance for one final curtain call. Curbishley agreed, and the interviewer, Aubrey Powell, filmed what would be the public's final view of him when it was later shown on BBC television. Even as death loomed, Reg still refused to say that he was sorry for murdering Jack McVitie. How could he, when the killing had become the basis of his precious legend? He had no regrets and would die proud of what he'd done.

But why had he killed him?, Powell persisted.

'Because he was a vexation to the spirit.'

Soon after the interview, it seems that as Reg grew weaker he changed his mind about who should be his pallbearers. Certainly Roberta believes he did. Clearly it suited the picture that she had of him, as someone who had changed completely from his past role as a violent murderer, if she could now believe that he no longer wished to be associated with the criminal fraternity. The Reg she knew and loved was not the man who killed McVitie. In her eyes he no longer belonged with other notorious criminals.

But as far as his legend was concerned, he and Ron would always be murderers or nothing, and to divorce them from their past would be to lose everything they stood for. By now, Reg himself was probably too weak to care, and both Roberta and Bradley were convinced that he no longer wanted any of the old guard to carry his coffin at the funeral. The row that followed all but wrecked what should have been his great farewell.

It started when Wilf Pine rang Foreman to inform him that Reg's death was imminent, and he in turn spoke to two other former pallbearers, Johnny Nash and Joey Pile. The three of them decided there and then to drive up to Norwich on that Sunday morning to pay their last respects. But this was no sentimental journey. For them their presence at this solemn moment was intended as a gesture of solidarity and an affirmation of their role as former criminals. It was also the final consecration of the cult of violence that Reg had lived by. According to Roberta, the way the trio burst in unannounced when Reg was at the very point of dying was a violation of their privacy, especially when these three friends rapidly proceeded to take over. Reg was beginning his death agony by now, but instead of having Roberta's presence to console him, he had Freddie Foreman, Joey Pile and Johnny Nash.

Freddie put his arm around him and whispered in his ear, 'Let go, son! Let go!' Shortly afterwards, Reg did let go – and died.

Immediately after Reg's death, Foreman gave an interview to a waiting reporter, describing not only Reg's death in detail but, more importantly, his last wishes. With his dying breath, so Freddie Foreman said, Reg had expressed the wish that he, Johnny Nash and Joey Pile should be his pallbearers. But Roberta soon denied this, saying that Reg could not speak by then, and that the old gangsters' invasion of her husband's death was a 'gross intrusion'.

By then, Roberta had made her peace with Reg's past. She had also come to terms with Reg's love for Bradley Allardyce. The night before Reg died, she and Bradley and his wife Donna held a candlelit vigil round the bedside, holding hands and drinking wine as Reg slipped in and out of consciousness. This, Roberta says, was how he had wished to go, and this was how she wanted to remember him.

But this was not the way the self-appointed 'aristocracy of crime' regarded Reg Kray's memory, nor were they prepared to accept Roberta's actions now without a struggle. Which explains, in part at least, what happened at the funeral.

Roberta was not only distressed at having her last precious moments with her husband taken over by these forceful members of the criminal fraternity. She now claimed that Reg was barely conscious during his last two days, and that earlier, when they talked about who should bear his coffin, he had firmly said he didn't want any ex-criminals to participate, apart from Bradley. But for the three former gangsters, this was not acceptable. Considerably more was at stake than sentiment and self-importance: Foreman put it, 'All we've got is our respect', and the Krays and the cult of violence around them had become central to their public image. According to Dave Courtney, Reg had been 'our Rock of Gibraltar. Since Ronnie died,' he said, 'he's been a living monument, the greatest criminal celebrity in the country.'

Besides this, serious money was at stake. Over the years, lesser men had fed off Reg's fame, living in his shadow and recycling his exploits. Without the Krays, the famous criminals from sixties London would have been utterly forgotten by now. There would have been no criminal biographies, no television rights, no movie deals, no interviews. Also, as Freddie Foreman would have put it, 'no respect'.

So when Freddie and his friends had made their presence so powerfully felt at Reg's deathbed, much was involved for all of them. Like disciples at the deathbed of some embattled medieval saint, they had been trying to ensure that Reg was theirs and that it would be their version of his life and legend and final words that would prevail.

But so was Roberta, and, worn and exhausted as she was, she was a match for all the criminals. Like it or like it not, she was also next of kin, and as such she insisted she would have her way, at whatever cost.

* * *

At least the autumn rains held off for Reg's funeral, which began at around 10.30 a.m. on 11 October, eleven days after he died. It cost £8000 and was his last and in its way his greatest self-indulgence.

Its start was as ritualised as the burial of a cardinal, as he lay in state in a private room at the back of Mr English's funeral parlour in Bethnal Green Road, his emaciated, all-but-shaven head on a satin pillow in the intricately carved and varnished coffin, in which his pallbearers would carry his wasted body, shoulder high, into St Matthew's Church for the funeral service.

Already the shiny black limousines for honoured guests were lined up round the corner. These days in Bethnal Green even the grandest funerals rarely exceed five, or at best, six limousines for mourners. Reg had stipulated thirty-three; Roberta settled for eighteen. Two coachloads of security men had driven up once more from Reading and were all in place to line the route. With their long black coats with scarlet armbands, shaven heads and dark glasses, they seemed as silent and inscrutable as castrated monks from some esoteric oriental order.

There were some fine examples of the florist's art in the banks of flowers that seemed to sprout from the roofs of the limousines – 'FREE AT LAST', 'BELOVED REG' – and even now one could not escape the dead man's favourite word. The floral tribute sent from a former Miss United Kingdom consisted of one word spelt out in two-foot-high white daisies – 'LEGEND'.

And there in the road outside were the six black horses who had haunted his dreams as he lay dying, each with a purple cross embroidered on its pale brown blanket, and a top-hatted groom in mute attendance. With their black ostrich plumes nodding in the wind, the horses stood as patiently as steeds from Hell, ready to draw the glass-sided hearse from Mr English's to St Matthew's Church. And there the deathbed dreams of Reg Kray ended.

Funerals don't thrive on repetition, and some of the police outside were looking bored and possibly a shade resentful at having their time wasted when it was clear that the massive crowds that had greeted Reg six months earlier at Charlie's funeral were not materialising. Nor for that matter were the celebrities Reg had hoped for. There were flowers from Barbara Windsor with a loving note, but no sign of her presence. No sign either of the fat cats who'd grown ever fatter on the legend of the Krays. Even their greatest fan and follower, Dave Courtney, seemed to have backed away. The nearest to a recognisable celebrity was Stephen Berkoff, who played George Cornell in the film *The Krays*. Wearing a blue-green velvet scarf and baseball cap in honour of the occasion, he was lecturing a reporter outside the church on the role of the Krays in establishing the mythology of the old East End.

The most serious absentees were the grand old men of English crime, who had decided to boycott the proceedings. Their places as pallbearers had been taken by Reg's solicitor Mark Goldstein, the lead singer from the pop group E17 Tony Mortimer, the promising young boxer Adam Myhill and, of course, Bradley Allardyce.

Had anyone entered St Matthew's Church that Wednesday morning, ignorant of whose funeral it was, he or she would have been hard pressed to work out the profession of the much-loved, seemingly devout Christian whose life and times the clergy and congregation were celebrating in this costly funeral.

There were fulsome tributes from those who knew him. Reg's lawyer, bespectacled young Mark Goldstein, began by saying that his departed client was a man of honour and what he called 'a twentieth-century icon'. The same thought was expressed more fulsomely in the short poem dedicated to Reg by Donna Allardyce:

It broke our hearts to lose you but you did not go alone,
A part of us went with you the day God called you home.

John Redgrave read some touching words on behalf of Roberta, expressing the deeply sentimental nature of their autumnal romance.

The chief testimonial to the piety and loving kindness of the dear departed came in the heartfelt words of Dr Ken Stallard, the Free Church Minister from Oxfordshire who had officiated at the marriage of Reg and Roberta three years earlier. In his role of self-proclaimed 'spiritual adviser' to both Kray Twins during their last seventeen years in gaol, he spoke first of Ron, as a humble child of God and a born-again Christian who, when he visited him in Broadmoor, had fallen on his knees before him. A far better man than those who had presumed to criticise him, Ron Kray had an unforgettable kindness, charity and deep belief that would, said Dr Ken, ensure his place in Heaven. It was the same with Reg, who had also undergone a similar conversion, thanks to Dr Ken. ' "I want to be like you, Ken," Reg told me as I held his hand. "I want to be a Christian. But don't tell anyone until I'm gone. I don't want anyone to think I've become a Christian just to get parole." '

Dr Ken waxed eloquent on the subject of Reg's essential kindness, purity of soul and generosity. Placing him among the poor and outcast of a cruel society, he did not mention how the convert gained the money that he gave away. What he did reveal, however, was the true inspiration of Reg Kray during his years of suffering. It was Winston Churchill – and here Dr Ken gave his own imitation of the statesman's words, 'Never, never, never give in.'

The peroration closed with an upbeat ending, in which Dr Ken told the congregation that after all Reg's sufferings on earth, 'This rare bird has flown his cage.'

Only as the service ended, with the singing of 'Abide with Me', might one have picked up just a hint of the 'rare bird's' past and occupation. As the priest swung a silver censer over the bier, clouds of incense rose above the coffin as they do at funerals in Sicily. Then, again as at Mafia funerals, holy water was sprinkled on the coffin and parting prayers were piously intoned as the bearers shouldered their burden and started on their way.

'Reggie, dear child, may the company of the Redeemed enfold you and bring you to the Heavenly City,' beseeched the Revd Ronald Vaughan.

'O Lord, may Reggie, set free from bondage on earth, be recreated in Thy heavenly image,' echoed the Revd Alan Green.

Then, as the congregation gathered their coats and shuffled after the coffin into the dank and windy street outside, for the last time the chords of Frank Sinatra's famous ballad, now the farewell anthem of the Krays, echoed through the church: 'I did it my way.'

Perhaps it was as well that Freddie Foreman had a prior appointment at New Scotland Yard to answer charges of perverting the course of justice over the murder of Frank Mitchell. And that tough old Joey Pile decided to sit in his car outside the church rather than endure such eulogies. One could even sympathise with Dave Courtney, who deposited his wreath of two handcuffed doves depicted in white daisies on a bed of red chrysanthemums at the gates of Chingford Mount Cemetery with words that summed up his feelings and those of at least one member of the congregation: 'Gutted. Nuff said,' he wrote.

* * *

After the obsequies in St Matthew's the favoured mourners in the limousines (who now included me and my wife) began the long trail to Chingford Mount Cemetery at ten miles an hour.

This apart, the cortège was something of an anti-climax. Reg in his coffin was no substitute for Reg triumphantly returning as the living person he had been just seven months earlier for the funeral of his brother Charlie. No celebrities sat in the limousines, apart from Mad Frankie Fraser, who had loved Reg and in spite of everything had wanted to attend his funeral. What crowds there were made do with clapping and cheering Mad Frankie when they saw him. Mad Frankie cheerfully responded.

Like a long black snake, the cortège crawled on its way through a new and prosperous East End, markedly different from the one the Twins remembered from their days of violent freedom – through gentrified Hackney, through multi-racial Chigwell, then into the cemetery, where Bethnal Green's most famous son was to take his place at last among the granite pink sarcophagi of long-dead East London worthies, in the marble heaven of Kray Corner. It was a homecoming of a sort.

Ron's last resting place had been prepared in readiness to receive the coffin of his brother. Reg had always known that in death he would be finally reunited with his brother. His arrival meant that at last the Kray family was together. Frances was just across the way, sharing her grave with Charlie's gay son, Gary. Violet and old Charlie were next door, with their eldest son, Charlie, in a recent grave beside them.

There was a sudden crush around the open grave as Reg's coffin was lowered into it, and everybody pushed forward for a final glimpse of it. In the midst of them all, a lonely figure in a black dress, stood Roberta, with the thin white face of a lost child, clutching the godfatherly hand of Wilf Pine. He stood as the pacifier between the two embattled sides, and his presence may have been the reason why the trouble simmering below the surface never quite erupted.

As at Ron's funeral, Reg had asked for a Battle of Britain Spitfire to fly past, dipping its wings at the moment of interment, but it never came. As his coffin was committed to the earth, all that flew across the leaden sky were starlings going home to roost in the high trees around the cemetery.

'In the midst of life we are in death; of whom may we seek for succour but of thee, O Lord,' said the Revd Alan Green.

A man with a blue chin in a tight grey suit handed out red roses to the women at the graveside and they started throwing them into the open grave on top of the coffin, partially obscuring Roberta's cross of white and scarlet roses. With solemn faces, the men followed suit with handfuls of earth which spattered on the coffin.

'Man that is born of woman hath but a short time to live, and is full of misery. He cometh up, and is cut down like a flower; he fleeth as it were a shadow, and never continueth in one stay,' said the Revd Ronald Vaughan.

Barely had the priest finished speaking when a brown-painted tipper truck, driven by one of the cemetery workers in a red-and-white checked shirt, came chugging through the mourners to the graveside. It reversed, backed noisily through the crowd, then raised its tail and neatly deposited its first load of heavy soil into the open grave. This brought a swift and very final end to the proceedings, and my last sight of Reg Kray's earthly presence was of his coffin, with Roberta's floral cross, being swamped beneath the rush of earth. Then, in an instant, it was gone.

TWENTY ONE

A Myth is Born

A legend is reality so enlarged by imagination that,
eventually, the image becomes reality.

J.K. Galbraith

Up to the very moment when the earth closed over the two
coffins and I knew that Reg was safely laid to rest with the
other members of his family in Kray Corner, I'd still been
regarding the Twins as criminal celebrities, and their violent
lives as a twisted but essentially old-fashioned cockney
success story. Like a pair of ambitious cockneys on the
make, by the time they died, they had clearly achieved
what they had set their hearts on – in their case celebrity
status, non-stop media attention and a place at the heart of
the East End counter-culture.

But now that their lives are over, I realise that, just as
they were almost totally unlike any other criminals, so they
were something more than ordinary celebrities. With most
celebrities, their fame dies with them, but long before they
died, the Twins were already as firmly part of criminal
mythology as Bill Sykes, Dick Turpin and Jack the Ripper.
More than thirty years after the gangland killings of two
otherwise unmemorable East End villains, public fascination with the Twins is showing no sign of diminishing, and
at Reg's death, the widespread interest of the foreign press
showed that this interest is by no means just confined to
Britain.

I have also come to realise how long ago it was that their 'legend' started. Even before they were arrested, on the eve of Reg's wedding, journalists were already hailing them as folk heroes of the old East End and Francis Wyndham was comparing the stories he was hearing about them with the legends told of outlaws from the American Wild West. It was then too that the Twins' visual image was indelibly established. The faces in the public eye are not the faces that I saw when I visited the Twins later on in Parkhurst or in Broadmoor; still less is the face of Reg that gaunt visage as he gave his final television interview when he lay dying. The picture everyone remembers of the Twins will always be that threatening high-fashion image which David Bailey created in the studios of *Vogue* Magazine not long before their murder spree began.

It is surprising how little else about them remains from this period that is anything like as memorable, apart from odd clips of contemporary television film and press pictures showing the Twins as dark-haired, sharply-dressed young cockney gangsters. After their trial, when they started their thirty years in maximum security, the pictures effectively ceased, as did their lives as active criminals. This meant that their public image did not change. Instead it remained frozen in the 1960s, just as their 'legend' was preserved in the aspic of the prison system. Slowly the mythic status of the Twins began in earnest.

The important thing to bear in mind about a myth is that it has no direct connection with the truth. According to the dictionary, a myth is essentially fiction, and as Philip Ridley showed when he wrote his extraordinary script for the film, *The Krays*, the important thing about a myth is that it can be endlessly reinterpreted and retold to exalt or terrify later generations – and therein lies its power. For myths survive in ways that media reports of even the most famous celebrities do not. As a phenomenon, this is actually far rarer than one might imagine, for the subject must be capable of endless reinvention, and what really counts will always be the need that people feel to establish contact with the image at the centre of the story. The more varied and powerful this need, the more lasting and recurring is the myth. Even in their lifetime, this clearly happened with the Twins: one of the most extraordinary things about them has been the constant public interest in them both since they were arrested over thirty years ago.

This reaction has varied right across the spectrum. For some people, the image of the Twins has changed little from that which was established at their trial – as criminals and murderers whose power and undoubted magnetism derives from the fact that they were abnormally evil and wicked men, and little else. But for others, and particularly for many present day East Enders and for members of the younger generation, the image of the Twins is different. For them they appear as exciting, often nostalgic figures, part of an old Bethnal Green now lost for ever. No one who witnessed the enormous crowds outside Mr English's funeral parlour, cheering the frail Reg Kray, brought back from prison for his brother Charlie's funeral, could ever doubt the power of this almost tribal feeling. For them the Twins always were and always will be 'their own', 'diamond geezers' who would help any fellow East Ender in trouble, who had also made it to the big time – and if they killed McVitie and Cornell, they did so in much the same spirit as when Jesse James gunned down his enemies, because they were in Reg's dying words, 'a vexation to the spirit'.

What is so fascinating in this whole phenomenon is the way in which the image of the Krays has also become for all of us the 'accepted face of violent crime', despite the fact that by the time of their arrest, the Twins, in realistic criminal terms, were fast becoming obsolete. The hard drug business was only just beginning, bringing with it a new breed of ruthless and dispassionate, international criminals. Crime as a branch of investment banking never appealed to the Twins, any more than murder as a corporate decision carried out by someone else.

The true nightmare of modern big-time crime lies in the fact that it is faceless, and this makes that Bailey portrait of the Twins now seem strangely reassuring. They could never have lived the life of modern big-time criminals, since in the last resort what truly mattered to the Twins was their image and their legend. Unlike the faceless men behind the anonymous crime that threatens all of us today, the Twins will always be the faces that everyone remembers.

From childhood we are all fascinated by monsters, provided they offer us no real threat at all, which is why I am convinced that their story, far from ending on that October day in Chingford Mount Cemetery, is only just beginning. They will be endlessly studied by criminologists and their students, as well as by criminal psychologists. There will be yet more films, more books, more highly coloured versions of their lives and crimes. For the Twins are now so firmly embedded in our subconscious that their story will always be recycled, and reinvented to satisfy the curiosity of later generations.

Since Reg's death this mythic process has been flourishing, with the promise of yet more books and a further film about the Twins, while endless rumours on the subject continue to abound. One of the strangest and most persistent of these rumours is one which I find particularly fascinating for the way it fits into the pattern of certain legends from the past. I have heard this rumour more than once, and, as with the return of the King in the Arthurian legends, or the stories of reincarnation that occur time and time again in the Greek myths, it centres on the possibility of the Twins' physical return. As with all folk mythology the story I was told may or may not be true but, according to the rumours, shortly before Reg died, one of his devoted followers took a sample of his sperm, thereby hoping to ensure for the Twins a sort of immortality. Although there was speculation at the time over who had done this, no one seemed to know for sure, but I was told that, somewhere in the frosty depths of a London sperm bank, the genetic essence of the Kray Twins is still very much alive. Such is the power of mythology around the Twins that already there are some who genuinely believe that, at some future date, the seed will be placed inside a willing womb and, as with their mythical progenitors, Castor and Pollux, not only will the legend of the Twins continue, but their physical presence will one day reassert itself. Whether it does or not, their myth will certainly live on as they both intended.

Index

Index

Index